Border Guard

BORDER GUARD

Also by Don Whitehead:

THE FBI STORY
JOURNEY INTO CRIME

Don Whitehead

BORDER GUARD

THE STORY OF THE UNITED STATES CUSTOMS SERVICE

McGraw-Hill Book Company, Inc.

New York   Toronto   London

BORDER GUARD

Library of Congress Catalog Card Number: 63-12134

Third Printing

69947

For Ruth and Gene Neilsen

CONTENTS

1
A SLIGHT CASE OF CONSCIENCE

One of the most serious problems confronting the Customs Service in this century is the control of the illegal importation of narcotics. Some of the difficulties involved in handling dope smuggling can be seen when it is realized that these drugs are being sent from all over the world, by every means of international transportation. The comparatively small number of Customs agents rely on patience, diligence and intelligence, and they are doing a remarkable job. Since this problem is so important, and so typical of the job the Service does, we will begin with the story of one successful case.

On the night of May 17, 1955, seventeen-year-old Truls Arild Halvorsen sat in an office in the Customs House in Boston, Massachusetts, blinking back the unmanly tears that threatened to spill down his face. He kept trying to swallow the dry lump of fear in his throat, but it wouldn't go away. And he had to concentrate hard to remember the answers to all the questions being asked of him by the men sitting about the room.

He was a tall, handsome youth. His blond hair was cropped in a crew cut. His eyes were as blue as the waters in the fjords of his native Norway which he had left for the first time only a little more than a year before. That was when he had shipped out as a seaman aboard the MS *Fernhill*.

He remembered the day he left home his father had said, "We are very proud of you, son." His mother had wept as she clung to him. His friends had gathered to shake his hand and wish him good luck on his first voyage. He had felt grown up and proud and excited—ready to cope with anything the future might bring.

But now . . . now he sat, a virtual prisoner, answering questions about his role in the plot to smuggle narcotics into the United States. It was a nightmare he wished he could forget, but he knew he never could. The men around him were members of the U.S. Customs' Special Racket Squad out of New York City, whose job it was to run down smugglers.

He heard the big, soft-voiced man sitting across the desk from him—the agent named Dave Cardoza—say, "Let's go over the story again, Halvorsen. This time it's for the official record. Tell it just as you did before—exactly what happened."

Halvorsen swallowed once more and nodded. He didn't need a translator to understand what Cardoza was saying because he spoke excellent English as well as German.

"Will you state your full name?"

The youth replied: "Truls Arild Halvorsen." And the recording began.

Q—What is your position on the ship?

A—Ordinary seaman.

Q—What vessel are you on?

A—The name of the ship is the *Fernhill*.

Q—How long have you been employed aboard the *Fernhill*?

A—Three trips, about fifteen months.

Q—How old are you, Mr. Halvorsen?

A—I am seventeen and a half years old.

Was it possible this had begun only a few weeks ago? It had begun that day in Hong Kong when he met the Chinese stranger aboard the *Fernhill* and, like a fool, he had listened to the man's talk about making easy money. That was when he should have walked away.

But he hadn't walked away. And that's why he was now in this strange room in Boston with these men who asked so many questions. . . .

Q—Mr. Halvorsen, on the 15th of March, 1955, where was your ship, the *Fernhill*?

A—It was in Hong Kong.

Q—And did you have any conversation with a visitor to the ship?

A—Yes, I was talking to him.

Q—Will you explain what conversation you had and with whom it was?

A—The man was a tailor and he said to me that he wanted to talk about some business down in my cabin.

Q—Had you ever met him before?

A—No.

Halvorsen recalled that he had talked to the Chinese tailor about the price of a suit. Several tailors had boarded the *Fernhill* to solicit orders as soon as the ship dropped anchor. Most of the ship's crew had placed orders for suits, but Halvorsen had decided the price was more than he could afford. It was after this that the tailor—a well-dressed man of medium height with a wart on the lobe of his left ear—whispered to Halvorsen that he would like to talk to him alone in his cabin.

Q—What did he say when he talked about this other business of smuggling?

A—He asked me if I wanted to make some money.

Q—What did you say?

A—Yes, I said.

Q—Then what did he say?

A—He said, "I can give you opium * if you will take the opium to San Francisco." He said that if I would do this for him he would pay me $1,200 American.

Q—What did you say then?

A—I was not sure if I wanted to do it or not, but I did not say no.

The tailor then wrote an address on a slip of paper—No. 54 Cameron Road—and pressed it into Halvorsen's hand. "If you decide you want the money, come to this address at seven o'clock tonight."

By six o'clock that evening, Halvorsen had reached a decision. The sum of $1,200 sounded like a small fortune to the boy who had never in his life had more than a few dollars at one time. It was more money than he could save in many months at sea—enough to buy an interest in a fishing boat back in Norway.

Halvorsen dressed in his best blue trousers and white shirt for the trip ashore. When he left the *Fernhill* he carried a briefcase which the Chinese had suggested he bring along. He hailed a rick-

---

* In the transcript of Halvorsen's story, the young seaman referred to the narcotics sometimes as opium and at other times as cocaine and heroin. The narcotics in each case was heroin, a derivative of opium highly favored by drug addicts in the United States.

shaw at the ferry slip near the Peninsula Hotel, and gave the address on Cameron Road. Then he sat back to enjoy the gaudy, East-meets-West sights of Kowloon as the coolie trotted through streets swarming with Chinese, most of them refugees from Red China.

After he stepped from the rickshaw and paid the driver, he stood uncertainly at the curb looking about for the number 54. A Chinese came up to him and said, "You looking for Number Fifty-four?" Halvorsen said he was, and the man said, "You follow me." . . .

Q—Where did he take you?

A—He took me inside the house and into a corridor. We turned right and there was a door. He knocked on the door.

Q—Was the house No. 54, Cameron Road, ground floor, Kowloon, Hong Kong?

A—Yes.

Q—Was there any number or anything written on the door of the corridor?

A—I don't remember.

Q—Then what happened?

A—Somebody opened the door and said, "Please, come in." He took my hand as in welcome. He said, "I am glad to see you," or something like that and in the room was the Chinese tailor I saw on the ship and another man. . . .

Halvorsen remembered sitting with the three Chinese at a small, round table. The room was dimly lit and dingy. One of the men offered him whiskey but he refused and instead asked for a glass of beer. A woman padded into the room and placed a bottle of beer on the table. And then he was aware that a Chinese girl was standing near him. But when he glanced at her, he was blinded momentarily by a flash of light and so startled that he started to rise from his chair.

The wart-eared tailor laughed and said, "Don't worry. It was only a flash from a camera. We need a photograph to send to our man in San Francisco so he will be able to recognize you when you arrive with the packages."

One of the Chinese, a short, fat man in shirt sleeves, took a slip of paper from his pocket and scrawled on it the words, "San Francisco." He tore the paper in half, handing one part to Halvorsen. "You keep this half," he said, "and we will send the other to our man in San Francisco. When you meet him, you give him your half of the paper and he can match the two halves to make sure you are the right man."

"Where will I meet him?" Halvorsen asked.

The man wrote on another slip of paper "Lew Gar Kung Saw, 854 Clay Street, San Francisco." He handed it to Halvorsen and said, "You deliver the packages of heroin to this man at this address. When you make the delivery, he will pay you twelve hundred dollars. Okay?"

Halvorsen nodded. "I guess it's okay," he said. Then he gave them the itinerary of the *Fernhill*. He told them the ship was scheduled to arrive in Boston on May 16. If possible, he would leave the ship there or in New York and travel by bus to San Francisco to make the delivery, after which he would return to Norway.

The fat Chinese left the room, and when he returned he was carrying ten cotton bags filled with heroin, each of them weighing about half a pound. He placed them in Halvorsen's briefcase. . . .

Q—What happened then?

A—Then he asked me if I saw the bags. I said, "Yes." He said that was what I was going to take ashore and he said, "You have to keep it on your body." And he showed me a white silk sash.

Q—Did he tell you how to use that white silk sash?

A—Yes. He said I was first to fold it double and put it around my waist and then I could put the white bags down in the folds of the sash. He said I should keep maybe two bags in front, two bags in the back and the others strapped to my legs.

After the Chinese put the heroin in the briefcase, Halvorsen left the house on Cameron Road. He returned to his ship and placed the briefcase in a ship's locker. He explained to the officer in charge that it contained souvenirs.

From Hong Kong, the *Fernhill* steamed to Djakarta, Indonesia, where Halvorsen hurried ashore with several crew members for a look at the city. After a time he wandered away from the others. He was alone, sipping a glass of beer in a bar near the Hotel Des Indes, when a Javanese approached and stood beside him.

"Have you got anything you would like to sell?" the Javanese said. "Any clothes or shoes? I can get you a good price."

Halvorsen looked at the man, a middle-aged Javanese with a jagged scar running from his left eyebrow to his chin. He said stiffly, "I'm not interested in small stuff."

The Javanese slid into a chair beside the youth. "You mean you've got something else you would like to sell?" he asked.

Halvorsen nodded, trying to appear casual and matter-of-fact.

"Maybe we can do business," Scar Face said. "What have you got to sell?"

Halvorsen said, "What would you pay for a pound of heroin?"

The Javanese was impressed. "You can get heroin? You are not fooling me?"

"I'm not telling a lie," Halvorsen said. "How much for a pound?"

Scar Face said, "If it's pure stuff, I'll take two pounds and pay you ten thousand dollars American money."

$10,000 for two pounds of heroin! Halvorsen was so startled that he blurted: "That's too much. Five thousand would be enough. I'll have to get the stuff from the ship."

Scar Face said, "You wait here. I'll be back." And he hurried from the bar.

In less than five minutes he was back with two other men, one of them dressed in a police uniform. They took Halvorsen to the dock, where they boarded a police launch which carried them to the *Fernhill*. Halvorsen took Scar Face to his cabin and told him to wait there.

Then he went to the ship's locker and removed two bags of heroin and brought them back to his quarters. The Javanese opened one of them. He took a pinch of the white powder and tasted it. "It looks and tastes like it's pure stuff, but I don't know. I'll have to get a doctor to make a test."

This precaution seemed reasonable enough to Halvorsen. He handed the two bags to the Javanese, who concealed them under his coat. They returned to the police boat which carried them back to the pier. And then he and Scar Face got into a car and drove to the outskirts of the city, where the car swung into a driveway beside a white frame house.

"This is the doctor's house," Scar Face said. "You wait in the car." He carried the two bags into the house.

In a few minutes Scar Face came back to the car. "The doctor says it will take time to test the heroin. I can't get the money until he makes the test. I'll bring it to you tomorrow."

With appalling innocence, Halvorsen said, "I guess that's okay." And as Scar Face drove him back to the waterfront, they agreed to meet on the pier the following morning.

The next day Halvorsen went ashore to meet Scar Face. He waited at the agreed meeting place for more than two hours. Slowly it dawned on him that he would never see Scar Face again. He had been duped. It was then that young Halvorsen felt more than chagrin. He felt enormously ashamed. He wondered why he had ever permitted himself to become involved in something so dishonorable as smuggling narcotics.

He felt, too, a growing, bitter anger toward the wart-eared tailor and his friends in Hong Kong and the scar-faced Javanese. He wondered how he could atone for this sin. And after a while he decided the best thing to do was to seek advice from someone older.

When the *Fernhill* reached Singapore, Halvorsen hurried to the home of a Norwegian minister whom he had once met in Baltimore. The youth poured out his story to the churchman. "What shall I do?" he asked.

"It is a bad business, my son," the minister said. "Let me go to the American Consulate and ask their advice. Perhaps they can help us." When the minister returned from the Consulate, he shook his head. "They can do nothing," he said, "because the matter is out of their jurisdiction. They said it would be best if you would take your story to the police agency called the FBI when you reach the United States."

But when Halvorsen reached his ship, he thought of his friend in New York City, the Rev. Leif Aagaard, pastor of the Norwegian Seamen's Church, 33 First Place, Brooklyn, in whose home he had spent the previous Christmas. On April 11, 1955, he wrote the Reverend Aagaard a long letter:

Dear Aagaard:
Let me get right to the matter. When we were in port in Hong Kong (March 15) I chanced to get in conversation with a tailor who came aboard to take orders. After the usual talk about everyday things he asked if he could get a word with me in private in my cabin. It proved he wanted me to smuggle four pounds of cocaine from Hong

Kong to Frisco. I was to get $1,200 from the man I was to deliver the goods to in Frisco. I said Yes!

He gave me an address in Hong Kong where I should come the same evening. There I was to get the necessary information as well as the cocaine. I arrived at the specified time. There a flash photo was taken of me in order that the contact in Frisco could identify me. I also received one half of a letter that was torn in two parts. The photo and the other half was to be sent to Frisco. The half which I retained was to serve as my pass in order to get in contact with these men. I also was given the name and address of the man I was to deliver the cocaine to in Frisco. Afterwards I received eight * small sack-like bags made of cotton, each containing one-half pound. They were placed in a brief case which I should bring them aboard in. I did everything they instructed me to do and locked it in my cabin, later to hide it in a safe place. I had, at that time, all intention of doing this rotten job. Later, however, when I had had the time to think more clearly about these things I cursed myself for having wanted to take part in such dirty things. I came to the conclusion that I would throw it all overboard, but at the same time a thought struck me that perhaps I could be of help to the American authorities by getting these people jailed in Frisco. When we arrived in Singapore I contacted Rossebo whom I knew from the time I was ashore in Baltimore. I told him the whole story and he promised to get in contact with the American Consulate there, and in a discreet manner try to find out about same. Now it was found, however, that they could not give any direct answer as to what the American authorities might do to me as a smuggler. They were very much interested, but said that that type of smuggling was something that came under FBI.

Will you now be so kind as to do me the favor of presenting the entire matter before the FBI in New York and say that I am placing myself entirely at their disposal in the case. Let as few as possible in on this. I am afraid that the persons I am dealing with on this are no small fry. I will now seal the goods and declare it on the manifest as four pounds of camphor. This I am doing so as not to have the ship and the captain mixed up in this affair, if it should get that bad. Now I ask that you or the authorities who will handle this matter send me a discreet telegram before May 10, which will assure me that I can safely count on avoiding any trouble from the authorities as a result of my smuggling. If I do not receive the telegram within the

---

* Actually, Halvorsen received ten sacks—but he could not bring himself to admit to Aagaard that he had been swindled of two of the bags in Djakarta.

specified date, I will throw everything overboard and remove every trace of everything that might implicate me. In case you do not want to have anything to do with the matter, please advise me as soon as possible. *Fernhill* is scheduled to arrive in Boston May 16th.

Well, now I hope that you will not judge me too harshly and that all will be well again.

> Warmest regards to you and your family.
> *Truls Arild Halvorsen*

When the Reverend Aagaard received the letter, he was shocked and dismayed. He remembered young Halvorsen well because the youth had come to his church in Brooklyn when his ship made port there. Aagaard had become so fond of the boy that he had invited him to his home the past Christmas for dinner with his family. He knew he was an intelligent youth and had never before been involved in wrong-doing.

The pastor got in touch with the Norwegian Consul General, Thor Brodtkorb, and the two men arranged a meeting with Supervising Customs Agent Lawrence Fleishman at his office at 21 Varick Street. At this meeting Aagaard and Brodtkorb reviewed the entire case as it had been told to them in the letter by Halvorsen.

After a further discussion with the U.S. District Attorney, it was agreed that if Halvorsen would turn over the narcotics to the master of the *Fernhill* while the vessel was still on the high seas, then young Halvorsen would avoid prosecution for possession of narcotics— simply because the narcotics would not be in his possession. It was agreed also that if Halvorsen were cooperative there would be no prosecution for conspiracy to smuggle narcotics into the country. The master of the vessel was to be held blameless in this case, since he had known nothing whatever of the smuggling plot, and there were to be no penalties assessed against either him or his vessel once the narcotics were turned over to the Customs officers.

As soon as it was learned that the *Fernhill* had cleared from Suez on its way through the Canal to the Mediterranean, a cable was dispatched to Halvorsen: ALL IN ORDER HERE. GIVE IT TO THE CAPTAIN.

A representative of the steamship company dispatched a message in international code to the captain of the *Fernhill* saying:

International signal book code only for the Captain. Confidential. Halvorsen will hand over packages. Keep them safe until arrival Boston. Cooperating with authorities here. Everything in order. Immunity on condition that you handle in accordance herewith. You must not discuss this with anybody else. Wire us following message in code to me: Have acted as per your instructions.

On May 5 the *Fernhill's* skipper radioed:

The packages have been placed for safekeeping in the safe until arrival Boston according your instructions. Receiver has photograph of Halvorsen and first half of papers of introduction. Receiver's address Lew Gar Kung Saw, 854 Clay Street, San Francisco. Consignor Shing Kee and Co., 54 Cameron Road, ground floor, Kowloon, Hong Kong. Signed, Captain Carlson.

Eleven days later Customs Agents Dave Cardoza, Oscar Polcuch and Edward Finnegan boarded a launch on the Boston waterfront and were carried into the harbor to meet the *Fernhill*. They were greeted by Captain Carlson, who took them to his cabin and handed over to them the sacks of heroin. Then he summoned Halvorsen to his cabin and introduced him to the agents.

Cardoza said, "I understand, Halvorsen, that you are willing to cooperate with us in breaking up this smuggling ring."

"I'll do anything I can to help, sir," Halvorsen said. "I'm sorry I ever got mixed up in this."

"We need your help," Cardoza said, "and you have nothing to worry about if you do as we say." He warned Halvorsen that a member of the smuggling ring might approach him when he went ashore in Boston—and he must do nothing to create any suspicion.

Cardoza drew a rough map of the waterfront and showed it to the youth. "You will get off the ship at this point," he explained. "Walk over to this corner and wait for a bus. When the bus comes along, get aboard and take a seat as near the driver as possible. If anyone approaches you about the heroin, tell them it is still aboard the ship and make arrangements to meet them later. But don't worry. Finnegan and I will be on the bus with you. Get off the bus at this street and you'll see a restaurant on the corner. Go in and order a glass of milk—and sit there until we come for you. Is this clear to you?"

"I understand," Halvorsen said. "I'll do as you say."

Cardoza instructed Agent Polcuch to hide the sacks of heroin under his jacket when leaving the ship and to take them to the Customs Bureau's laboratory at 408 Atlantic Avenue for an analysis. "Tell them it's a rush job, Oscar, and we would like to know the results as soon as possible. They can reach us at the Customs House this afternoon."

It was almost noon when Halvorsen walked down the gangway alone and strolled over to the bus stop. The youth boarded the bus and did not even glance at Cardoza and Finnegan when they brushed by him. No one spoke to him on the bus nor did anyone approach him as he sat in the restaurant sipping a glass of milk.

Cardoza and Finnegan lounged in the doorway of a building opposite the restaurant, from where they could see Halvorsen seated at a table. When it seemed apparent that no one had followed him from the waterfront, they took Halvorsen to the Customs House for questioning. The longer they talked to him, the more certain they were that he was telling the truth.

During the afternoon, Cardoza received a telephone call from Acting Chief Chemist Melvin Lerner at the Bureau's laboratory. "The stuff is heroin, all right," Lerner said. "It's a very high grade. What do you want us to do with it?"

"Make the usual report," Cardoza said, "and hang onto those sacks until we decide what to do next. We may need them in making a case against the buyer. And thanks."

The questioning of Halvorsen continued until after midnight. When the session was over, the penitent young man knew that his personal nightmare was nearing an end and that there was a way to atone for what he had done. The whole sorry mess could be washed out by helping the Customs agents trap the receiver in San Francisco—the man named Lew Gar Kung Saw.

Agent Finnegan accompanied Halvorsen from the Customs building to the *Fernhill* and left him. It was agreed he would remain aboard the ship until it reached New York harbor. By that time a decision would be made on the next move.

On May 23, one week after the arrival of the *Fernhill* in Boston harbor, Agents Cardoza, Polcuch and Finnegan met with their chief, Lawrence Fleishman, at their headquarters at 21 Varick Street in New York City. Fleishman was a lean man with graying hair who had been doing battle with gangs of smugglers, crooked importers, and international con men for almost thirty years. Long ago he had lost count of the number of crooks he had helped send to prison, and the millions of dollars involved in these cases. But he had never lost his enthusiasm for matching wits with those he called "the bastards."

At this moment, Halvorsen was seeing the sights of New York in company with a young Customs agent. He had been taken from the *Fernhill* when the ship reached New York harbor and he had registered in a midtown hotel to wait for the next move in the game.

Fleishman said of Halvorsen: "The kid can never make the delivery in San Francisco alone. He's too nervous and it is too risky. Polcuch had better go with him. We'll rig up a story that Polcuch is Halvorsen's shipmate and that they have been working together on the deal."

Fleishman told them it wasn't practical to use the original eight sacks of heroin as a decoy in trapping the receiver in San Francisco. He agreed with officials in Washington that there was too much danger of the heroin being lost or stolen and being put back into the illicit market. Also there was the difficulty of obtaining legal clearances for transporting that amount of heroin across the continent.

"We'll have to ask the laboratory to find a substitute to put in those bags," Fleishman said. "It will have to be something that looks, feels and tastes like heroin. We can blow this whole case if we're not careful."

Fleishman knew the San Francisco receiver would become suspicious if Halvorsen didn't show up soon. He picked up the telephone and asked his secretary to call the chief chemist in the Bureau's Boston laboratory. . . .

When Acting Chief Chemist Melvin Lerner put down the telephone after talking to Fleishman, he sent word to the laboratory that he wished to see Chemist Paul Leavitt. Lerner was a tall, brown-haired young man who had been with the Bureau for fourteen years.

Lerner called for Paul Leavitt because this remarkable man had an uncanny sense of taste—and if anyone could find a material which tasted like heroin, it was he. Leavitt could identify accurately an enormous number of materials simply by tasting them, an odd sort of sensory skill which he had had since childhood. It had been a valuable asset in the laboratory, where he had spent almost forty years as a chemist.

The problem was to find a light, white, powdery substance with the same bulk and weight as heroin and the same bitter taste. The taste was particularly important because it was characteristic of narcotics buyers to taste heroin before accepting it in any large amount.

When Leavitt came into the office, Lerner outlined the problem that had been dumped into their laps and he gave him the details of the Halvorsen case.

"How much time do I have?" Leavitt asked.

Lerner said, "It's a rush job, Paul. They want it in New York on the first plane tomorrow—in the same cotton bags which are out there in the vault. We'll have to remove the heroin from the bags and refill them with a substitute material."

Leavitt knew that sacks filled with milk sugar or ordinary sugar would never fool a veteran trafficker in narcotics because the sugar would weigh ten times more than heroin. The substitute had to have the same bulk density as heroin.

For hours the chemist worked on the problem, testing different materials, but each of them was either too dense or did not meet the specifications in appearance or taste. It seemed that the agents in New York had tossed the laboratory a problem that simply could not be solved in so short a time.

Leavitt was still in the laboratory late in the evening pondering the problem when he remembered that several months earlier the laboratory had made a routine test of a white, light, powdery, silica compound produced by the Johns-Manville Company as a filter agent. Somewhere in the laboratory there was a sample of this product.

Leavitt found the sample in a storage room. He also found the product had the bulk density, weight and appearance of heroin. The remaining step was to make the stuff taste like the narcotic— give it the same bitter flavor.

At last Leavitt found the solution in a mixture of quinine and strychnine added to the filter powder in just the proper proportions. The amount of strychnine he used was in safe limits, even if a man should swallow a large amount of the stuff.

The following morning, Lerner supervised the job of emptying the sacks of heroin and filling them with the harmless substitute. He took the sacks to his secretary, Miss Alfhilde Norrman. "I've got a job for you, Alfy," he said. "Can you re-sew these bags so no one can tell they've been tampered with?"

"I think so," Miss Norrman said. Using the same threads with which the bags had been sewn in Hong Kong, Miss Norrman stitched them shut. She was careful to insert the needle in the old thread-holes left in the material. When the job was finished, the eight sacks appeared exactly as they were when young Halvorsen accepted them from the fat Chinese.

Less than twenty-four hours after Fleishman's call to Lerner, the sacks of phony heroin were on their way to New York by plane. The following day, Agent Polcuch and Halvorsen flew to San Francisco, where they checked into a seaman's hotel near the waterfront. After dinner, they carried the brief case containing the heroin substitute to the Greyhound bus station and checked it in a locker.

That same evening they met with agents from the San Francisco Customs office to make plans for the delivery of the sacks to Lew Gar Kung Saw—a name that meant nothing to the San Francisco agents, who knew every suspected narcotics trafficker on the West Coast. Very likely the name was an alias.

It was agreed Polcuch should carry a concealed radio transmitting device to the building on Clay Street. Two agents would be hidden in a small delivery truck parked on the street to record the conversation with the receiver. They would come to help Polcuch and Halvorsen if trouble should develop.

If possible, the receiver was to be lured to Polcuch's room at the seaman's hotel to accept delivery of the sacks. Two agents would be concealed in an adjoining room to help with the arrest in case more than one man were involved.

At 10 A.M. the following day, May 27, Polcuch and Halvorsen left their hotel and took a taxi to San Francisco's Chinatown. They stepped out in front of a four-story building which appeared to be a Chinese rooming house. They walked up three flights of stairs without encountering anyone. On the fourth floor they saw a Chinese man walking down the hallway.

Halvorsen said, "Can you help us?" He showed the Chinese the note bearing the name of Lew Gar Kung Saw. The Chinese pointed to the end of the hallway. The room appeared to be a clubroom. There were lounging chairs, a large sofa, and several tables with chairs. At one of the tables sat an elderly Chinese reading a Chinese-language newspaper. The man looked up as Halvorsen and Polcuch entered.

Halvorsen handed him the slip of paper and said, "We're trying to find this man. We were told to meet him here." The Chinese glanced at the name and nodded. He told them to sit down and then he went to a wall telephone, where he began dialing several numbers. He seemed to be having trouble locating Lew Gar Kung Saw.

Polcuch glanced at Halvorsen and winked. "Nervous?" he said in a low voice. Halvorsen grinned for the first time in days. "Yes," he said, "aren't you?"

Polcuch nodded and lit a cigarette. "You're doing fine. Just keep it up and everything will be all right."

Polcuch knew how the kid felt. No matter how many times you played this game, you never knew what was going to happen next. One false move and you blew the whole case, often without knowing why. Halvorsen was old enough to know the dangers. Now that the pressure was on, he was handling himself even better than Polcuch had reason to expect. His hands trembled a bit, but that was the only sign of inner excitement and fear. He hoped the boy would be as steady later as he was now. He had been coached on what to say and what to do under every possible contingency—but this was tricky business even for a veteran agent.

Perhaps the best of the agents were good because they had something of the ham actor in them. Day after day they were called on to assume false identities and to act the part of an underworld character in the drama of the hunters and the hunted. The only difference between this sort of acting and the theater was that this was not to amuse or to entertain the audience. A part was played to protect the people and the Treasury of the United States from thieves, looters, corrupters and chiselers. If you made one false move or spoke one unconvincing line, then the curtain came down. The play was over.

There was the time when one veteran Customs undercover agent worked his way into the confidence of a gang of big-time narcotics dealers whose operation was a multi-million-dollar business. He gave up his own identity and his own life to play the role of a narcotics dealer. He played his part so well that he gained the confidence of the man suspected of being the mastermind of the operation in New York.

Then came the day when it looked as though the weeks of acting would pay off. The man who was Mr. Big agreed to sell the agent a large supply of heroin. That evening they met in an East Side bar and had a few drinks before going to the place where the delivery was to be made. The agent insisted on paying for the drinks and then they walked outside to hail a taxi. Suddenly Mr. Big mumbled something about having forgotten an important date.

"We can't get the stuff tonight," he said. "I'll see you later." Mr. Big ducked into a taxi and that was the last time the agent was ever able to get within shouting distance of his man.

What had happened? What had gone wrong? Where had the agent made the false move that blew the case? He reviewed every word that had been said and every move he had made without finding a clue. He never knew the answer until months later when Mr. Big finally was trapped by other agents. He was asked why it was that he had walked out on the undercover agent that night at the East Side bar.

Mr. Big said, "We had two or three drinks at the bar that night and everything was fixed to get the stuff. Then this guy insisted on picking up the tab. He gives the bartender a sawbuck and when he gets the change he leaves a two-bit tip. Hell, I know right then he's a government man because only a government man would leave a lousy two-bit tip. That's when I checked out."

Polcuch knew as small a slip by him or Halvorsen could wreck the case. While the Chinese was making the telephone calls, he left the table and strolled over to the window looking out on Clay Street. He saw a panel truck parked near the entrance and knew the agents were inside.

At last the elderly Chinese hung up the receiver and came to the table. He said, "You come back at twelve o'clock."

Polcuch and Halvorsen left the building and whiled away the time looking in shop windows. When they returned to the clubroom the Chinese man was still engrossed in his newspaper. He saw them enter the room, and went immediately to the telephone and dialed a number. There was a brief conversation in Chinese, after which the old man said, "In five minutes he come. You wait."

They sat at the table waiting, and at 12:35 a well-dressed Chinese entered the room. He wore a neat brown suit and a figured brown tie. He looked to be a man about fifty years old, and on one pudgy finger he wore a diamond ring. He smiled as he walked over to shake hands with Polcuch and Halvorsen.

Halvorsen held out the slip of paper bearing the name Lew Gar Kung Saw. "Are you this man?" he asked. The Chinese glanced at it and said, "Yes, yes. That's my name." But actually, agents learned later, his real name was Lew Doo—long suspected of being a trafficker in narcotics.

Lew Doo produced the photograph of Halvorsen and after that the half of a torn slip of paper bearing the words "San Francisco." He matched his half with the half handed to him by Halvorsen.

"Have you got the stuff with you?" he said.

"No," Halvorsen said. "It's in a locker at the bus station. Have you got the money?"

The Chinese showed them a wallet stuffed with currency. Halvorsen said, "You come to my hotel and bring the money. We'll get the opium and do business there."

Lew Doo exclaimed, "No! No! This place is safe. I do business here all the time. The hotel room is no good."

Halvorsen said, "We can't go walking around the street carrying that stuff. We might get caught."

"Don't worry," Lew Doo said. "It's safer here."

Polcuch sensed it would be a mistake to insist on going to the hotel room. He said, "Maybe the guy's right, Truls. This place looks safe enough. Let's do what he says."

Halvorsen agreed with apparent reluctance. And then the youth said, "I want the money we spent for bus fares, too." He explained to Lew Doo that it had cost $138 to come from New York by bus and he thought this money should be repaid.

Lew Doo made no protest. He agreed to pay the extra money. Halvorsen and Polcuch left the place and headed for the waterfront in a taxi. When Polcuch was certain they were not being followed, he gave the driver the name of their hotel.

Polcuch explained the situation to the agents at the hotel. It was agreed they would go to Clay Street and conceal themselves near the entrance to No. 854, where they could see the clubroom windows. They were not to make a move until Polcuch signalled from the windows or called for help over the concealed radio transmitter. While it appeared Lew Doo was working alone, he might have confederates with him when they returned to the clubroom. It was best to have help near in case there was trouble.

From the hotel, Polcuch and Halvorsen went to the Greyhound bus station and took the brief case from the locker. They returned to No. 854 at approximately 2 P.M., and Halvorsen was carrying the brief case when they walked into the clubroom where Lew Doo was sitting alone.

The Chinese said, "Let me see the stuff." He took out a sack and examined it closely, even to the stitching. He pulled a penknife from his pocket and slit a small hole in the bag. He poured out a pinch of the powder and tasted it—and then he nodded in satisfaction.

Lew Doo lifted the other sacks from the brief case and said, "I paid for ten bags and you have only eight. Where are the others?"

Polcuch tensed. This was a critical moment—and the question he had been waiting for the Chinese to ask. He glanced at Halvorsen.

"I'm sorry," Halvorsen said evenly, "but two of the bags got wet on the ship and we had to throw them overboard. The stuff was ruined."

For several seconds Lew Doo stood and looked first at Halvorsen and then at Polcuch as though trying to read their minds. Polcuch, the veteran, knew the entire case was hanging by a thread. If Lew Doo backed out now, the mission was a failure. If he didn't take the final step and hand over the money, there wouldn't be enough solid evidence to hold him for twenty-four hours. It was now—or perhaps never.

Suddenly the Chinese shrugged and the muscles around his eyes relaxed. He reached into his pocket and pulled out his wallet. He counted out $1,338 onto the top of the table and then began placing the sacks into the briefcase.

Polcuch picked up the money and counted it. His hand darted beneath his jacket and he pulled a snub-nosed revolver from a shoulder holster to cover the startled Lew Doo. "Don't move," Polcuch ordered. "I'm an agent of the U.S. Treasury Department. You are under arrest." Slowly he backed to the window overlooking Clay Street and signalled to the agents below. Within a few seconds they came pounding up the stairs and into the room. But there was no fight in Lew Doo.

Lew Doo was charged with conspiracy to violate the narcotics laws of the United States. He pleaded not guilty, but he was convicted and sentenced to four years in prison. In Hong Kong, British police raided the room on Cameron Road and smashed the ring operating from the Crown Colony.

This was the end of the ordeal for Halvorsen, the young man who had brought himself to a halt on the edge of a chasm of crime. But it was a happy and prosperous ending because the U.S. Customs Bureau awarded him a check for $1,000 for his role in helping smash the smuggling ring.

The case of Truls Arild Halvorsen is only one of countless thousands of smuggling cases recorded in files which now are gathering dust in the archives of the Customs Bureau, the oldest agency in the Federal government.

The Bureau of Customs—or the Customs Service, as it is often called—is the nation's border guard. For more than 170 years it has had the primary responsibility for policing the foreign trade, collecting tariff duties on imports, and exposing conspiracies which would defraud the Treasury of the United States.

The Customs Service was organized hurriedly in the first days of the Republic, when the original Thirteen Colonies voluntarily surrendered certain rights to the Federal government in order to "form a more perfect Union." One of the most important of these rights was the collection of duties—for without this income the new-born government could not have existed.

The need for revenue was so great in the nation's beginning that Congress rushed through legislation authorizing a Customs Service even before the organization of the Treasury Department. And when Alexander Hamilton assumed his duties as the first Secretary of the Treasury, he found the month-old Customs Service already at work collecting revenues. The Service was incorporated into the Treasury Department as a division of the Secretary's office, and it continued as a division until 1927 when it was given the status of a bureau, directed by a commissioner appointed by the President.

Since the day in July, 1789, when George Washington submitted to the Senate the first list of Customs collectors, the nation's overseas trade has grown from a mere trickle to a multi-billion-dollar flood. The administration of the Bureau has become more complicated and its operations more diverse as the commercial intercourse between nations has grown.

In size, the Customs Bureau is one of the smaller Federal agencies, having approximately 8,500 employees. But being the senior service in the Federal government, its past is a mirror of the nation's history. It is a history tinged with violence and intrigue, because there has never been a time when its agents were not engaged in a running war with smugglers—from Jean Laffite and his band of cutthroats in the bayous of Louisiana to the criminals who direct today's multi-million-dollar traffic in contraband.

Because it deals with commerce and travel, the operations of Customs touch every man, woman and child and every item of merchandise entering this country—from the tourist returning from Zamboanga to the aardvark headed for a zoo.

Customs has been damned as a nuisance and a bumble-headed bureaucracy. It has been praised as one of the most efficient and necessary units in the Federal government. Despite its long history, few Americans know anything about Customs beyond the fact that they must submit to an irritating baggage examination by an inspector upon arriving home from abroad.

What is Customs? Why was it organized? What are its duties? And why is it necessary?

Customs is a slender, dark-haired expert sitting in a small room in New York appraising the value of a treasure in diamonds. It is a chemist in a laboratory checking the quality of a foreign import—and its dutiable value—and arriving at a decision which may mean life or death for an American business in a highly competitive market. It is an inspector at an airport or on a pier examining the luggage of passengers to be sure they have complied with the law.

Customs is a tall man with a wind-burned face lying in the mesquite above the Rio Grande, watching patiently for the smuggler of heroin or marijuana he knows is coming his way. It is a burly man lowering himself into the dark hold of a ship to check the cargo and to search for contraband. It is a man giving an expert appraisal of the antiquity of a tapestry or the authenticity of a painting to be certain an importer is not being defrauded. It is a man checking the contents of a mountain of parcels arriving from overseas.

Customs is a man explaining to a tourist what he can do to save time and avoid trouble in his travels. It is volumes of complex rulings by the courts and laws passed by Congress governing the huge import-export trade. It is a lawyer standing in a courtroom arguing that an import is subject to much higher duties than its importer claims.

In the long years past, Customs was James Madison standing in Congress and urging his fellows to adopt a tariff act quickly in order to save the government from financial ruin. It was a band of men slipping through the bayous in search of Jean Laffite and the mountain of loot he was smuggling into New Orleans.

Customs was a small army of men whose collection of duties symbolized an issue which threatened to touch off a civil war long before Abraham Lincoln entered the White House. More recently it was an angry maid exposing a distinguished judge and Hollywood stars caught in a tangled web of intrigue. It was, unfortunately, also a thief who rocked the country with a scandal, and weak-willed men who could not resist the temptation of an underworld bribe.

The Customs Service is and was a thing of many parts, involving the lives and fortunes of many people. And that is the reason for this story.

2
A TIME OF CRISIS

The problem of tariffs is one with which governments have contended from the beginning of recorded history.

The Old Testament mentions customs duties and indicates that in those ancient times a well-established system of duties existed.

In the early chapters of Ezra is to be found the story of Cyrus, a king of Persia, who permitted the captive Israelites to return to Jerusalem from Babylon in order to rebuild the city and their temples. But there were those who opposed the return of the Israelites. The scriptures say these opponents "weakened the hands of the people of Judah, and troubled them in building, and hired counsellors against them, to frustrate their purpose."

This dispute carried over into the reign of King Artaxerxes, who succeeded Cyrus. Those who opposed the Israelites returning to Jerusalem wrote the king a letter in which they said, "Be it known now unto the King, that, if this city is builded and the walls finished, they will not pay tribute, custom, or toll. . . ." But the king searched the records and found that there was precedent for imposing a tribute or a customs toll. He replied to the letter, "And I decreed, and search hath been made, and it is found that . . . there have been mighty kings also over Jerusalem, who have ruled over all the country beyond the river; and tribute, customs, and toll was paid unto them."

The New Testament indicates that Matthew was a collector of customs at the city of Galilee. It says that Jesus called Matthew from "the receipt of customs."

The first recorded history of customs being collected in England is found in the code of laws enacted by King Ethelred in 979 A.D. The law read, "Every small vessel arriving at Billingsgate shall pay to the tax gatherer one obolus; if of greater tonnage and mast rigged, one denarius. If a ship shall arrive and anchor there, four denarii shall be paid to the tax gatherer. Vessels laden with timber shall pay one log to the tax gatherer."

In the Magna Charta is found the following: "Cap. XXX. All Merchants, if they are not openly prohibited before, shall have safe and sure Conduct to depart out of England, to come into England, to tarry in and go through England, as well by land as by water, to sell and buy, without any manner of evil tolts, by the old and rightful customs, except in time of war. xxx"

The collection of customs on the North American continent was first made by the Dutch in 1651 when the governor ordered that all imports from foreign countries entering the harbor at New York should pay a duty. The method of collecting was later outlined in a document which reads as follows:

Instructions for Mr. Cornelius Van Ruyven, collector of the customes in ye City of New York, by order of Colonell Francis Lovelace,
governour, May 24, 1668.

You or your clerk are to be daily at ye Custome House from nyne
untill twelve at noone. There to receive ye customes both in and out,
as the Merchants shall come and enter, ye Merchant is to make foure
Bills and sign them with his hand, writing his name on them, and ye
same time, when you have signed ye Warrant, or one of ye Bills, you
are to demand ye Custome, either in kinde at 10 P Cent inwards or
double ye vallue of its first Cost in Holland, in Beaver. And likewise
outwards for Peltry you are to receive 10½ P Cent according to ye
value in Beaver, for Tobacco one half penny for Per pound which
is noe more than all Englishmen doe pay. xxx You to tell ye Merchante
you are not to give credit. xxx If they do not like your propositions,
you are not to pass their Bills. xxx

And Lastly pray lett ye Books be kept all in English and all Factoryes
and Papers, that when I have occasion to satisfy myself I may better
understand them.

When the city came under British rule in 1664, the system of
tariffs set up by the Dutch was continued. Almost one hundred
years before the Boston Tea Party and the beginning of the Revolution, there was an uprising in New York against the British collection of customs. Religion played a role in this rebellion, which
was touched off when England's Catholic King James II was succeeded by the Protestant William of Orange and his wife Mary.

When the news of King James' overthrow reached New York,
a Captain Jacob Leisler, who had lived in New York for about
thirty years and was a deacon in the Reformed Dutch Church, decided that he would not pay customs duties to a king's representative who was himself a Catholic. Leisler was in the business of importing liquors and other merchandise into New York. One of his
vessels came into the harbor on April 29, 1689, loaded with wine
from Europe. Leisler refused to pay the $100 customs duties. He
argued that the collector, named Plowman, was a Catholic and was
not qualified to receive the customs under the new Protestant re-
gime in Britain. Leisler's stand threw the city and military officials
into a dither. There was a hastily called meeting of the counsellors,
alderman and military officials in the city to discuss this development. The majority ruling was that the system of collecting duties

would continue as it had in the past until other orders were received from William of Orange.

Leisler would have no part of this ruling. He told the assembly he would not pay the tax and he stalked out of the meeting room to discover he was not alone in his opposition to the customs duties. Other merchants saw an opportunity in this situation and joined his side. The result was that Captain Leisler and his friends organized an uprising against Lieutenant Governor Nicholson.

Leisler reached such a position of power that he drove out those in charge of the Customs service and appointed his own man, Peter DeLansy, as a collector. The British finally hanged Captain Leisler for his role in this revolt and in April, 1696, appointed the Earl of Bellomont as Governor General over New York and New England.

The Earl was not a man to brook any nonsense such as the nonpayment of customs to the royal treasury. He restricted the Colonies' trade with New York and Albany and forbade the shipment of merchandise up the Hudson River unless duties were paid at New York.

The collectors appointed by the Earl of Bellomont had a rather difficult time of it. The merchants of New York were, to be charitable, unreliable when it came to the payment of customs duties. In fact, smuggling was a popular practice. In one instance a cargo of merchandise from the East Indies was ordered seized but the officers who went to make the seizure simply disappeared. Then it was learned that the sheriff himself was hiding the merchandise in his own home.

From the viewpoint of King George III's counsellors, the actions of the Americans in smuggling and otherwise evading the payment of the customs duties were no less than thievery from the treasury of Great Britain. Such nonsense had to be stopped. And so it was that, after Canada came under British control in 1763, the British adopted a tougher policy toward the Colonies. In 1764 the Parliament passed the Sugar Act, which called for the payment of duties on lumber, food stuffs, molasses and rum brought into the Colonies. This in itself was enough to enrage the American merchants, but then the Sugar Act was followed by the Stamp Act in the same year. This act required revenue stamps to be purchased on all imports. The receipts were to be used to help defer the cost

of British troops stationed in the Colonies. In short, the Americans
were to pay to have British troops quartered in their towns and
cities. When news of the passage of the Stamp Act reached New
York, more than 200 merchants gathered for a protest meeting at
Burn's Tavern. They signed an agreement not to import goods
from England.

Judge Robert R. Livingston wrote at the time: "England will
suffer more by it in one year than the Stamp Act, or any other,
could ever recompense. Merchants have resolved to send for no
more British manufactures, shopkeepers will buy none, gentlemen
will wear none; our own are encouraged, all pride in dress seems
to be laid aside, and he that does not appear in homespun, or at
least a turned coat, is looked upon with an evil eye."

The U.S. Customs Service came into being on July 31, 1789,
in a time of crisis. It was an organization put together by Congress
and President George Washington to save the struggling young central government from financial collapse through the collection of
duties on imports.

The formation of Customs thus became the first step to be
taken by the original thirteen states toward a practical, working
partnership after the adoption of the Constitution. For in agreeing
to a uniform tariff, to be collected by the central government
through its Customs Service, the states voluntarily gave up an
important state's right which each had guarded jealously—the right
to collect and retain its own customs duties.

For this reason, August 5, 1789, is an important though little-
known date in history. On this day Captain James Weeks sailed his
brigantine, *Persis,* into New York Harbor with a miscellaneous
cargo of merchandise from Leghorn, Italy. The cargo was assigned
to Mr. William Seton, who paid the Collector of Customs a total of
$774.71 in duties—the first payment of duties destined for the
Treasury of the United States.

Captain Weeks' payment was a modest one, but at least it was a
prop under the financially shaky young government. And for the
next 124 years—until the income tax amendment to the Constitution was adopted in 1913—the Federal government's primary
source of revenue was to be the money collected by Customs on
merchandise and materials brought into the United States from
abroad.

Until they were bound together by the Constitution, the thirteen states were not a nation. They had fought for more than six years for freedom from political, economic and military domination. They had struggled through incredible hardships, physical and financial. They had won their victory. But they were not a nation.

Throughout the struggle, they were linked together in a loose confederation in which each state was entirely independent of the others. The move toward confederation came on September 5, 1774, when state delegates gathered in Philadelphia to organize the congress known as the Continental Congress. Each state was represented by one delegate, and each delegate had one vote. Peyton Randolph of Virginia was elected president of the Congress—and it is to be noted that he was not referred to officially or unofficially as the President of the United States.

The members of this Congress hammered out the Declaration of Independence and signed it on July 4, 1776. But not until two years later were the Colonies joined together by a formal agreement, the Articles of Confederation and Perpetual Union Between the States. In these Articles the Colonies called themselves the United States of America, but they remained a union of independent states. Having gone to war to free themselves from a strong central government with an autocratic ruler, the Colonies distrusted centralized authority and each was jealous of its sovereignty.

The result was that the central government was reduced to the status of a pleader for money. It had no power to levy taxes directly. It could only appeal to the states to contribute to the expenses of the central government in proportion to the assessed value of their land. As a matter of fact, whenever the central government did ask the states for funds, as likely as not the states simply ignored the request.

In 1781, during the final months of the exhausting revolution and while the outcome still was in doubt, the central government was in need of $9 million for operating expenses. The Congress thought it possible to raise this amount by borrowing $4 million and then asking the states to contribute the additional $5 million. But the states responded to the urgent appeal with only $442,000. North and South Carolina, Georgia and Delaware contributed nothing. At times it seemed that if the British didn't defeat the Revolution, an empty treasury would.

During and after the American Revolution, the tariff situation was an unholy mess. Each state had its own tariff laws, with the exception of New Jersey, which had none. The states often set up tariff barriers against each other, sometimes for protection and sometimes for reprisal. The dickering amongst them was continual and the maneuvering for advantage fierce.

On one occasion, New York, Connecticut and New Jersey plunged into a three-way fight that to later generations might seem little more than hilarious comedy—but there was nothing comic about it at the time for those involved. It began when the New York legislature reached the conclusion that the Connecticut Yankees and the New Jerseyites were taking too many dollars out of New York City, and giving too little in return.

It was true that Connecticut merchants supplied most of New York's firewood, for a tidy profit. And the farmers of New Jersey were sending boatloads of chickens, eggs, vegetables and fruit across the river, selling them, and taking back dollars. The imports from Connecticut and New Jersey were running ahead of the exports to these two states by too great a margin—or so the gentlemen in the New York legislature figured. The legislature passed a tariff law which imposed a tax on every stick of Connecticut wood and each New Jersey egg, chicken, duck, goose and cabbage brought into the city. The chicken peddlers from New Jersey had to get clearance papers and pay taxes on each pullet or hen, each basket of eggs and each head of cabbage. Stovewood had to be measured and counted at the Customs House and taxes paid on the spot.

Naturally this state of affairs irked the New Jersey folk, whose legislature promptly looked around for a means of retaliation and, in so doing, spotted the City of New York's lighthouse standing on Sandy Hook. It was solemnly agreed by a majority that this lighthouse should not stand out there flashing an untaxed warning to ships headed for the New York Harbor. And so the legislature voted to place an $1,800-a-year tax on the lighthouse.

In Connecticut, the merchants were no less aroused than the farmers of New Jersey. It was agreed that a boycott of New York products was justified. Whereupon the merchants formed themselves into an association dedicated to the proposition that no loyal Connecticut merchant would either buy or sell anything in the City

of New York. Any member who violated the agreement was subject to a fine.

Again, the British in 1783 decided that only British vessels
would be permitted to handle cargoes in the West Indian trade.
This proclamation so enraged New Yorkers that they retaliated by
laying a double duty on all cargoes arriving in British vessels. New
Hampshire, Rhode Island and Massachusetts were equally in-
censed—and declared that no cargoes could leave their harbors if
carried in a British ship.

But these tremors of righteous outrage did not stir the Connecticut Yankees. They saw the situation as holding the promise of fat
profits. The ships of Great Britain were invited to use Connecticut
ports, duty free. And then Connecticut further enraged its neighbors by imposing a tariff on goods coming into the state from
Massachusetts.

Virginia and Maryland also were having their troubles. Virginia
owned the lighthouses on both sides of the Chesapeake Bay entrance and demanded fees from every vessel entering the bay.
Maryland, on the other hand, claimed the entire width of the Po-
tomac River, citing old land charters to the effect that even if a
vessel were tied to the Virginia shore, it still was in Maryland
waters.

Connecticut, on the basis of a royal charter of 1662, laid claim
to the Wyoming Valley, which Pennsylvania regarded as her own.
The two states were on the verge of open war before cool heads
prevailed and Pennsylvania's claim was recognized as the more
valid.

With such discord between the states, even in time of war, the
winning of the Revolution and the survival of the Union approached
the miraculous.

Merchants in Philadelphia and then in Boston decided to follow
the lead of the New York merchants. Orders went out to English
shippers not to ship more goods to America as long as the Stamp
Act was in effect. In this tempest the seeds of revolution were
broadcast, and it was a tempest that would not subside until the
Colonies had won their freedom from Great Britain.

Despite the jealousies and the conflicts between the Colonies
during and after the war, the people realized that only in unity
could there be any real hope for survival. This realization moved

leaders among the thirteen states to call the Constitutional Convention of 1787. And here it was they hammered out the Constitution which was to become the foundation for the United States of America and a blueprint for freedom.

The Convention met in New York City on May 14, 1787. The delegates chose George Washington as presiding officer of the Convention. The document produced at this convention by no means won the unanimous approval of the representatives from the various states. There were disagreements and reservations to the Constitution. A total of sixty-five qualified delegates were certified by the states to attend the Convention but ten of these did not attend. When the document was completed there were only thirty-nine who actually signed on September 17, 1787. Sixteen failed to sign, and some of those who did sign had reservations. This document was sent by George Washington to Congress, and Congress sent it to the various legislatures for their consideration.

The greatest fear at the time was that a central government would become too powerful. Having thrown off the yoke of one oppressive government, the Colonies wanted no part of another.

Washington reflected these fears when he sent the newly drafted Constitution to Congress. He was sensitive to the fact that the states would have to surrender some rights if they hoped to have an effective central government. In a letter to the president of the Congress, dated September 17, 1787, he said in part:

... It is obviously impractical in the Federal government of these States to secure all rights of independent sovereignty to each, and yet provide for the interest and safety of all. Individuals entering into society must give up a share of liberty to preserve the rest. ...

The Constitution went into effect on March 4, 1789, and Congress acted with remarkable swiftness on measures which would insure the financial stability of the young government. On April 8, 1789, James Madison arose in the House of Representatives and said:

I take the liberty, Mr. Chairman, at this early state of the business, to introduce to the committee a subject which appears to me to be of the greatest magnitude; a subject, sir, that requires our first attention, and our united exertions . . .

The deficiency in our treasury has been too notorious to make it necessary for me to animadvert upon that subject. Let us content ourselves with endeavoring to remedy the evil. To do this a national revenue must be obtained; but the system must be such a one, that, while it secures the object of revenue, it shall not be oppressive to our constitutents. Happy it is for us that such a system is within our powers; for I apprehend that both these objects may be obtained from an impost on objects imported to the United States.

After some discussion Madison proposed a resolution to impose a flat fixed duty on rum, liquors, wines, molasses, tea, pepper, sugar, coffee and cocoa, with a percentage tax on all other imported articles, the tax to be based on the value of the imports at their time and place of importation. The resolution also recommended a tonnage tax on all vessels doing business at American ports.

Madison's resolution touched off a fight between those who favored free trade and those who favored heavy duties to protect the interests of their particular region. There were those who wanted a heavy tonnage tax on vessels so that the American shippers would be given an advantage over foreign vessels. There were those who wanted to protect industries in their own states from the European competition. Congressmen from the agricultural states leaned heavily toward free trade.

Thomas Fitzsimons of Pennsylvania came forward with an amendment to the Madison resolution in which he asked that the duties be placed not only on the imports suggested by Madison but also on beer, ale, porter, beef, pork, butter, candles, cheese, soap, cider, boots, steel, cables, cordage, twine, malt, nails, spikes, tacks, salt, tobacco, snuff, blank books, writing, printing and wrapping paper, pasteboard and cabinet ware, buttons, saddles, gloves, hats, millinery, castings of iron, leather, shoes, slippers, coaches, chariots, carriages, nutmeg, cinnamon, cloves, raisins, figs, currants, and almonds.

Madison argued that his proposal was only a temporary one and that as far as possible the trade should be free. He said, "If my general principle is a good one, the term commerce ought to be free, and labor and industry left at large to find its proper object, the only thing which remains will be to discover the exceptions which did not come within the rule that I have laid down. . . ."

It was Madison's belief that the cheapness of land in the United

States, compared with the cost of land in other nations, gave this country a great advantage in agricultural trade. He said that so far as manufacturing was concerned, "Other countries may and do rival us." But then he added, "We may be said to have a monopoly in agriculture; the possession of the soil, and the lowness of its price, give us as much a monopoly in this case, as any other nation or other parts of the world have in the monopoly in any article whatever; but with this advantage to us, that it cannot be shared nor injured by rivalship."

Nevertheless, while favoring free trade, Madison conceded that if America did leave her ports entirely free then the country would suffer. He said, "If America was to leave her ports perfectly free, and make no discrimination between vessels owned by her citizens and those owned by foreigners, while other nations make this discrimination, it is obvious that such policy would go to exclude American shipping altogether from foreign ports, and she would be materially affected in one of the most important interests."

Despite sharp and often bitter differences, the young Congress was aware that sectional interests were secondary to the absolute necessity for action in collecting revenue. Within a short time it had put together the first Tariff Act. It was titled "An Act for laying a duty on goods, wares and merchandise imported into the United States." And on July 4, the thirteenth anniversary of the signing of the Declaration of Independence, President Washington signed into law the act which was the second to be passed by the Congress.

Then Congress quickly set up the machinery for the collection of the tariff. This was done in the Fifth Act, "To regulate the collection of the duties. . . ." The bill was sent to President Washington for his signature on July 31, which fell on Friday. On the following Monday the President sent to the Senate a list of about one hundred appointments to Customs offices. The Senate advised and consented to about half this list but on the following day gave the President an unexpected jolt. The Senate, without warning, refused to consent to the appointment of Colonel Benjamin Fishbourn to be Naval Officer (auditor) at the Port of Savannah. Fishbourn had served with distinction in Washington's command during the Revolution and apparently had a spotless reputation in civilian life.

Washington did not make a fight over Fishbourn's rejection even though the Senate action no doubt seemed to him to be a petty and totally unwarranted assertion of veto power. He did send a message to the Senate which called to mind later clashes between Chief Executives and Congress, pointing out that at least the Senate might have done him the courtesy of inquiring into his reasons for appointing Fishbourn.

Perhaps under different circumstances Washington would not have been so mild in his reaction to the Senate veto. But the need to establish an organization for collecting revenue was imperative, and Washington perhaps felt this was no time for a fight over executive and legislative prerogatives. The most pressing need was unity in the government.

And so was the Customs Service created to help bring financial stability to the nation at a critical time. Despite all the trials and difficulties, the Customs Service collected more than $2 million for the Treasury in its first year of operation.

3

A PRESIDENT IS BAMBOOZLED

There was little cause for gaiety in any part of the nation in the summer of 1808. Gloom hung over the country and particularly over Washington, where even the new capitol building had not been completed and the problems of getting the young government firmly established sometimes seemed insurmountable.

The reason for the gloom was the worsening relations between the United States and Great Britain and the threat of American involvement in the brawling affairs of Europe, where the British were at war with the French.

In a desperate move to avoid being drawn into the conflict, President Thomas Jefferson had called the previous year for an embargo on all overseas shipping. He felt such drastic action necessary because British warships had been seizing American vessels headed for France. Even worse, the British had been forcing American sailors from the ships on the high seas and impressing them into British naval service by the hundreds.

Under these circumstances, Jefferson decided it would be better to withdraw American shipping from the seas and deny American supplies to the combatants, rather than risk plunging the nation into another war. His proposed embargo had been fought over bitterly in Congress. But in December, 1807, the Embargo Act had been passed and shipping had come to a halt. Even trade with Canada would be stopped with the enforcement of a land embargo—except for the commerce carried on by smugglers defying Federal Customs officers.

Now, seven months after the start of the embargo, the nation was in deep trouble. New England was practically paralyzed. Ships which had engaged so busily in world commerce a few months earlier stood rotting at the wharves. The number of unemployed was alarming. Businessmen who depended on overseas trade were going bankrupt. There was scarcely anyone in the country who did not feel the depressing effects of the embargo. The nation's economy had sunk to its lowest point since the Revolution.

President Wilson was to say of this period: "The States themselves suffered from the Act more than the nations whose trade they struck at. America's own trade was ruined."

Onto this gloomy stage in mid-July, 1808, strode the so-called Chinese mandarin, Punqua Wingchong, and before two months had passed this Oriental fraud had half the country hooting with derisive laughter and the other half red-faced with rage.

Punqua Wingchong. It's a name to remember in American history because he helped to bamboozle a President of the United States in one of the gamiest confidence games ever pulled against a trusting Chief Executive. But he was only the puppet; the man who pulled the strings behind the scenery was John Jacob Astor, the merchant prince.

The hoax began to unfold in June, 1808, when Astor and the Boston firm of J. & T. H. Perkins applied to the government for permission to send a ship to Canton to bring back certain property allegedly owned by the applicants. The government refused to lift the embargo for such a venture and as a matter of policy rejected the application.

The rejection would have discouraged the average merchant, but John Jacob Astor did not build his fortune by being an average man. Soon after the application was refused, Senator Samuel L. Mitchill of New York was told a disturbing story. An anonymous informant advised him that a distinguished Chinese mandarin, who divided his time between New York City and Nantucket, was the unfortunate victim of the shipping embargo. It was said that the mandarin, Punqua Wingchong, had made the long and arduous voyage from Canton to collect several large debts owing to his grandfather's estate. Then he had been caught by the embargo and had been unable to return to his homeland to participate in mourning rites for his venerable grandfather, who had died suddenly.

It was suggested to Mitchill that the situation was one which quite possibly could create ill feeling between the governments of the United States and China if Wingchong chose to blame the Jefferson administration for the predicament he found himself in, being a virtual prisoner in a foreign land. Wingchong was reputed to have considerable influence among the government class of China, and this influence could be used against American traders in the future if he were not permitted to return home.

The journals of the time were not clear as to whether the Senator ever met Wingchong face to face. In all likelihood he did not. But he was moved to such sympathy by the pictured plight of the hapless mandarin that he penned a personal appeal asking President Jefferson to intervene. The Senator had a distinguished background in science and literature and was a professor of natural history in the College of Physicians and Surgeons in New York City. It was later to be said that Senator Mitchill was "strangely deficient in that useful commodity called common sense," but his motives seemed sincere enough when he wrote to the President on July 12, saying:

Sir:

Punqua Wingchong, a Chinese merchant, will be the bearer of this note of introduction. He came to New York about nine months ago, on business of a commercial nature, and has resided during that time, part time, partly here and partly in Nantucket. Having completed the

object of his visit to the United States, he is desirous of returning to
Canton, where the affairs of his family, and particularly funeral ob-
sequies of his grandfather, require his solemn attention.

This stranger is represented to me as a man of respectability and
good standing in his country; and is consequently entitled to a corre-
sponding regard and treatment in ours.

The chief object of his visit to Washington is to solicit the means
of departure, in some way or other to China, but he feels at the same
time a strong desire to see the chief executive officer of the United
States. He will be accompanied by Mr. Palmer, an inhabitant of New
York, who will aid him in stating his request and explaining his meaning. This gentleman, in addition to many other valuable qualities,
possesses admirable skill in acquiring languages; and he is perhaps
already master of more living tongues than any person among us—
as an evidence of which he has already made considerable progress
in China.

While I recommend these two persons to the notice of the President I beg leave to accompany the recommendation, with the highest
expression of my high and respectful consideration.

Sam'l L. Mitchill.

Armed with the Mitchill letter and dressed in the finest of silks
and brocades, Punqua Wingchong journeyed to Washington and
no doubt created a stir of excitement throughout the city, where
visitors from the Orient were not a common sight. Unfortunately,
or perhaps otherwise, Wingchong and his companion, Mr. Palmer,
found they could not deliver the letter to the President in person.
Mr. Jefferson had left the city for a rest at Monticello.

The Mitchill letter was then forwarded to Monticello along with
a note signed by Punqua Wingchong "praying permission to depart" from the United States with his retinue and his belongings
in a vessel of his own choosing.

President Jefferson was moved by Wingchong's appeal. Not only
did he feel sympathy, but he felt the situation presented an opportunity to establish better relations between his government and
the rulers of China, which was becoming an increasingly important customer in foreign commerce. On July 25, the President
wrote to Secretary of the Treasury Albert Gallatin saying:

Dear Sir:

. . . Punqua Wingchong, the Chinese Mandarin, has, I believe, his
headquarters at New York, and therefore his case is probably known

to you. He came to Washington just as I had left it and therefore wrote to me praying permission to depart for his own country with his property in a vessel to be engaged by himself. . . . I consider it as a case of national comity, and coming within the views of the first section of the first Embargo Act. The departure of this individual with good disposition may be the means of our making our nation known advantageously as a source of power in China to which it is otherwise difficult to convey information. It may be a sensible advantage to our merchants in that country. I cannot therefore but consider that a chance of obtaining a permanent national good should outweigh the effect of a single case taken out of the great field of the embargo. The case too is so singular that it can lead to no embarrassment as a precedent. . . .

(signed) Th. Jefferson.

Gallatin detected an odor of intrigue in the situation because Wingchong requested permission to make the trip to China in the *Beaver*, a "full-bottomed ship of 427 tons with a capacity for 1,100 tons of cargo," and the *Beaver* had been constructed especially for John Jacob Astor. Gallatin was well aware of the fact that scarcely a month had passed since Astor had been denied permission for a Canton voyage. But Jefferson had issued his instructions and Gallatin was a loyal lieutenant.

On August 3, 1808, Gallatin wrote to David Gelston, Collector of Customs in New York City, ordering him to make an exception and lift the embargo. His letter said in part:

Sir,

Punqua Wingchong, a respectable Chinese, who had with the leave of his government come to the United States for the purpose of collecting debts due to his father's estate, having obtained the special permission of the President of the United States to engage a vessel to carry himself together with his attendants and property to his native country, and having made arrangements for that purpose with the owner of the ship *Beaver* of 427 tons or thereabouts; you would be pleased to permit that vessel to depart for Canton on the following terms and instructions. . . .

The conditions, previously outlined by Jefferson, were that the vessel could sail with equipment and provisions for crew and passengers. Punqua Wingchong was to be permitted to be accompanied by his "attendants" along with their baggage and personal effects and also about $45,000 . . . "either in specie or in furs, cochineal, ginsang, or any other specie of merchandise of his choice."

After giving these instructions to Gelston, Gallatin wrote a cautious letter to Jefferson saying that he had carried out his orders and Wingchong "has engaged Astor's vessel to which we had on general grounds refused permission." Then he added: "Had I had any discretion as to the application itself I would have hesitated; for I apprehend that there is some speculation at bottom; and every deviation from general rules is considered a favoritism and excites dissatisfaction."

He also warned Jefferson that to lift the embargo for one vessel would open the way for others to make direct appeals to the President for special treatment. Jefferson did not agree with his Secretary. He insisted that important diplomatic and commercial benefits might accrue from the courtesies shown Wingchong and they were "likely to bring lasting advantage to our merchants."

Gallatin was right. The uproar came when Collector Gelston authorized the voyage and workmen began swarming over the *Beaver* to prepare her for the long sea voyage. With other vessels standing idle and deserted, such a burst of activity could hardly be kept secret along the waterfront. In all the United States, this lone ship was the only one being prepared for a voyage.

The first protest came from a group of Philadelphia merchants who wrote to Secretary Gallatin on August 10 suggesting that "avarice and perjury" were being used to obtain the special dispensation for the voyage of the *Beaver*. As for Punqua Wingchong, the merchants said they were satisfied he was an impostor "and an insignificant instrument in the hands of others." He was unknown to Philadelphia traders who had been stationed in Canton as agents for years. At best he was only a petty shopkeeper without credit and not a wealthy member of the mandarin class, they insisted. It was pointed out to the President that the mandarins of China never left their own country.

New York newspapers, getting wind of the *Beaver*'s voyage, described Wingchong as "a Chinaman picked up in the port," "a common Chinese dock loafer," "a Lascar sailor," and even as "an Indian who had been dressed up in Astor's China silks and coached to play his role in the affair."

The New York *Commercial Advertiser* on August 13 said in a page-one story:

A first rate merchants' ship, which will be navigated by about 30 seamen, is preparing for sea, and is expected to proceed on a voyage to Canton, in a few days, under special permission from the President of the United States.

The ostensible object of this voyage is to carry home a person who is said to be a Mandarin of China.

It is, however, well known that the person for whom permission has been obtained, is no Mandarin; is not even a licensed or security merchant;—that his departure from China was contrary to the laws of that country; that if he arrives in China he will be put on shore privately, and that the obscurity of his condition in life affords him the only chance he has of avoiding punishment.

It is also believed that the owner of the ship would not accept all the property of all the Chinese in this country as a compensation for the voyage, and it is known that he has offered to contract for bringing home goods or freight. . . .

Neither Gallatin nor the President retreated before this barrage. Gallatin wrote the Philadelphia merchants that their plea had come too late and besides he had no authority to detain the *Beaver*. He delayed his reply until September 17—the same day on which the *Beaver* sailed.

Six days later, Jefferson admitted that he had no means of judging whether the charges by the Philadelphia merchants were true or false. He said he acted as he did because of "the application having come to me grounded on his character as a settled fact." He added "nor are the jeers of the Federalists any proof of the contrary." Then he made the rather lame statement that if the *Beaver* had not yet sailed perhaps "she should be detained till the facts . . . are inquired into."

But the *Beaver* was gone. She was to return a year later with a cargo of teas, silks, and other valuable merchandise which allegedly brought Astor a net profit of $200,000.

The December embargo on shipping had been followed in March by the Land Embargo, which became effective just before Lake Champlain was free of ice and open for normal navigation. The Land Embargo came as a shock for the people of northern and northeastern Vermont. Over the years they had developed a brisk trade with Canada, shipping timber, potash, coal ashes, and other exports into Canada in return for Canadian merchandise. The embargo had the effect of shutting off this lucrative trade for the Vermonters.

The Act was not popular with the citizens or with most Customs officials along the border and as a result there was lax enforcement. Smuggling operations reached such proportions that Customs Collector Jabez Penniman wrote to Secretary of the Treasury Gallatin, complaining that he could not enforce the law unless the Federal government supplied troops.

Penniman's communication spread alarm in Washington. Gallatin personally carried the letter to the White House to discuss emergency steps with the President. Jefferson called in Senator Robinson and Congressman Witherell of Vermont to obtain their advice. The Vermonters told him that the smuggling could not last for long, probably no longer than early May. Then the Richelieu river would subside from its spring flood stage and would not be navigable for the big rafts used to carry smuggled timber and other products.

Despite the assurances from Robinson and Witherell, Jefferson was convinced that strong Federal action had to be taken immediately, to set a precedent if for no other reason. The President directed Gallatin to authorize Collector Penniman to equip and arm "such vessels as might be necessary" to put down the smuggling. Penniman also was authorized to engage crews for these vessels "voluntarily, by force of arms, or otherwise, to enforce the law." Then if further aid were necessary, the Secretary of State was to authorize the United States Marshal to form a posse to "aid in supressing the insurrection or combination."

These measures would seem sufficient to discourage any normal smuggler. But, apparently caught up in the enthusiasm of stamping out the evasion of the Embargo and the payment of Customs duties, the President went even further. He declared that in case the armed vessels and the posses should not be able to do the job, then the Secretary of War was to move Federal armed forces to the scene. The Secretary himself was asked to go to Vermont "and lend the aid of his counsel and authority." Also the aroused President informed Secretary Gallatin that he was going to have two gunboats built at Skenesborough (Whitehall), New York, to halt the flow of illegal traffic between Vermont and northern New York and Canada.

Many Vermonters were surprised and indignant at the President's use of the word "insurrection" to describe the situation. But in May, 1808, the good citizens of Vermont (and those not so good) were thrown into further uproar by a Presidential proclamation which appeared without warning in *Spooner's Vermont Journal*. It said information had been received by the White House that "sundry persons are combined or are combining and confederating together on Lake Champlain and the country thereto adjacent, for the purpose of forming insurrections against the authority of the laws of the United States, for opposing the same and obstructing their execution." The President sternly warned against any person engaging directly or indirectly "in any insurrection" and he ordered "such insurgents and all concerned in such combinations, instantly and without delay to disperse themselves and retire peaceably to their respective abodes."

The citizens of St. Albans for some reason must have felt that the President was aiming his shafts at them. At any rate, a town meeting was held in St. Albans at which it was "positively and unequivocally" the consensus that the conduct of the citizens of the district had never given President Jefferson cause to issue such a proclamation. It was the sense of the assembly that the President's proclamation "must have been issued in consequence of erroneous and unfounded representations, made and transmitted to the executive department of the United States by some evil minded person or persons." Then the citizens let their personal sympathies leak into the matter when they added that even if individuals "finding themselves and their families on the verge of ruin and wretchedness" had tried successfully to evade the embargo, nevertheless this did not justify the President in proclaiming to the world that the district was guilty of insurrection and rebellion.

People living along the Canadian border, whose livelihood depended on the trade with Canada, did not regard this trade as being the evil which Jefferson declared it to be. For them it was a matter of economic survival. Soon after the Land Embargo became a law, smuggling rings had begun operations along the border. Dress goods and other merchandise were carried to the border on the Canadian side, where it was picked up by men and transported through the woods into the United States. The contraband was hidden until such time as it could be taken by wagons or boats to the merchandising centers.

It was openly rumored that the merchants in Troy and Albany were hiring gangs to bring foreign goods into the country in this fashion. Some Customs officers tried to stop the traffic, though most were in sympathy with the smugglers. In one case a Customs officer leaped aboard a smuggling craft to seize the cargo and arrest the crew. He was carried across the boundary line, and then dumped unceremoniously overboard in water which, fortunately, reached only to his chin.

One method of getting Vermont goods across the border into Canada was this: dozens of wagons or sleds would be loaded with barrels of pork, flour, and other commodities. They would be driven to a hillside point on the American side of the border. A hut would be built in such a way that, when a stone was kicked from the foundation, the hut would collapse, the floor would tilt and the contents would roll down the slope of the hill into Canada, where men were waiting to receive it. Who was guilty of smuggling if barrels of merchandise, of their own momentum, suddenly rolled across the border into Canada?

Many Vermonters, however, applauded the action of the President and supported Customs Collector Penniman in his efforts to halt the illegal trade across the border. A group of citizens in Franklin County publicly applauded the action of the President and the Collector. They said that the lumber and potash merchants were determined to carry on their "nefarious schemes" of smuggling by armed force if necessary and that threats had been made to kill the Collector if he attempted to enforce the laws. There were hints also of a citizens' agreement for an uprising if any troops should kill anyone in the process of law enforcement.

Soldiers were stationed along the border at Windmill Point on the western shore of Alburg under the command of Major Charles K. Williams, who later was to become Governor of Vermont. The Customs officers themselves had a twelve-oared cutter called *The Fly,* which they used near the outlet of the lake to intercept smuggling operations.

One of the most famous of the boats used by the smugglers was known throughout the area as the *Black Snake*. This boat was originally built for ferry service between Charlotte and Essex, New York. It was 40 feet long, 17 feet wide, and had seven oars on each side in addition to a sail. After being smeared with tar, the boat was almost invisible at night. It was said to have a capacity of 100 barrels of ashes, and for a single run across the border the owners received $5,000 to $6,000.

The *Black Snake* would sneak into St. Albans Bay at night, take on a cargo of potash, and then slip through various creeks and inlets into Missisquoi Bay, across Cook's Bay, and into Canada at a point about one mile north of Alburg Springs.

Customs officers tried without success for months to halt the operations of the *Black Snake*. At last, in August, 1808, government officials detailed Lt. Daniel Farrington, Sgt. David D. Johnson, and twelve infantry privates to board the Customs boat, *The Fly*. Their orders were to pursue the *Black Snake* until its capture.

On the night of August 2, the *Black Snake* moved into the Onion River to take on a cargo of potash. The commander of the craft was Truman Mudgett of Highgate, a burly, thick-chested man whose defiance of the Customs officers had made his craft famous.

Mudgett knew that *The Fly* was in the area seeking his hiding place, and throughout the night he and his crew oiled and tested their rifles at their camp site on the bank of the river. They also test-fired their small artillery piece, a gun 8 feet long with a bore of 1¼ inches which fired fifteen 16-ounce slugs of lead. They had long poles for fending off a boarding party, 3-foot-long clubs, and baskets filled with stones the size of a man's fist.

The poles were to be used first to prevent anyone boarding the *Black Snake*. If this did not succeed, then the crew were to use the clubs and stones. As a last resort, they were to defend themselves with the guns.

At daybreak on August 3, a lookout came racing to the camp to warn the smugglers that *The Fly* was moving up the Onion River. Within a few minutes the revenue cutter came into view and closed on the *Black Snake*.

Mudgett shouted at Lieutenant Farrington: "I'll blow the first man through who lays his hand on the *Snake!*"

Farrington coolly ignored the warning. He leaped from *The Fly*

onto the *Black Snake* and ordered Sergeant Johnson to come
aboard with six men and commandeer the outlaw craft.

"You'll never get out of this river alive," shouted Mudgett as
he turned and ran back into the woods to rejoin his men.

Farrington sent four soldiers ashore to search for the crew of
the *Black Snake* and then he returned to the helm of the cutter
and started downstream with his prize. They had gone about half
a mile when the smugglers opened fire from behind an embank-
ment above the river. Farrington ordered Pvt. Elias Drake to take
the helm of the cutter, but as Drake reached for the helm a bullet
tore through his head and killed him instantly.

As gunfire raked the cutter, Farrington ordered his men to
lie flat in the boat. He grabbed an oar and maneuvered the craft
ashore below the smugglers' hiding place. Then he and his men
leaped ashore and started to move against the smugglers.

They had advanced only a few yards when the attackers fired
the blunderbuss artillery piece. Two men fell dead under the hail
of lead, and Farrington was badly wounded. Sergeant Johnson
rallied the men and succeeded in capturing all but two of the *Black
Snake's* crew. They were lodged in jail at Burlington, and later
the two smugglers who escaped were rounded up.

Cyrus B. Dean, one of the smugglers, was convicted of murder
and sentenced to be hanged. A crowd of ten thousand gathered
in Burlington to witness the execution, and some historians say
that Dean was the first man to die of capital punishment in Vermont. Others of the gang, including Mudgett, were convicted of
manslaughter and sentenced to prison.

The smuggling did not stop when the United States went to
war with Great Britain in 1812. The British army in Canada was
willing to pay high prices for cattle and other provisions at that
time. The Customs officers were almost helpless in trying to halt
the traffic across the border. Huge herds of fat oxen and cattle
were driven through the woods to the border and turned over to
Canadians. The militia were called out to halt the traffic in cattle,
but even the militia were unable to man all the crossing points
along the border.

Customs officers seized cattle, horses, provisions of all kinds,
merchandise, furs, and other articles from the smugglers. It also
was found that some Vermonters were making contracts with the

British to supply them with masts and spars for their naval vessels. And it was whispered that a prominent Vermont businessman was the backer of a smuggling gang which was selling materials to the British navy. There were gun battles between Customs men and the smugglers.

The War of 1812 had been underway for two years when Sir George Prevost, Governor General of Canada, wrote to Lord Bathurst in the British Foreign Office reporting that "two-thirds of the army in Canada are at this moment eating beef provided by American contractors, drawn principally from the States of Vermont and New York."

Secretary of War Armstrong was informed by one of his generals that the only way that intercourse with the enemy could be halted was to line the border with troops—which obviously was impossible. The General reported: "Like herds of buffaloes they pressed through the forest, making paths for themselves. Were it not for these supplies, the British forces in Canada would soon be suffering from famine, or their government be subjected to enormous expense for their maintenance."

The young Customs Service now had fought gun battles on land and "at sea" in an effort to enforce the law. This was a fight that still would be going on a century and a half later.

4

THE PIRATES OF NEW ORLEANS

On November 24, 1813, most citizens of New Orleans were chuckling over a new proclamation, bearing the signature of Gov. W. C. C. Claiborne, which had been posted on bulletin boards throughout the city. They were not so much amused because the Governor had accused a pirate of attacking a U.S. Customs officer (although this was amusing enough to many), but because Claiborne actually expected someone to take seriously his offer of a $500 reward for the capture of the pirate Jean Laffite.

Invade the pirate hideout in the swamps and capture Jean Laffite—or even his brother Pierre—for a mere $500? And Claiborne was naive if he thought that most of Louisiana's politicians and merchants had any desire to halt the smuggling of pirated merchandise while a war was being fought against Great Britain. Any kind of merchandise was hard to obtain.

Two days after the posting of the proclamation, a wave of raucous laughter sounded in the coffee houses, taverns and drawing rooms of New Orleans. The laughter exploded over a proclamation posted throughout the city which was a parody of the Claiborne document. It offered a reward of $1,500 for the arrest of Governor Claiborne and his delivery to the pirate hideout at Grande Terre in the bayou country south of New Orleans. The proclamation was signed by Jean Laffite.

Laffite's arrogance was no laughing matter to government officials in Louisiana and Washington. Not only were the pirates openly defying Federal and state authority, but a legitimate merchant had little chance to compete against those who purchased their goods at the pirates' auctions. The auctions were held regularly on islands in the swamps near New Orleans. Hundreds of thousands of dollars' worth of merchandise—captured on the high seas—could be bought cheaply and with no payment of Customs duties.

The enemies of the Laffites and their cutthroat crew were in the minority. Everyone knew—including Claiborne—that a majority of the people were sympathetic to the Laffites. The general view was that the pirates actually were performing a patriotic service when they attacked ships of the enemy countries, England and Spain, and then made their booty available to Louisiana citizens at ridiculously reduced prices.

Before Claiborne issued his proclamation, the general attitude of the citizenry was fairly summed up in a letter received by the *Louisiana Gazette* and signed "The Agent of the Freebooters." There had been a complaint against piracy and smuggling in the newspaper, and the freebooter (perhaps it was Jean Laffite) wrote a reply saying:

Gentlemen:

Your paper of Wednesday contained a letter written by some idiot
... (who) makes a great outcry against a few honest fellows of us,
who are using extraordinary exertions to punish the common enemy,
the British and their allies, the Spaniards.... Does he wish to discourage our profession and put an end to trade altogether? ...

Cannot the booby perceive that without us there would not be a
bale of goods at market; and does he not see, by the open manner
in which our business is done, that the government of the United States
has no objection either to the fitting out of our prizes and the sale of
their cargoes, without troubling ourselves about the payment of duties;
which I assure you we would find extremely inconvenient when we
sell so low for real cash in these hard times. ...

The legislature paid little attention to Governor Claiborne's
appeals for help in suppressing piracy and smuggling because too
many of its members were profiting from the operations of the
smugglers or were close friends of Jean and Pierre Laffite.

Honest merchants, competing at great disadvantage against those
who bought their goods from the pirates' stores, were the first to
raise a clamor for Claiborne to do something to halt the smuggling.
As a result of these demands, Customs Officer Walker Gilbert in-
vaded the pirate country with a company of armed men. As they
moved through the marshes south of New Orleans, they encountered Laffite convoying a shipload of contraband goods toward
New Orleans. Gilbert and his men attacked the pirates and there
was a brief, savage skirmish. Laffite and his group fled from the
ship, leaving Gilbert in possession. But before Gilbert could re-
organize his forces the pirates counterattacked. One of Gilbert's
men was badly wounded. The Federal officers were driven off.
The pirates took over the ship and resumed their journey to New
Orleans to sell their booty. It was this episode which caused
Claiborne to issue his proclamation that stirred so much amusement.

Piracy and smuggling, after the turn of the century, had become
profitable for two prime reasons. The first of these was the worsening relations between the United States and Great Britain, which
brought about the embargo on shipping in 1807 and later the War
of 1812. Any kind of merchandise was hard to come by and could
be sold for a handsome profit. The second reason was the U.S.
government's efforts to outlaw the traffic in slaves.

With the passage of the embargo on slave trade in 1808, the price of Negro slaves in the United States skyrocketed. Slaves could be bought in Cuba for about $300 each and sold for three or four times that amount on the illegal markets in the United States. But then the pirates found it more profitable simply to by-pass Cuba and waylay the slave ships at sea. They found a ready market for the slaves in the lower Mississippi Valley, where huge cotton and sugar plantations were being developed and where plantation owners were willing to bid against each other for this cheap labor.

The pirates found Barataria Bay near New Orleans an ideal place from which to operate. In this maze of canals, marshes, bayous and meandering waterways at the mouth of the Mississippi were many hiding places. In addition, the location furnished easy access to the markets of New Orleans.

The Baratarians had a loose organization headed by an Italian named Gamby. The outlaws were forever quarrelling among themselves and Gamby was not strong enough to control them, an internal weakness which was more serious for the pirates than the opposition of Governor Claiborne.

At this time (1810) Jean and Pierre Laffite were living in New Orleans with their younger brother, Antoine, whose name was never to figure in any of their piratical exploits of later years. The elder brothers, all reports agree, were striking-looking men with great personal charm and wit.

Pierre was of medium height, well-built, and handsome, although an illness had affected the muscles in the left side of his face and one of his eyes was slightly crossed. Jean stood 6 feet 2 inches tall, had blue eyes, and black hair. Like his brother, he was shrewd and fearless.

The brothers operated a blacksmith shop in the very heart of the city on St. Philips Street, not far from Bourbon Street. Even on the sultriest, hottest days of summer they kept the bellows blowing on the red-hot coals of the smithy fire. The anvil rang with the blows of their hammers beating lengths of iron into light, strong chains—chains to which slaves would be manacled before being brought to the auctions in the city.

Almost always there were groups of Baratarians lounging in the smithy, rough men with cutlasses at their waists and pistols stuck into their belts. They advised the Laffites on how they wished the chains to be made. And they also talked of their raids on English and Spanish ships, the booty they had brought to their hiding places in the swamps, and the wild parties they had after seizing a ship's stores of rum, wines and liquors.

For years, the Laffites acted as the "fences" for the pirates, handling slaves as well as other merchandise. It can only be assumed they listened to the tales of adventure, excitement and stolen riches—and became envious of the wealth acquired with such ease by men who were not as intelligent as they. At any rate, Jean Laffite left the smithy regularly to make trips to the pirates' hideout at Barataria, where he studied their operation.

After a time, Jean won the confidence of the ruffians to such a degree that he was invited to become their leader—despite the mumbling of Gamby. But this gentleman proved to be no problem whatever. He abdicated without a fight after he saw Laffite coldly shoot down one man who questioned his authority.

Laffite had exceptional executive abilities, along with a bold courage. Under his command the pirates of Barataria reached new heights in prosperity and arrogance. Men flocked from New Orleans to his pirate hideout to enlist their services. The stores of stolen goods sometimes were worth hundreds of thousands of dollars. Regular auctions were held on islands near New Orleans.

While he brought piracy to a new height in the Gulf, Laffite perhaps organized it too well. He made it so efficient that some historians believe he was responsible for its downfall sooner than otherwise might have been. This may well be true, because the pirates achieved such great power under Laffite that the government of the United States could not forever condone their brazen disregard of revenue laws, the slave trade embargo, and the authority of government.

At one period, Laffite had from 800 to 1,000 men under his command—an outlaw army which was equipped with the best artillery and huge stores of powder and ammunition. His artillerymen had no peers in any army in the world. His storehouses were filled with stolen merchandise. On one day 400 Negroes were sold during an auction—which meant a gross business of approximately $500,000 in slaves alone.

Laffite had his choice of the best wines of the Old World. He dined on silverplate. In New Orleans, he and Pierre were seen on the streets, in the coffee houses, and in the taverns in the company of many of the city's leading businessmen, merchants and lawyers.

Jean Laffite did not like the name of pirate. He called himself a privateer. But in the New Orleans of that day his occupation did not bar him from the society of the leading citizens of the city.

In the summer of 1812, Capt. Andrew Hunter Holmes was sworn in as a Customs officer and led an expedition against Laffite and his men. Captain Holmes took a group of thirty or forty men in small boats and proceeded toward Barataria. But Jean Laffite was forewarned of the expedition by his brother Pierre. According to the records of the times Jean Laffite laughed uproariously when he learned that Holmes was heading for Barataria with such a small company. Laffite took his boats loaded with merchandise through devious waterways and avoided Holmes and his men rather than get involved in a skirmish which could end only in disaster for Holmes.

But Holmes was not to be outwitted so easily. In the fall, Holmes returned with a larger force, surprised Jean and Pierre Laffite with contraband merchandise and took them to New Orleans as prisoners. The brothers were released on bail and neither showed up for trial. Six writs of arrest were issued for Jean and Pierre but all were returned with the notation "Not found in New Orleans." It seemed reasonable to assume that no one seriously wanted to find them.

The acceptance of piracy and smuggling as elements of legitimate trade in New Orleans was not so astonishing as it might seem because Louisiana commerce for many years prior to this time had been built on such a foundation. Smuggling to avoid tariffs and then selling at cheap prices, as one historian said, "had become a part of the habits of life there." The people were satisfied for the most part because the smuggled goods were cheaper than they would have been had duties been paid. Merchants were satisfied because they were able to obtain scarce merchandise and make a good profit. Men such as Laffite were regarded as performing a necessary function for the community at no little personal risk— and only a minority attached any moral stigma to the trade.

The confidential and intimate relationship between the pirates and their customers reached its peak on New Year's Day, 1814.

Handbills were boldly scattered in public places and prominently displayed throughout New Orleans announcing that the brothers Laffite, on January 20, would offer at auction at "The Temple" a quantity of slaves and merchandise.

The Temple was a favorite market place for the Laffites. It was an ancient Indian mound of white shells where, legend had it, Indians of the area had gathered to give human sacrifices to appease their gods. The pirates had built a platform at the edge of the water, onto which they could unload their boats. There they spread their merchandise for all to see who came from New Orleans. Since it was easily accessible, there was never any lack of buyers when the auctioneer went to work.

Claiborne was infuriated by the distribution of handbills announcing the auction. The pirates were offering for sale 415 slaves in addition to a supply of "fine foreign merchandise." Claiborne called in the U.S. Collector of Customs to discuss what could be done about this outrageous disregard of the laws of the United States. Both must have known that there was not much that could be done. Nevertheless the Collector ordered a small force to proceed to The Temple to "defeat the purpose of the law infractors."

Jean Laffite and his companions attacked the Customs men, killing one man and wounding two others fatally. Nine of the officers were held as prisoners by the pirates while they proceeded with their auction as planned. It was reported that buyers came from many parts of Louisiana. They bought all the slaves that were put on the block. And the Laffites considered the auction a great success.

The Collector wrote to Governor Claiborne: "It is high time that the contrabandists, dispersed throughout the State, should be taught to respect our laws, and I hold it my duty to call on your excellency for a force adequate to the exigency of the case."

Claiborne could have dispatched a state militia against the pirate gang, but he hesitated to do this because he already had had one embarrassing experience with the militia. He had ordered a company of troops to move against the Baratarians, but Jean Laffite had met this problem by the simple expedient of bribing the entire expeditionary force. It has been recorded that "the brave leaders of the Baratarians had spared their lives, loaded them with costly presents and had allowed them to return safely to New Orleans."

Again Claiborne pleaded in a letter to the legislature for action, saying: "The evil requires a strong corrective. Force must be resorted to. These lawless men can alone be operated upon by their fears and the certainty of punishment. I have not been able to ascertain their numbers . . . but they are represented to be from 300 to 500, perhaps more. . . . So numerous and bold are the followers of Laffite, and, I grieve to say it, such is the countenance afforded him by some of our citizens, to me unknown, that all efforts to apprehend this high offender have hitherto been baffled." As is the history of many complaints to legislatures, the matter was referred to a committee, where it died quietly.

Failing again to get any action from the legislature, Claiborne resorted to another course. He arranged to have a grand jury, friendly to his views, chosen from the city's merchants and bankers. Witnesses were called who, in the strictest secrecy, swore to knowledge of piratical acts by the Laffites and their men. Before the news of this grand jury's meeting spread through the city, Pierre Laffite was arrested. He was taken to jail and bail was denied. Jean Laffite, when he heard of Pierre's arrest, hurried secretly to the city to talk with friends about releasing his brother. But this time nothing could be done.

It was while Pierre was in jail, on September 3, 1814, that His Britannic Majesty's brig *Sophie* sailed into the narrow strait off the island of Grande Terre and dropped anchor. A small boat was lowered and two officers were rowed ashore by sailors. The British were met on the beach by a tall, dark-haired man whom they asked to lead them to Monsieur Laffite. Their guide led them across the beach onto the porch of a breeze-swept house. And then the guide turned and said, "Messieurs, I myself am Laffite." The visitors were Captain Lockyer from the *Sophie* and Captain McWilliams of the Royal Colonial Marines. They had brought a most unusual offer.

Laffite refused to discuss business until lunch had been served. They ate their lunch from silverplate. It was an excellent meal, the officers recalled, with fine wines and good conversation. When the meal was finished, the men lit cigars and then Laffite was ready to hear what they had to say. Captain Lockyer disclosed that he brought an offer from Admiral Sir William H. Percy, commanding the British squadron at Pensacola. In brief, the British were offer-

ing Laffite $30,000 if he would bring his ships, guns and men to
the side of Britain in the war against the United States. Laffite
asked them to leave the Admiral's letters with him and to give
him fifteen days in which to study the proposition. Then, he said,
"I will be entirely at your disposal."

But Jean Laffite, pirate and cutthroat though he was, had no
intention of betraying the United States. He hastily wrote a letter
to his friend Jean Blanque, in New Orleans. He enclosed the letters handed to him by the British, together with a personal message for Governor Claiborne. Laffite said in his letter to Blanque:
"Our enemies exerted on my integrity a motive which few men
would have resisted. They have represented to me a brother in
irons, a brother who to me is very dear! of whom I can become
the deliverer ... from your enlightenment will you aid me in a
circumstance so grave."

And then he enclosed this letter to be delivered to the Governor:

MonSieur:
... I offer to return to this State many citizens who perhaps have
lost to your eyes that sacred title. I offer ... their efforts for the defense of the country.

This point of Louisiana that occupies great importance in the present
situation, I offer myself to defend it ... I am the lost sheep who de-
sires to return to the flock ... for you to see through my faults such
as they are....

In case, MonSieur Le Gouverneur, your reply should not be favorable
in my ardent wishes I declare to you that I leave immediately so not
to be held to have cooperated with an invasion.... This cannot fail
to take place, and puts me entirely on the judgment of my conscience.

I have the honor to be, MonSieur Le Gouverneur,

Laffite.

Jean Laffite had put loyalty to the United States before profit
in this time of peril. But even as Captain Lockyer conferred with
Laffite, Claiborne was going forward with plans for a land-sea
operation against the pirate stronghold.

After receiving Laffite's letter, Claiborne called his military advisers into conference. These were Major General Jaques Villere,
Commodore Patterson of the U.S. Navy, and Colonel Ross of the
regular U.S. Army. The questions they discussed were whether

the documents sent by Laffite were genuine and whether the governor should enter into correspondence with Laffite. Villere thought the documents genuine and that the Governor should reply immediately to the Laffite letter. However, Ross and Patterson voted against Villere. The majority favored an attack on the pirate stronghold.

Peculiarly enough, the morning after this meeting at the Governor's mansion, newspapers carried notices that Pierre Laffite had mysteriously escaped from jail. A notice was posted offering $1,000 reward for his capture.

Eight days after Laffite wrote to Claiborne, the Ross-Patterson expedition set out for Barataria. Three barges were loaded with men and ammunition. It left the levee at New Orleans before dawn and drifted silently downstream with the current. Near the mouth of the river, the barges joined forces with Colonel Ross' fleet of six gunboats and the schooner *Carolina*. The pirate hideout on the islands of Grande Terre and Grande Isle was sighted on the early morning of September 16.

There were indications at first that the Baratarians were going to resist. They began placing cannon into position and arming themselves. But then apparently they saw the American flag on the approaching ships. They broke ranks and ran. Without firing a shot, the expeditionary force captured the pirate fleet, guns, and stores of merchandise valued at more than $500,000.

When news of the attack on Barataria was received in New Orleans, there was much criticism of the expedition. And there was even more indignation when it was learned that the expedition was launched after Laffite had offered his services and those of his companions to the government in the defense of New Orleans against the expected attack by the British.

The British bribe offer to Laffite came as General Andrew Jackson arrived in New Orleans to arrange for the defense of the city. Claiborne sent copies of Laffite's documents to Jackson on the chance that they were genuine and contained military information which would be important. Jackson made it quite clear he wanted no traffic with "this hellish banditti" and he rebuked Claiborne for having permitted Laffite and his men in the past to visit the city.

At last Jean Laffite made a secret trip to see Jackson himself.

There is no record of what went on between the two men and what was said in that conference. It became known that Laffite offered to put in Jackson's hands a supply of 750,000 pistol flints and some of the most skilled artillerymen in the world, including Laffite's lieutenants, Dominique You and Beluche.

Jackson relented and accepted Laffite's offer of help. The General made You and Beluche captains and they were given command of batteries on the right side of the American line.

On January 8, 1815, the decisive battle of New Orleans was fought. As dawn was breaking, Jackson visited the troops along the front lines and stopped at a battery where the Baratarians were making coffee in an old iron pot.

"That smells good," Jackson said. "It's better coffee than we get. Where did it come from? Did you smuggle it in?"

Dominique You grinned. "That may be," he said, and he ordered a cup filled for the General. As Jackson sat on his horse sipping the strong, black coffee, he remarked to an aide, "I wish I had fifty such guns on this line, with five hundred devils such as those fellows behind them."

The British advanced on the American positions to be mowed down by withering fire. At the height of the battle, Jackson again visited Dominique You's battery to see how things were going.

"Ah, we do not make much damage," You said.

"Why is that?" Jackson demanded.

"The powder!" You replied. "It is not good. The cannon balls, they fall short."

Jackson said, "I'll remedy that!" He ordered an aide to see to it that the Baratarians received the best ammunition possible. The General was heard to say later, "Were I ordered to storm the very gates of hell with Dominique You as my lieutenant, I would have no misgivings as to the outcome."

Jean and Pierre Laffite acquitted themselves with honor in the battle for New Orleans. They and their men were given Presidential pardons, clearing the slate of past crimes, and for some time after the city was saved, they were great heroes. They were wined, dined, and cheered wherever they went.

Perhaps the brothers became bored with respectability. At any rate they drifted back into piracy. They pulled out of their old haunts and moved to Galveston to set up operations, and for sev-

eral years they carried on business in the slave trade. In 1820,
Jean Laffite boarded his favorite boat, *The Pride,* and sailed away
into legend. There were stories that he died in Yucatan. Some
claimed that he carried on his piracy in the Mediterranean. Still
others said that he settled in France and lived to be an old man.
All recorded history of Jean Laffite ended when he sailed from
Galveston. Pierre Laffite was said to have lived in Louisiana to
an old age and to have died a poor man.

The quality and the quantity of piracy subsided along with the
fortunes of the brothers Laffite. But not smuggling. Smuggling
was to continue to plague the Customs Service, and some of the
smuggling would make the Laffites look like amateurs.

5

THE DARK YEARS

Slavery was the issue which exploded into the Civil War in 1861,
but twenty-eight years before the first shot was fired on Fort
Sumter, the nation was on the edge of open war over a dispute
involving the Federal government's right to force the collection
of customs duties.

The spirit of revolt flamed high in South Carolina in 1832–
1833. It was fed, too, by sympathy in Virginia and Georgia and
other agricultural states which bitterly opposed the system of pro-
tective tariffs as being oppressive to the farm states.

Did the central government have the Constitutional right to force
the collection of duties in a state which opposed such collections?
No! said the "Nullifiers," who favored striking down the Federal
tariff laws. They insisted that any state had the right to withdraw
from the Union if it so desired.

The Nullifiers gained control of the government of South Carolina and a call was issued for a convention to meet and abolish by formal state action the collection of duties. There also were loud demands from some state leaders for mobilization of South Carolina troops to oppose any Federal intervention. Customs officers, more sympathetic to the state of South Carolina than to the Union, refused to collect duties. This convention call was the aftermath of a previous convention at which a grim resolution was adopted saying in part: "The state looks to her sons to defend her in whatever form she may proclaim to *Resist*."

The tariff collection issue became so divisive that reports reached President Jackson in August and September, 1832, that the loyalty of army officers in command of Federal troops at Charleston was suspect.

It was reported to Jackson that in event of Federal "aggression" against South Carolina to enforce tariff collection and oppose secession, these officers were ready to surrender their troops to the state rather than fight to protect the Charleston forts. These same reports said overtures had been made "perhaps not without success" to switch the allegiance of the naval officer in command at Charleston, in order to prevent a Federal blockade of the port.

Jackson advised his Secretary of State, Edward Livingston, that "the Union must be preserved, without blood if this be possible, but it must be preserved at all hazards and at any price." He changed the garrison at Charleston and sent Maj. Gen. Winfield Scott to take over the command. He warned Secretary of War Lewis Cass that a surprise attack would be made on the Charleston forts by South Carolina militia and directed that such an attack must be "repelled with prompt and exemplary punishment."

While taking these precautions, Jackson argued that if the doctrine of nullification of customs duties by the states were ever established, then every Federal law for raising revenue could be annulled by the states. He denied the right of secession, declaring that "to say that any state may at pleasure secede from the Union is to say that the United States is not a nation."

The controversial tariff laws had been a national issue long before Jackson entered the White House in 1828. The major issue in the Presidential campaign of 1823–1824 revolved around tariffs and the use of Federal funds for such internal improvements as roads, harbors, and like projects. The leading candidates for the

Presidency that year were John C. Calhoun of South Carolina, Henry Clay of Kentucky, John Q. Adams of Massachusetts, William H. Crawford of Georgia, and finally, Andrew Jackson—with Jackson and Adams emerging as the showdown antagonists.

Adams won the election when Henry Clay threw his support to the New Englander. Under the leadership of Clay and Daniel Webster a high-duty system of tariffs was adopted, which was termed the "Act of Abominations" by its opponents.

When Jackson entered the White House in 1828 the tariff issue was still the most important and also the most divisive issue of the day. In January, 1830, Senator Robert Y. Hayne of South Carolina launched a strong attack in the Senate against the excessively high tariffs. The young Senator sought a coalition between the West and the South, the agricultural areas, to oppose the duties favored by the industrial states.

Hayne's argument rested on the states' rights questions which were to plague the nation for many years to come. Hayne contended that "no evil was more to be deprecated than the consolidation of this government." He argued for the right of any state to set aside "oppressive" Federal legislation, including tariffs.

Daniel Webster picked up the argument against Hayne. He contended that "the Constitution is not the creature of the state government. The very chief end, the main design, for which the whole constitution was framed and adopted was to establish a government that should not . . . depend on the state opinion and state discretion." He said it was folly to support a doctrine of "liberty first and union afterwards," and he spoke the famous line: "Liberty and union, now and forever, one and inseparable."

By 1832, the South Carolina Nullifiers were openly led by Vice President Calhoun. The extremists were in control in South Carolina to push events toward the crisis which forced Jackson to rush back to Washington from Nashville. The state's legislature proclaimed that any effort by Federal authorities to collect the duties after February 1, 1833, would cause South Carolina to secede from the Union.

When news of this proclamation reached Jackson, he ordered seven revenue cutters and a warship dispatched to Charleston. Maj. Gen. Winfield Scott set his men to work preparing harbor defenses against attack from the land. The situation was at the

stage where only recklessness was needed to set off a conflict. At
this time Jackson wrote a friend that "no state or states has the
right to secede ... nullification therefore means insurrection and
war; and other states have a right to put it down. . . ."

Jackson issued a proclamation warning the citizens of South
Carolina not to follow the Nullifiers, whose "object is disunion."
He warned that "disunion by armed force is treason" and that
those who followed this path must suffer the "dreadful conse-
quences." The proclamation spread excitement throughout the
country. Many men volunteered for military duty in case of a conflict. Several state legislatures met to denounce nullification. But
in South Carolina Robert Y. Hayne—who had resigned from his
Senate seat to become governor of the state—issued his own proclamation in which he vowed to maintain South Carolina's sovereignty or else to perish "beneath its ruins." Hayne called for the
organization of "Mounted Minute Men," which, he said, would
permit him to place "2,500 of the elite of the whole state upon
a given point in three or four days. . . ."

The only concession held forth by Jackson in this cold war was
his approval of a bill for introduction in the House which would
call for a reduction of tariff rates. His willingness to go along
with this measure did not eliminate the threat of a shooting conflict.

While holding an olive twig of compromise in one hand, Jackson held a sword in the other. He sent a request to Congress asking authority to use Federal troops if necessary to collect the customs. Even as the cheers and curses sounded over this move, Jackson sent a letter to Gerald R. Poinsett, a Unionist leader in South
Carolina, outlining his plans to use strong measures to enforce
Federal authority. No doubt he intended his letter to reach the
hands of the Nullificationists. He said should Congress fail to act
on his request for authority to use military force, and should South
Carolina oppose with armed force the collection of the customs
duties, then "I stand prepared to issue my proclamation warning
them to disperse. Should they fail to comply I will : . . in ten or
fifteen days at fartherest have in Charleston ten to fifteen thousand
well organized troops well equipped for the field, and twenty or
thirty thousand more in their interior. I have a tender of volunteers
from every state in the Union. I can if need be, which God forbid,

march 200,000 men in forty days to quell any and every insurrection that might arise. . . ."

Not only would he take these measures against South Carolina, Jackson added, but if the governor of Virginia should make any move to prevent Federal troops from moving through the state against South Carolina then "I would arrest him. . . ." The President also was prepared to call on Pennsylvania, New York, Virginia, North Carolina, Ohio, Tennessee, Alabama, Georgia and South Carolina to furnish 35,000 troops to carry out his orders.

Jackson's request of Congress for authority to use troops in forcing the collection of customs was immediately called the "Force Bill." To the extremists it was known as the "Bloody Bill." Vice President John Calhoun said darkly that if the bill should pass then "it will be resisted at every hazard, even that of death."

It was at this point that the Great Compromiser, Henry Clay, moved to seek the solution which would avoid bloodshed and perhaps civil war. He introduced in the House his own bill to lower tariffs by 20 per cent over a period of ten years. The Clay bill was pushed through Congress along with the Jackson Force Bill and both were sent to the President for his signature. Jackson won his demand for authority to send troops to South Carolina to put down any move toward secession or nullification of the tariff laws, and he signed the compromise tariff bill even though it was, in a measure, appeasement of the Nullificationists. Clay's tariff bill was a face-saving measure for South Carolina. The head-on conflict between Federal and state forces was averted—at least for the time being.

In Jackson's administration there was one man whose name appears mostly in the footnotes of that turbulent period, but it is a name that deserves special mention in this chronicle. The man was Samuel Swartwout, Collector of Customs in New York City during Jackson's two terms in the White House. He rates special mention and a shadowy niche in American history because he was the first and only man to steal a million dollars from the Treasury of the United States. In fact, he stole $1,250,000.

Swartwout was a young man when he plunged into New York politics. He was a dark-haired, personable man who made himself useful by running errands for the political bosses until he reached a position of backroom fixer and schemer with no small amount of influence. He was the bluff, hearty type who made friends easily. And while he never was a central figure in the making of history, he was one of those men whose names continually cropped up in the affairs of the men who did make history in his time.

Swartwout was a protege and confidante of Aaron Burr during the period of Burr's shady adventure in the West when he was accused of treason in an alleged plot to establish an empire in the southwestern United States. And when Jackson's star began to rise as a Presidential candidate, Swartwout attached himself to the cause of the Tennessean.

Many of Jackson's friends and followers resented Swartwout's close association with Jackson because they regarded him as a doubtful character smeared by the tar of the Burr affair. But when Jackson entered the White House in 1828, Swartwout was among the honored guests at the celebrations.

Jackson's friends were concerned when it became known that the New Yorker had easy access to the office of the President and was seen coming and going as though he were one of Jackson's intimate advisers—which he wasn't. The concern became dismay when rumors spread that Swartwout had come to town seeking from Jackson the nomination as Collector of Customs for New York City, a post of no little prestige and political influence in those days. Jackson's Secretary of State, Martin Van Buren, was so upset by the reports that he refused to admit Swartwout to his office or to enter into correspondence with him.

Jackson must have felt he owed a political debt to Swartwout because on April 25, 1829, during a recess of Congress, he handed the New Yorker the political plum he had been seeking. Swartwout continued in the office until March 29, 1838, with never any public suspicion that he was involved in thefts of money collected by the Customs House in New York. Only when the records were checked by his successor was the discovery made that his accounts were short by $1,250,000.

The scandal which followed broke like a storm over the young Customs Service. Demands were made in Congress for safeguards to prevent any such future looting of the Treasury. Enemies of Jackson attacked the "spoils system" of appointments and centered much of their assault on Customs.

As for Swartwout, he had foreseen the storm that was to come.

He had bade his friends farewell and boarded a ship for Europe several weeks before the shortages in his accounts were discovered. He was in France, safely out of reach of the law, when the scandal broke—and he didn't bother to return.

By 1849, the Customs Service spanned the continent. It reached the coast of California in the person of John Collier, who was appointed as the first Collector of Customs for San Francisco just as the state was clearing the way for entry into the Union. Collier reached San Francisco on November 13, 1849, after a perilous trip across the country. He arrived at the beginning of the gold rush to find the city and the customs situation in a state of disorganization and confusion.

Collier was overwhelmed by the amount of business being carried on in San Francisco, by the number of vessels arriving and leaving the harbor, by the smuggling which was going on, and by the high prices he found in the city. He advised Secretary of the Treasury W. M. Meredith in a long, rambling letter: "I am perfectly astounded at the amount of business in this office. . . . The amount of tonnage . . . on the 10th instance in port, was 120,317 tons; of which 87,494 were American, and 32,823 were foreign. Number of vessels in the harbor on that day, 10th instance, 312, and the whole number of arrivals since the first of April, 697; of which 401 were American, and 296 foreign. This state of things, so unexpected, has greatly surprised me. . . ."

He found that Customs clerks were being paid from $1800 to $3000 per annum but that the salaries were not particularly attractive in a city gripped by the get-rich-quick fever. Flour was selling for $40 per barrel and pork for $60. Board was $5 a day and a room with a single bed was $150 a month. Wood was $40 a cord and prices for other necessities were equally shocking to a man as obviously thrifty as Collier.

Collier moved into the Old Spanish Custom House to set up shop. It was a dark and gloomy building. The roof leaked. Some of the doors were off the hinges. There was no vault in which to place the money he collected. He confided to the Secretary that "owing to the rates for rents, I am afraid to lease a building. One for myself, containing four rooms, two below and two above, without fireplaces, was offered to me on yesterday at $2400 a month. . . ."

He continued: "To enforce the revenue laws in this district, and to cut up and prevent smuggling, which has been and is now carried on to a great extent, it seems to be necessary that an additional cutter should be sent out or that the *Ewing,* now in this port, should be assigned to that duty."

In a later letter to the Secretary, Collier wrote: ". . . San Francisco . . . must become to the nation what New York is to the Atlantic. . . . It is impossible to estimate the extent to which her commerce may reach. It is now large and it will be constantly on the increase. These facts are stated for the double purpose of putting you in position of what may be anticipated from duties, and of impressing upon Congress the necessity of doing something—doing much for California, and that without delay. The responsibilities that rest upon the Collector, in the absence of any legal tribunal, any legal adviser, to which he might resort for redress or advice weigh heavily upon me."

The troubles experienced by Collier and other early-day collectors along the borders of the growing nation were soon to be submerged in the conflict between the states. At the outbreak of the Civil War most Southern Customs officers simply resigned and accepted appointments to similar posts in the Confederate government.

President Lincoln ordered a blockade of the South on April 19, 1861. At that time the United States naval fleet consisted of only 42 ships carrying some 555 guns. Of this total many were tenders and store ships and among them were old fashioned sailing ships and frigates. For a time, business went on as usual in the Southern ports.

Many in the South laughed at the idea of a blockade. One Southerner in a letter from Charleston, South Carolina, printed in the New York *Illustrated News* on June 15, 1861, said:

We are now in the enjoyment of a very pleasant spring, and are now as quiet as a brood of chicks under the parent's wing. For all that, however, our head men are not asleep. Everything is going nicely. You have heard, no doubt, old Abe has blockaded our port.

A nice blockade indeed. On the second day a British ship, the *A & A* ran the gauntlet and got in safe. She leaves in a few days with a snug freight of $30,000. Today two vessels passed safely in, both British, I understand. A captain told me that one of them can carry more cotton than the *A & A* and that she is engaged at 5¢ a pound, which will give a freight of $35,000 to $40,000. . . .

Under the guns of Admiral Farragut and the troops of General Butler, New Orleans remained securely in the hands of the Northern forces, shutting off this port to the Southern cause. After a short while Galveston fell to the Union and the flow of cotton and smuggled goods from this area was sharply reduced.

In England, the Liverpool firm represented by Thomas E. Taylor owned some fifteen ships which were engaged in blockade running. Among Taylor's swiftest and most elusive runners was a steel vessel called the *Banshee,* one of the first—if not the first—ship built for the express purpose of evading the Union blockade for the Southern ports. Nassau, in the Bahamas, was the primary staging point where the blockade runners fueled and stocked for the run to the American coast.

The blockade had been underway for two years when Taylor brought the *Banshee* into Nassau. Workers removed everything aloft except the two lower masts, and the ship was painted an off shade of white which the blockade runners had found made their ships almost invisible at night, even from a distance of only a few yards.

Moving cautiously out of Nassau, the *Banshee* sailed along the Bahama shores and then began the run toward Charleston. From a crosstree in the masts, a lookout was rewarded with a dollar each time he sighted a sail on the horizon before it was seen from the deck. If someone on the deck spotted the sail first, then the lookout was fined five dollars. It was a system that encouraged alertness by the lookouts. As soon as a ship was sighted, the *Banshee* turned its stern to the stranger and waited quietly until the vessel was out of sight.

On the fourth day the *Banshee* reached the American coast some fifteen miles north of Cape Fear and the mouth of the Charleston River. When darkness came she began easing cautiously toward the blockading Union ships, running as close to the pounding surf as the skipper dared. No lights were permitted, not even the glow of a lighted cigar. Tarpaulins covered the engine-room hatchways. And the *Banshee* was a gray ghost slipping silently through the water while the men aboard talked only in whispers. Occasionally the ship stopped for a seaman to take soundings.

Taylor later recalled one tense moment in these words: "...
Suddenly Burruss (the pilot) gripped my arm—'There is one of
them, Mr. Taylor, on the starboard bow.'... A moment afterwards
I could make out a long, low, black object on our starboard side,
lying perfectly still. Would she see us? That was the question: but
no, though we passed within a hundred yards of her, we were not
discovered and I breathed again. 'Steamer on the port bow,' and
another cruiser was made out close to us. Still unobserved, we
crept quietly along, when all at once a third cruiser shaped herself out of the gloom straight ahead and steaming slowly across our
bow.

"Burruss was now of the opinion that we must be inside the
squadron and advocated making the land. So 'ahead slow' we went
again, until the low-lying coast and the surf line became dimly visible.... It was a big relief when we suddenly heard Burruss saying,
'It's all right, I see the big hill!'...."

The Big Hill was near the Confederate-held Fort Fisher at the
mouth of the Charleston River. As dawn came, the *Banshee* was
sighted by the Union blockaders and they moved against her with
guns blazing. But then the *Banshee* slipped under the protecting
guns of Fort Fisher and safety.

The owners of the *Banshee* made 700 per cent on their investment before the ship was captured on her ninth round trip between
Nassau and Charleston.

The blockade runners, British and Confederate, supplied the
armies of Gen. Robert E. Lee with desperately needed arms, clothing and food supplies in the early years of the war. For a time the
blockade appeared impotent, while Southern privateers harassed
the shipping of the North and captured much booty at sea.

While Lee was winning battles on the land, the Confederates
could never gain mastery of the sea. The Union blockade could
not be broken, and slowly the superior sea forces of the North
strangled the commerce of the South, shutting off her armies from
vital sources of supplies overseas.

Soon after the war began, it became evident to President Lincoln, to his Cabinet, and to members of Congress that the revenues
collected by the Customs Service were not enough to finance the
mounting costs of the massive conflict. The loss of tariff revenues

in the Southern states, the South's raids on the shipping of the North, and the breakdown of normal commerce had reduced Treasury receipts drastically. The President was forced to seek new sources of revenue.

In this emergency, the administration turned for the first time to an income tax. Congress passed a law imposing a tax of 3 per cent on incomes between $600 and $10,000, and a tax of 5 per cent on incomes above $10,000. Later, the taxes on those two income brackets were raised to 5 per cent and 10 per cent.

The income tax collected throughout the struggle—and until the law expired in 1872—helped carry the nation through its money crisis. Then the collection of duties by the Customs Service once more became the country's primary source of revenue.

But during most of the war and for many years afterward, the venerable Customs Service's cloak of respectability was at best a tattered and stained garment. It had become, particularly in New York City, the symbol of the political spoils system which had been encouraged by that partisan old fighter, Andrew Jackson.

The office of the Collector of Customs at the Port of New York had become a prize second only in political prestige and influence to a Cabinet appointment. The man receiving this office was in a position to dole out lucrative jobs to hundreds of the party faithful, to collect tribute for his party's campaign chest, and to use his influence in shaping the affairs of his city, county and state. To a lesser degree, the same situation existed across the country.

Under such blatantly political management, it was hardly surprising that the Customs Service in New York should become the target of bitter charges of graft and corruption. The charges became so loud and persistent in 1863 that the administration ordered an investigation into the management of the New York Customs House.

A report from the Treasury's solicitor said in part: "As to the accessibility of many of those employed in the Customhouse to corrupt influences, the evidence is conclusive and startling.... The statements herewith submitted seem to justify the belief that the entire body of subordinate officers, in and about the Customhouse, in one way or another, are in habitual receipt of emoluments from importers or their agents.... It is shown that a bond clerk, with a salary of $1,000 per annum, enters upon a term of eight years with nothing, and leaves it with a fortune of $30,-000. . . ."

Until Congress slammed the door on such practices in a reform move generated in the 1870s, Customs officers were legally permitted to receive half of any fines and forfeitures resulting from the seizure of imports which had been undervalued or underweighed by an importer, even though the methods of determining dutiable value were complicated and subject to dispute.

However, the law encouraged collectors, appraisers and inspectors to seek out discrepancies in values and weights and to give themselves the benefit of any doubt. In one case, the great Phelps, Dodge & Co., metal importers, was charged with an attempt to evade duties by undervaluing a shipment worth $1,750,000.

The company's attorneys argued in vain that there had been no attempt to defraud the government; that if a mistake had been made it was an honest error, and that even with the benefit of a doubt, the most that the government could fairly claim in unpaid duties was $1,600.

With the entire shipment subject to forfeiture, the company finally agreed to settle for $271,017.23—50 per cent of which was divided among the Customs officers. Records of the time showed that one of the Customs officials who received an award of $56,120 was Chester A. Arthur, who later would become President of the United States.

Arthur was active for years in Republican politics in New York City, working his way up through the ranks until he became a member of the New York State Republican Executive Committee. He was rewarded for his labors in 1871 with an appointment as Collector of Customs in New York City.

Under Arthur, the Customs House became the center of such open and partisan political activity that it eventually led to conflict between Arthur and President Rutherford B. Hayes. Hayes championed a strong civil service with appointment of Federal employees on a basis of merit rather than political allegiance. The President asked Arthur to resign, and when he refused Hayes removed him from office in 1879.

But this Presidential rebuke by no means dimmed Arthur's political star. Two years after his removal, he was elected Vice

President of the United States, running with James A. Garfield. Garfield was fatally wounded by a disgruntled office-seeker, Charles J. Guiteau, only four months after his inauguration. He died on September 19, 1881, and Arthur took the oath as President. Ironically, once he was in the White House, Arthur became a supporter of a stronger civil service.

Reforms came slowly to the Customs Service in the years that followed the Civil War. But they came, spurred by the efforts of Hayes and then of President Grover Cleveland to establish a civil service and to break up a spoils system in which the "rascals" were thrown out of their jobs with every change in administration.

The demands for further Customs Service reforms were particularly loud in the early years of the twentieth century. One of these resulted in the formation in 1909 of the Customs Court of Appeals, to bring uniformity to the legal decisions governing the huge import trade and to speed up the hearing of Customs cases.

From the earliest days of the Republic, disputes over the appraising of imports had been carried to the U.S. Circuit Courts. The result was a continual conflict in judicial opinions which left importers and Customs officers confused. In 1908, the Secretary of the Treasury reported that the law had made "each of at least 120 judges a possible final judge of Customs appeals, a condition which experience has demonstrated will inevitably result in numerous irreconcilable conflicts of authority."

In addition to the legal conflicts, the U.S. Circuit Courts had become jammed with Customs cases. It was not unusual for importers to have to wait almost five years to get a judicial settlement of their cases. But the creation of the Customs Court of Appeals by the 1909 Tariff Act removed most of the inequities and brought order out of the judicial chaos.

In this period, the reformers also centered their attention on the system which had permitted pork-barrel legislators to have their towns and cities designated as ports of entry with almost total disregard of the need for such services.

At Saco, Maine, the port's receipts for fiscal 1910 amounted to $15, while expenses totalled $662—a cost of more than $41 to collect $1. At St. Mary's, Georgia, the cost of collecting $1 in duties was more than $45. At Annapolis, Maryland, the government paid $309 to collect $3.09. And there were dozens of similar examples throughout the country. The major function of many ports of entry, it was evident, was to give jobs to the workers in the political vineyard.

Congressional investigators also found that the system of paying collectors, surveyors and other Customs officials was a fiscal nightmare—in which thirty-five different methods were used for compensating employees. For example, collectors along the Canadian border were permitted to charge ten cents for each entry blank they executed. Some of them were pocketing, legally, as much as $17,000 a year.

In 1912, Congress authorized the President to overhaul the Customs operation. The day before he stepped out of office, President William Howard Taft issued an executive order establishing 49 Customs districts to replace the existing 126 districts and 36 independent ports. Collectors were placed on a salary basis. Many of the political appointees were dropped from the government payroll.

It was during the early years in this century, too, that the Customs Service relinquished to the Internal Revenue Service its role as the prime collector of revenue in the Federal government.

This change was foreshadowed on December 19, 1907, when a tall, gangling Democratic Congressman from Tennessee arose from his seat in the House of Representatives in Washington, D. C., and called for the attention of Speaker Joe Cannon, the thin, wiry political leader who ruled the House with iron-fisted discipline.

"The gentleman from Tennessee is recognized," the Speaker intoned dryly.

Then it was that Cordell Hull, a freshman Representative from the foothills of the Cumberland mountains, boldly introduced a bill calling for a Federal tax on all incomes. He long had felt that tariff duties bore too heavily on the consumers of the country and that the wealthy were not paying a fair share of the cost of their government.

Bold though it was, the Tennessean's move created scarcely a ripple in the capital. The House droned on with its business. The newspapers hardly made mention of the bill or of the new Congressman. It was as though a rock had been tossed into a lonely mountain pool to sink rapidly from sight, leaving no trace after the first plop on the quiet surface.

But Cordell Hull's action on that cold December day marked the beginning of a long and bitter fight which would end six years later with an amendment to the Constitution authorizing Congress to enact an income tax law. With the passage of this law, the Customs Service became a secondary producer of Federal revenue.

The reforms of these years, together with those which came in the Tariff Act of 1922, established Customs on its present base. It was a leaner and more efficient service which shouldered the increased burdens imposed by the outbreak of World War I.

During the war years, the Customs Service was responsible for the enforcement of the neutrality laws in shipping. Its officers acted also as local agents for the Bureau of War Risk Insurance, insuring vessels, cargoes and seamen against the hazards of war at sea.

When the United States entered the war on April 6, 1917, Customs agents moved quickly to seize seventy-nine German and Austrian ships in American ports. Customs officers enforced the import and export licenses issued by the War Trade Board.

Two years after the Armistice in 1918, the country was swept by the nostalgic longing for a "return to normalcy"—and Warren G. Harding was installed in the White House. But there was nothing normal about the 1920s for the Customs Service. Its agents were to become involved in fighting the greatest wave of smuggling the nation had known since the days of Jean Laffite.

6

BOOZE AND BRIBES

Lawrence Fleishman had gone to sea at the age of sixteen, when most youths his age hadn't yet put on long pants. He had enlisted in the Navy and served in convoy duty on the Atlantic in the final months of World War I. When the armistice was signed between the Allies and Germany, he had decided to remain in the Navy and he had achieved the rating of Chief Petty Officer. Still, he had no desire to spend the rest of his life at sea. When the opportunity had come, he had applied for a job with the Customs Service. He had been accepted after passing the Civil Service examinations.

Sodus Point had seemed a quiet enough haven. It was a resort center and coal shipping port on Lake Ontario, only a few miles removed from Rochester. The people were friendly and the work was pleasant. He had expected to remain for some time undisturbed, getting accustomed to the idea that his roving days were over.

Then an official-looking letter had arrived—marked "Confidential"—and within a few hours Fleishman was enroute to New York City under orders to tell no one of his destination. He was to report to Customs Agent Gregory O'Keefe in Room 501 at the Prince George Hotel.

Fleishman checked into his room at the hotel and then called O'Keefe. "Come to my room as soon as you can," O'Keefe said. "We're waiting for you."

When Fleishman went to the room, he was introduced by O'Keefe to a deputy collector of customs and to another young employee named Frank Gallagher.

"We called you two down here," O'Keefe said, "because you are new in the Service and no one around here knows you—not even the Customs people."

O'Keefe explained that the Customs Service was under fire in Congress. Rep. Fiorello La Guardia had charged that the Port of New York was so "wide open" that a circus could be smuggled past Customs officers and New York City port authorities. He claimed that bribery and corruption were rampant in the administration of the debonair Mayor "Jimmy" Walker, and that illicit whiskey was pouring into the city. He demanded that something be done about a scandalous situation.

La Guardia's charges had stirred Secretary of the Treasury Andrew W. Mellon to order an immediate inquiry. Customs officials had denied that conditions were as bad as La Guardia said they were. Nevertheless O'Keefe was directed by his superiors to undertake an investigation.

Fleishman got the impression in this meeting that the Cus-

toms people honestly believed that an investigation would clear
the Service's skirts and prove La Guardia to be wrong. Many apparently felt that the accusations were based more on political
inspiration than on facts.

O'Keefe said, "You two are being assigned to the Special
Agency Service. Everything is arranged for you to report for duty
day after tomorrow as Customs guards on the North River piers.
When you get your uniforms, badges, buttons and insignia, I'll give
you more specific instructions."

Fleishman and Gallagher were assigned to work as partners on
the piers handling the cargoes of the trans-Atlantic liners. In less
than a week each was accepted as "one of the boys" and they
listened to Customs guards, inspectors, stevedores, seamen and
other waterfront employees openly discussing their success in
smuggling liquor and other merchandise from incoming ships.
The standard pay-off for permitting a case of whiskey to cross the
pier unmolested was $1 per bottle.

They sat in on smuggling plans and watched the pay-offs being
made. They accepted their share of the money—and then met in
secrecy to mark the bills to be used as evidence in court. In only
eighteen working days these two alone had gathered evidence of
corruption involving twenty-three Customs and city waterfront
employees.

Instead of proving La Guardia wrong, they found that his
charges only touched the surface of a serious breakdown in law
enforcement. They found that many waterfront workers were
merely the tools of the mobsters. Whiskey smuggling was big
business and the pay-offs were tempting to government employees whose average pay in the 1920s was less than $100 a
month. Customs inspectors were earning only $4 a day and pier
guards $75 a month. The Bureau of Labor Statistics had reported
that the minimum salary on which a family could live decently
was $2,260 a year—or $1,124 more than the average government wage. Forty per cent of the Customs employees in New
York worked at night at whatever they could find to supplement
their pay. The conditions were ripe for corrupting influences to
flourish.

One night Fleishman and Gallagher were standing guard at
Pier 57 aboard the French lineship *DeGrasse*. An underworld tip-

ster had reported that the ship carried 1,500 cases of liquor which were to be smuggled ashore that evening. As they stood on the stern deck of the ship, a man dressed as a longshoreman walked up to Gallagher and asked for a light. Gallagher handed him a match and as the man touched the flame to his cigarette, the two agents saw well-manicured fingers and the gleam of a large diamond ring. Then they recognized their visitor as a hoodlum known as "Mike the Barber." Whenever there was a waterfront murder at that time, the name of Mike the Barber was certain to be mentioned sooner or later in the police list of those to be questioned.

Mike the Barber had said suddenly to Gallagher, "You're a new man, aren't you?"

Gallagher said that he was, and the hoodlum said, "Where do you come from?"

Gallagher replied, "I've been working as a subclerk at the post office over in Paterson, New Jersey."

Mike the Barber nodded. "Is that so? I happen to have a good friend over at Paterson. He is the assistant postmaster over there. You know his name, don't you?"

Gallagher was evasive. He began to make excuses for not being able to recall the assistant postmaster's name. Mike the Barber growled, "Oh, yeah? Look, you son-of-a-bitch, you forget everything you see here tonight or you're liable to get killed." And with that the hoodlum walked off into the darkness.

Fleishman and Gallagher knew their usefulness was over. Within minutes every member of the gang on the pier would know they were officers. Fleishman said to Gallagher, "You walk down the pier and walk down the middle of it—don't get to the side where there is any cargo or anything else. Walk right down the middle in clear sight. I'm going after a taxi."

Fleishman luckily was able to hail a cab, and he and Gallagher jumped in. As the cab wheeled from the pier a black sedan roared from the shadows to give chase. The frightened taxi driver finally shook off their pursuers and Fleishman and Gallagher returned to their rooming house.

The information they had gathered was turned over to the Department of Justice and prosecutions were begun. The crack-

down didn't halt the smuggling by any means, but it was a jolt to
the underworld.

Then, on August 30, 1928, Lawrence Fleishman sat at his desk
fingering a letter which the mailman had left at his office a few
minutes earlier. The letter was postmarked Washington, D. C.,
and across the front was written the word "Confidential."

Slowly he tore open the letter and began reading:

Sir:
You will report at the earliest date possible to Detroit, Michigan.
As soon as you arrive in Detroit, you will register at the Barlum Hotel.
. . . You are to work strictly undercover and you are to report to me
daily by mail as to your findings.

You will report any dishonesty or irregularity on the part of any
Customs employee, securing wherever possible such evidence as is
obtainable. . . .

(Signed) *Elmer J. Lewis*

Fleishman tossed the letter onto his desk and felt the excitement building up inside. The order really came as no great surprise, although he knew that it would be something of a shock for
his wife to learn they were leaving immediately for Detroit. Their
plans for the future hadn't included any sudden, mysterious
journeys to a city neither of them had ever visited before.

Fleishman knew the assignment would be dangerous. Yet he
saw no reason why he shouldn't take his bride along. He could
rent an apartment and the stay in Detroit could be pleasant for
both of them as long as business was separated from their home
life.

This wasn't an era for Fleishman or anyone else to be surprised over reports of graft and corruption in law enforcement.
The papers were full of stories of prohibition agents and other
officers being involved with gangsters in liquor smuggling. If Congress wasn't ordering an investigation of a breakdown in law
enforcement, others were. Bootlegging and racketeering had
grown to be a multi-million-dollar industry. It was hardly surprising that an underpaid police officer was tempted when he could
make $100 merely by looking the other way while a cargo of
liquor was being unloaded.

There were times when Fleishman and his fellow agents were not proud of their agency. But the Customs Service was by no means the only enforcement agency tainted by crooks and weaklings. There was corruption rampant throughout the United States. The Federal government itself was only beginning to recover from the shocking scandals in the administration of President Harding. It was all a part of the revolution in manners and morals which had swept the country after the close of World War I. It seemed after the war that the vast majority of the citizens of the United States were eager for prohibition. Congress had voted overwhelmingly for the Nineteenth Amendment to establish prohibition throughout the United States. The dry forces had easily won ratification of the amendment when it was placed before the various states.

Then came the revolt. As soon as Congress passed the Volstead Act, to enforce the prohibition amendment, the country developed a prodigious thirst. Bootlegging became one of the country's major industries. Revenue from the sale of illegal whiskey provided mobsters with unbelievably rich treasuries. It made millionaires out of bums. The gangsters were better armed, better disciplined, and better organized than the average law enforcement agency throughout the country. The cynicism of the period was summed up by Franklin P. Adams, who wrote in the New York *World:*

> Prohibition is an awful flop.
> We like it.
> It can't stop what it's meant to stop.
> We like it.
> It's left a trail of graft and slime,
> It's filled our land with vice and crime.
> It don't prohibit worth a dime,
> Nevertheless we're for it.

In Chicago, the pudgy gangster named Al Capone fashioned a crime empire from the profits made on smuggled booze, prostitution and other rackets. At one time he and his mob controlled— literally—the city of Cicero outside of Chicago. They elected its officials, controlled the appointment of police officers, and dictated the affairs of the entire community, with the threat of the

Thompson submachine gun to enforce their rulings. City governments—and even the Federal government at times—seemed powerless to cope with the marauders.

In Detroit the Purple Gang came to power, and among the major hoodlums was a man named Pete Licovoli, whose name usually cropped up whenever there was a gangland murder, violence, or a report of widespread corruption. He was a man whom Lawrence Fleishman would get to know well.

This was the state of affairs in September, 1928, when Fleishman and his wife loaded their belongings into their shiny new Model A Ford sedan and set out for Detroit.

On arriving in Detroit, they registered at the Barlum Hotel as Supervising Agent Elmer Lewis had instructed. The following morning Fleishman went to Lewis' room in the hotel to be briefed on his mission. He was eager to meet Lewis, who was one of the Bureau's veteran agents with a reputation for being tough, honest and efficient.

Lewis answered Fleishman's knock on his door. He took Fleishman's hand and Fleishman felt like a schoolboy as he looked at the big, broad-shouldered, sandy-haired man who towered above him. Lewis was 6 feet 4 inches of bone and muscle.

Lewis introduced Fleishman to Sumner C. Sleeper, the chief of the Detroit Customs Patrol. He was a man of medium height who had spent many years in the Service. The glasses he wore gave him the look of a schoolteacher.

Quickly Lewis got down to business and sketched the assignment Fleishman was to undertake: There were rumors, true beyond doubt, that some members of the Customs Patrol were deeply involved with the gangsters in smuggling whiskey into Detroit. The situation had reached the point where something had to be done to check the bribery and corruption, but there could be no effective prosecution until the Bureau had solid evidence that bribes were being offered and accepted.

Lewis explained that arrangements had been made for Fleishman to join the Patrol as a rookie. If offered bribes, he was to accept them and make a record of the serial numbers of the bills. He was to report daily in writing to Lewis, detailing everything that happened, along with the names of those involved in any wrongdoing. Only four men knew of his assignment—and he was to discuss his activities only with them. The four were Lewis, Sleeper and two assistant collectors.

"We hope," Lewis said, "that within three months you can get enough evidence to break this thing wide open."

It was agreed that as a "cover" Fleishman would tell anyone who was curious that after leaving the Navy he had found a job as bookkeeper for a large New York State gambling syndicate but the syndicate had been broken up by police, forcing him to find another job. The story sounded reasonable enough, because the newspapers had carried stories that summer of a big gambling combine which had been smashed by New York State police.

At the close of the conference, Lewis gave Fleishman a final bit of advice: "If you ever think they are suspicious of you, get to a safe place fast—and call me."

Within a few days, Fleishman and his wife were settled in a modest apartment on Van Dyke Street not far from Detroit's main downtown section. And on September 22, 1928, Fleishman reported for duty at the Customs Patrol headquarters at the foot of DuBois Street on the Detroit River. The Patrol offices were in an old wooden building enclosed by a high wire fence. There was an adjoining garage and a slip for the patrol boats alongside a boat repair shop. In addition to the office, there was a squad room for the patrolmen, where each of them had a locker.

During his first week on the job, Fleishman knew he was being watched with suspicion. He was never given an assignment with any of the night patrols. Each morning he was assigned to head-quarters duty—which meant sweeping out the offices, tending the coal fires, carrying out ashes, filling cars with gas and oil, and sprinkling water on the sand pile in the front yard to prevent the sand from blowing into the offices.

At odd moments, Fleishman sat around watching the older men shoot craps in the locker room and joining in their talk. Slowly the wall of suspicion began to crumble, and during the second week he was assigned to a 12 midnight to 8 A.M. patrol with a senior officer named Raleigh Hampshire, a big, flabby man who looked as though he slept in his uniform.

In the first hours of the night they drove aimlessly along Woodward Avenue, parking occasionally to get a cup of coffee at an all-night restaurant, or just to sit and watch the traffic. From time to time, Hampshire questioned Fleishman about his background. Fleishman told him of his years in the Navy and his experiences in strange ports of the world. He even confided to Hampshire that he had been a bookkeeper for the New York State gambling syndicate—but this job had blown up when the police smashed the operation.

"Maybe you heard about it," Fleishman said. "It was in all the papers."

Hampshire obviously was impressed. "Yeah," he said, "I read about that."

This conversation apparently resolved any doubts that Hampshire had about his companion. After a time he said, "Let's go see what we can find." He wheeled the car from the curb and drove to a residential area which Fleishman later learned was the Lake St. Clair section, a respectable neighborhood of attractive homes.

Hampshire drove into the driveway of a large house with a tree-shaded lawn, and Fleishman assumed they were going to visit one of Hampshire's friends. He followed Hampshire to the door, and when he knocked a man's voice said, "Come in."

They stepped through the door into a scene that Fleishman would always remember as one of the strangest he had ever witnessed. Stacked to the ceiling in what should have been the living room were cases of whiskey and sacks of ale. On an overturned beer keg sat a man cleaning a pistol. Six other men, using an overturned crate for a table, were playing blackjack. A young woman stood watching the gamblers while sipping from a bottle of ale.

No one showed any surprise at the appearance of the two uniformed officers. They only glanced at Fleishman and nodded when Hampshire introduced him as a new man on the job.

"Have a drink?" their host said.

"I'll take a bottle of ale," Hampshire said.

Fleishman nodded. "I'll take the same."

The hoodlum took a knife from his pocket and flipped open a blade. He ripped one of the sacks and took out two bottles. When he opened them, the warm ale spewed out on the floor. They sat and chatted for several minutes and then Hampshire signalled it was time to go. They bid everyone goodnight and returned to their car. As they drove from the house, Hampshire said, "It isn't everybody that would give a new guy a break like this."

"What do you mean, a break?" Fleishman asked.

"I mean introducing you to the guys back there," Hampshire said. "You never can tell when you might be working with a special agent. But I figure you're all right."

"Thanks," Fleishman said dryly. "I appreciate it more than you know."

This was the break Fleishman had been waiting for. He knew that he had passed the first test and he figured that Hampshire now would pass the word to others that he was "okay." When he returned home that morning he wrote a long report of the night's events and mailed it to Elmer Lewis at the Barlum Hotel.

And then his reports became more and more interesting. . . .

October 1, 1928. (Fleishman reported that he had made friends with a patrolman named Bill Tompkins, who lived only a few streets beyond his apartment. He became friendly by giving Tompkins a ride home after work.) Tompkins opened up wide this morning. He said: "Don't let any of these guys give you the runaround. If you see them talking to bootleggers and they don't let you in on it, or if they leave their boats or cars or act suspicious in any manner, you can be sure they are getting theirs and you are not. Just don't let them put anything over on you. Every time they make a run it is good for a hundred each." . . .

October 10, 1928. I reported for duty at base at 1 A.M. Detailed to land patrol with Inspector G. Slater. . . . Our first stop was at the foot of Orange Street in Wyandotte where the picket boat was tied up . . . Slater talked to O'Rourke while I drove to a restaurant at Slater's request. When I returned . . . Slater said, "Well, it's all fixed. We ought to be good for $125 apiece tonight." . . . We drove down to the foot of 23rd Street and parked the car and went to sleep. . . . We woke up at 6:15 and a bootlegger named Hamilton came along. He said, "Is it all right to work?" Slater said, "Yes." . . . He then told us he would see us around 8:30. We then left from the foot of 23rd Street and went to a restaurant on West Fort Street and had coffee. Left and drove over to the foot of Orange Street and Wyandotte. We were there about 7 o'clock. Bill O'Rourke . . . handed Slater a roll of bills. Slater walked over to the picket boat and another boat was tied up there having a propeller fixed. . . . All I saw of this transaction was O'Rourke giving Slater a roll of bills. We then drove down to the River Rouge. In the car Slater gave me a roll of bills and said, "Count it." I did and found $50. At the River Rouge we went to Peajack's. We met his lieutenant who got out of a car, came over, and dropped a roll of bills in Slater's lap. . . . After driving away Slater gave me another roll of bills containing $50. Slater said, "I bet you feel funny going into the base carrying $100." I admitted that I did feel uncomfortable. Slater gave me quite a bit of interesting data. The night's payoff when they work the River Rouge is $970. They all work at once and the boat crews and the land crews must all be fixed. In addition Border Patrol must occasionally be fixed, nightwatchmen and policemen must be fixed, and recently the prohibition agents have to be paid off to discontinue their activities on the river. Slater also told me a number of fellows were very suspicious of me . . . I said, "Why are they so suspicious of a new man every time?" Slater said, "Because every new man might be a special agent or a DJ (Department of Justice) man. But even if you are a special agent you are as guilty as I am because you have taken money too." . . . Near 23rd Street Slater turned up a side street. . . . Then I saw Hamilton rounding the corner. He came over to the car and dropped a roll of bills in my lap. I handed it to Slater when we drove off. . . . This made $115 for my share of the evening's profit. (Each bill Fleishman received he listed in his report, giving the denomination and serial number of each.) . . . Returned to base at 10 A.M. and made out report: "No activities noted." Slater made out a similar report. . . .

By mid-November, Fleishman had been admitted to membership in the Patrol's crooked inner circle. He was automatically included in the pay-offs made by the mobsters. He had found many of the patrolmen were honest men—but they were helpless with so many avenues for rumrunning left open around them.

Occasionally, Fleishman slipped at night into the Barlum Hotel to discuss the progress of the investigation with Elmer Lewis. The evidence of graft and corruption was piling up daily, yet Fleishman was troubled because he hadn't been able to link the pay-offs to any of the higher-ups in the rumrunning syndicates.

"You're doing all right," Lewis assured him. "Just be sure you don't get into any trouble."

Fleishman said, "There's one guy in this racket I would like to nail—Pete Licavoli. He's responsible for a big part of this mess."

Lewis nodded. "You're not likely to get close to Licavoli. He plays it smart."

Then one night Fleishman was detailed to the land patrol with Patrolmen James Mack and Shell Miller. They climbed into a Buick coach with Miller at the wheel and Miller headed the car out Fort Street to Military Road.

"Where are we going?" Mack asked.

Miller said, "I've found something worthwhile that I want to show you."

He turned onto Jefferson Avenue and after a time he drove slowly by a lumber yard beside a railroad track. "That's it," he said. "I got a tip they're handling booze in there by the carload. But they don't ship it until it's watered down. We'll come back later and pay them a visit."

The three men rode aimlessly around Ecorse until mid-morning and then Mack drove back to the lumber yard. They walked into a building where several men were making boxes. Suddenly Mack said, "Here comes a friend of mine."

Fleishman saw a big, handsome man emerge from an office. He recognized him instantly from his pictures. He was Pete Licavoli, and very plainly Licavoli was upset.

"For God's sake," the hoodlum said in disgust, "where did you come from?"

"We just thought we'd pay you a visit," Mack said. "Nice place you've got here."

"Beat it," Licavoli snarled. "Beat it and I'll fix you later."

Mack said, "Okay, boys, let's get out of here."

As they drove from the lumber yard, Mack said, "This thing is too good to put off. I'll arrange for us to see Pete tonight."

It was 5:40 when Mack and Miller picked up Fleishman at his apartment. They drove to Jefferson Avenue, where Mack parked the car. They walked down a long alley and Mack knocked on a door. They were admitted into an elaborately furnished restaurant which proved to be the private restaurant and hangout of Licavoli and his mob. The furnishings were in excellent taste. There were leather lounging chairs, a bar and the general atmosphere of a country club. Licavoli was seated at a table with one of his lieutenants, Sam Georges. He waved his visitors into seats.

Fleishman left the talking to Mack and Miller as they discussed how much Licavoli should pay to operate unmolested at the lumber yard shipping plant.

"This is the first time we've worked in a week," Georges complained, "and we're losing money."

Miller said, "Do you expect me to cry for you?"

The discussion continued through dinner and several rounds of drinks. Finally it was agreed Licavoli should pay $400 a week to be left alone. The mobster pulled out a fat wallet, counted out the money, and handed it to Mack. He stood up and put his hand on Fleishman's shoulder. "You boys come around any time," he said. "The drinks are on the house." And then he left.

In dividing the $400 pay-off, it was agreed that Fleishman would receive $110 and Mack and Miller $120 each, with $50 to be paid to the tipster who had pointed out the Licavoli operation to Mack. The money was divided as the men sat at the table.

In the days that followed, Fleishman's letters to Lewis were filled with reports of gangster pay-offs. The evidence piled up so rapidly that officials of the Treasury and Justice Departments, Customs Service, and the Prohibition Bureau met in Washington to discuss when and how a crackdown should be made. Elmer Lewis was called from Detroit to take part in the conference.

Lewis urged the conference to keep a tight lid of secrecy on the meeting. He warned that any disclosure that a Customs agent was working undercover in Detroit would be certain to endanger Fleishman's life. Sooner or later the hoodlums would discover he was an undercover man—and the Purple Gang gunmen would be after him.

But such news is difficult to keep bottled up in Washington. Part of the story, at least, was leaked to reporters. The following morning newspapers were carrying reports that a "big case" was expected to break soon over bribery and whiskey smuggling in Detroit. There was speculation, too, that a shakeup was coming in the Customs Patrol.

When Lewis read these reports, he arranged to take a train back to Detroit. He knew the news stories would be telegraphed to the Detroit newspapers.

At midnight on November 18, Fleishman reported for duty as usual. He was assigned to a patrol with two inspectors to cover the customary run along the River Rouge and the Wyandotte area. They visited the usual haunts, looking for any of the hoodlums who might be seeking an "all clear" signal for moving their whiskey across the river. None of them at the time had read the dispatches from Washington printed in the Detroit newspaper.

Shortly before dawn, the three men stopped in a Wyandotte restaurant for a bowl of soup and a sandwich. The restaurant was operated by Joe Rosen, one of the mobsters, and after a while Rosen came to the table. He whispered into the ear of one of the patrolmen and then hurried from the room.

"What's going on?" Fleishman asked. "Are we going to get some action?"

The inspector said, "Finish your sandwich and let's get out of here."

When they returned to the car, the inspector said, "Joe says at least three undercover men are working on the force and they've put the finger on about forty men. The mob is trying to find out who the stool pigeons are. Nothing's going to move until they do."

For the next two hours, Fleishman's companions talked of little else except the bribes they had turned down, and how honest they had been. Fleishman knew their talk was solely for his benefit. They were not good enough actors to conceal their anxiety.

When they finally stopped at a restaurant for a cup of coffee, Fleishman excused himself on the pretext that he had to call his wife. Instead he called the Barlum Hotel and asked for Elmer Lewis.

Lewis answered the phone. Fleishman explained what had happened. "This doesn't look good to me, Mr. Lewis," he said.

Lewis said, "Your job's finished. Now go home and pack your things. Get over here with your wife as fast as you can. You'll both be safer here."

Fleishman moved with his wife into the Barlum Hotel and only then did she learn of the role her husband had been playing for more than two months. A few days later, they slipped from the hotel and headed back East in their Model A Ford.

On November 30, eighteen hoodlums were arrested, along with

nineteen patrolmen. Two-score other patrolmen resigned. The cleanup was a newspaper sensation.

Pete Licavoli was among those sentenced to prison. The mob leader over the years had escaped conviction on charges ranging from sluggings to murders. But this time he pleaded guilty to bribing a Federal officer. He was fined $1,000 and sentenced to two years in Leavenworth prison.

While Fleishman was uncovering the evidence to convict Licavoli and the others in Detroit, another young agent—Chester A. Emerick—was making some interesting discoveries on the West Coast. A big, easy-going man, Emerick had developed sources which disclosed to him that much of the liquor bootlegged on the Pacific Coast was being shipped by a combine of Canadian liquor interests. Emerick learned that the Canadian liquor interests had formed the Pacific Forwarding Company of British Columbia to exploit the American liquor market. The company loaded its whiskey on ships at Vancouver for shipment ostensibly to Papeete, Tahiti. Once the liquor arrived in Tahiti, the Tahitian customs bond was cancelled and the shippers were not required to pay taxes on the liquor exported. Then the liquor was moved from Papeete to Rum Row off Southern California, off Long Beach and off the Washington coast. Rum Row was the nickname given by newspapers to the line of ships which stood at anchor in international waters, three miles offshore and just out of reach of U.S. maritime jurisdiction.

The Canadians did not merely bring the liquor to Rum Row. They had a well-organized force of salesmen operating in San Francisco, Los Angeles and Seattle, selling whiskey to bootleggers and guaranteeing delivery on a wholesale basis. The money collected by these salesmen was deposited in several banks along the Pacific Coast to the credit of the "Gulf Investment Company"—a company owned and controlled by the Canadian liquor interest. No one knows how many hundreds of millions of dollars in profit was realized by the Canadian conspiracy.

Emerick doggedly followed up the original leads obtained during prohibition and pressed for Federal action against the Canadian liquor dealers. In the spring of 1934—two years after the repeal of prohibition—two officers of the Canadian interests, Henry and George Reifel, arrived in Seattle. They were placed under arrest. The warrants had been issued secretly, and only four or five Customs officials knew of the action that had been taken. Service was obtained on warrants against the corporation which they represented, and a Federal action was brought in the District Court at Seattle, Washington. Before the case was concluded the Canadian interests had agreed to settle all liabilities by paying the U.S. government $3 million. This payment was accepted by the government and the case was closed.

There never were and perhaps there never will be again smuggling operations of such a magnitude as those which developed during the days of prohibition. Booze leaked across the borders from Canada and Mexico in streams. High-powered speedboats brought cases of liquor from supply ships riding at anchor in international waters. The Coast Guard and Customs were engaged at times in a shooting war with the rumrunners, and in the Detroit area alone, Customs had thirty speedboats engaged in around-the-clock blockade operations.

No authoritative study is available on how many ships and boats were engaged in rumrunning during the Twenties. But it was a formidable fleet, and there had been nothing quite like it since the blockade runners assembled their fleet to challenge the Union's blockade of the South during the Civil War.

One of the largest hauls of bootleg alcohol made by Customs came in 1926 with the seizure of the freighter *Cretan,* which was found to be carrying more than 70,000 gallons of Belgian alcohol easily worth $4 million on the retail bootleg market.

The *Cretan* was purchased by a "front" man for a group of Philadelphia and New York racketeers. Early in 1926, the *Cretan* steamed to the Bay of Fundy, where it made a rendezvous with the British ship the *Herald.* The *Herald*'s cargo of alcohol, a total of seven hundred 100-gallon drums, was transferred to the hold of the *Cretan.* Then several tons of baled waste paper were piled on top of the drums to conceal them in case the ship was boarded by Coast Guard or Customs officers.

The *Cretan* headed for Philadelphia with its valuable cargo of 190-proof spirits, but the mobsters weren't satisfied with the arrangements for unloading the cargo in Philadelphia. A message was sent to the *Cretan*'s captain ordering him to proceed to Boston and take on more baled waste paper. A decision would be made later on where to unload the alcohol.

The *Cretan* steamed into Boston harbor on schedule and tied up at an isolated pier. It began to take on more waste paper, with no one suspecting its true cargo. But a Customs officer observed several well-dressed men coming and going from the ship. He also noticed that two strange automobiles, both bearing New York license plates, were parked nearby. And he began to wonder what it was aboard the vessel that would bring the strangers all the way from New York to Boston—men who didn't seem to be seafaring types.

He reported his suspicion to Deputy Collector of Customs Thomas F. Finnegan. Finnegan decided to send a special duty squad aboard the ship to determine the nature of the ship's cargo. The squad boarded the *Cretan* but found they could not get into the holds. However, when they entered a coal bunker next to the holds, they detected the unmistakable odor of alcohol.

Finnegan ordered an immediate halt to the loading of waste paper. He posted guards at the gangway to prevent anyone from leaving the ship, and arranged for a lightering firm to unload the bales of waste paper from one hold. When the paper was removed, the drums of alcohol were uncovered. The *Cretan* and its cargo were forfeited to the government and sold at public auction. The alcohol was sold to drug companies which had Federal permits to dispense alcohol.

Some of the rumrunning craft were equipped with armor plate and bullet-proof glass around the pilot house area. They had underwater exhaust mufflers installed in order to slide silently through the water at night and evade the Coast Guard and Customs patrols. Most of them had two high-speed motors, each with a shaft and propeller. The conversion work on the boats was done by the rumrunners themselves or by small boat builders.

The *Whatzis,* operating out of Rhode Island, was believed to be the first rumrunning speedboat with four high-speed motors—two in tandem in each engine bed with a reduction gear between the motors. Each set of motors had one shaft and one propeller. This powerful craft was seized by the Coast Guard off the Massachusetts coast and later was inspected by several naval architects interested in its unusual power plant. Some insist to this day that the *Whatzis* was the craft that gave naval designers their idea for the rugged crash boats used at seaplane bases, and later for the PT boats which won renown in World War II.

The Twenties was a time of violence and turmoil for all the nation. And no agency of the government was more actively involved than the Customs Service, which, with other agencies, had the impossible task of trying to throw up a dike against the flow of illegal whiskey into the United States. Many good men tried, honestly and diligently, to enforce the law. But the great majority of the people simply didn't want prohibition.

In this period, Customs developed a tough and experienced corps of law enforcement agents and supervisors who were to serve the country well in future years.

7

THE ENFORCERS

Customs now has 240 special agents who police the Atlantic, Pacific, and Gulf of Mexico coastlines and the borders between Mexico and Canada. Their work is supported by 487 Customs enforcement officers (port patrolmen) and 2,551 Customs inspectors and supervisors.

Pressures for a special investigative force to combat smuggling and fraud developed after the Civil War, when normal trade was resumed between the United States and other nations of the world. Violations of the Tariff Act and a loose morality in administrative offices became so flagrant in those postwar years that in May, 1870, Congress passed a law providing: "The Secretary of the Treasury may appoint special agents, not exceeding 53 in number, for the purpose of making examinations of the books, papers and accounts of Collectors and other officers of the Customs, and to be employed generally under the direction of the Secretary, in the prevention and detection of frauds on the Customs revenue . . ."

With this act, the Secretary of the Treasury gathered under his direction for the first time a special police force to combat smuggling and frauds.

The need for such a force actually dated back to the first days of the Republic. But over the years, the enforcement work had been handled by inspectors, guards and other untrained personnel. In 1922 Secretary of the Treasury Andrew W. Mellon transferred the Special Agency Service from his personal direction to the Customs Administration, which was then a division of the Treasury Department. In 1927, the Customs Division was given the status of a bureau by Congress, with direct control over its own investigative force.

This force now operates under a Division of Investigations, headed by the veteran enforcement officer Chester A. Emerick, former Collector of Internal Revenue in Tacoma, Washington, who joined the Customs Service in 1920. Emerick has the title of Deputy Commissioner, and he is responsible to the Commissioner of Customs in the operation of his division.

The responsibilities of the Customs agents were not clearly defined in the early days of their operation. But a clear directive was issued in 1933 to dispel any lingering doubts. This directive read: "(a) Customs agents shall be employed generally in the prevention and detection of frauds on the Customs revenue and all matters involving such frauds requiring investigation shall be referred to them. They shall investigate and report upon all matters brought to their attention by the Commissioner of Customs, Collectors, Appraisers, Comptrollers, and others relating to drawback, undervaluation, smuggling, personnel, Customs procedure, and any other Customs matters.

"(b) undivided responsibility for the investigation and reporting to the proper authority of all irregularities concerning any phase of Customs administration or misconduct on the part of Customs employees, by whatever means brought to its attention, rests with the Customs Agency Service. This injunction, however, is not to be construed as abridging or modifying the responsibility of the principal field officers to maintain discipline and efficiency in the Customs personnel. There shall be no differentiation in the treatment of chief administrative officers of Customs and their subordinates in the matter of investigating accusations of alleged official misconduct. Collectors and other chief officers of the Customs shall cooperate in making this policy effective."

Jerome Dolan is a handsome, black-haired young Irishman. It was, literally, a swift and embarrassing kick in the pants which started him on the road to becoming a Treasury agent.

It began for Dolan when he was a twelve-year-old living on Selby Avenue in the Lexington Parkway area of St. Paul, Minnesota. The street was a quiet, comfortable, tree-shaded thoroughfare lined with the homes of middle-income families. The Dolan home was near a shopping center and only a brisk walk from the neighborhood school.

There were playgrounds not far distant and vacant lots where youngsters could play baseball after school and during vacations. But in the perverse way of small boys, Dolan and his pals found it more fun to play ball on the streets, much to the annoyance of the residents and Officer "Red" Schwartz, who frequently cruised through the area in Patrol Car 309.

Schwartz was a large, muscular man standing 6 feet 2. He was forever breaking up the ball games with gruff commands for the boys to get off the streets. If there was any backtalk, Schwartz was likely to box the ears of the impertinent rebel, or to boot him in the behind. Then he would growl that he wasn't going to have anyone killed by an automobile on his beat if he could help it.

Dolan and his friends usually kept a sharp lookout for Schwartz, the enemy. But one day they were careless and Car 309 came rolling down the street into the midst of a noisy game. Officer Schwartz came boiling from behind the wheel of the car. He laid two heavy hands on Dolan and another youth who hadn't been nimble enough to escape. He shook them until their teeth rattled and then he booted them in the backsides with the broadside of a large shoe—just hard enough to give emphasis to his words.

"Maybe that will teach you a lesson," Officer Schwartz called to the retreating youths. "And don't let me catch you again."

It never occurred to Schwartz to complain to the youths' parents. This was his beat. It was his responsibilty to maintain law and order, and to protect the lives of those in his charge. He also felt it was his duty to discipline the youths who showed a lack of proper respect for authority.

"I'll get even with that red-headed cop," Dolan vowed. "Just you wait and see."

"How are you goin' to get even?" his friend asked.

Dolan considered the problem. At last he said, "Well, I'm going to be a policeman and when I'm his boss, I'll fix him."

As a sophomore in high school, Dolan had forgotten his vow to "fix" Schwartz, even though he often looked from the window of his classroom to see Car 309 cruising by the schoolyard. But he had not lost his determination to become a law enforcement officer. In writing down his ambition for the class yearbook, he wrote: "I want to be a Federal law enforcement officer."

One reason Dolan had fixed his sights on a career in Federal law enforcement was the fact that the father of his friend, Sam Hardy, Jr., was an FBI agent. Sam Hardy occasionally came to the school and talked to the students about the work of the FBI. These talks only strengthened his desire to become a Federal agent.

After graduating from high school in the spring of 1950, Dolan entered the Army. He was assigned to the Army's security section and he travelled throughout the Far East as a courier. When he was mustered out of the service, he enrolled in St. Thomas College in St. Paul and worked part time as an investigator for business firms.

He was graduated from St. Thomas in 1958 and became chief security officer for the Golden Rule Department Store in St. Paul. Then he joined the city's police department.

One morning Dolan reported for roll call at the main police headquarters in the Public Safety Building. After inspection the lieutenant read off the list of assignments for the day. He said, "Dolan, you will work Car 309 with Officer Schwartz."

Dolan climbed into the car beside Schwartz and all the old memories came flooding back of how he once hated this gruff policeman who had booted him in the pants. He remembered wryly his vow to one day get revenge.

Now "Red" Schwartz's hair was sprinkled with gray. He was heavier and the lines on his face were deeper. His hands, though, were just as big and powerful as Dolan had remembered, and he had the same stern air of authority about him.

Dolan said nothing about the remembered indignities, and the older man apparently did not recognize the rookie as one of the youngsters who had given him such a bad time out on Selby Avenue. He could not know, either, that he had had such a strong influence on the youth who sat beside him.

They made their rounds without incident that day until late in the afternoon when the car radio said: "Car 309 . . . Hague and Dunlap . . . a child has been struck by a car. . . ."

Schwartz picked up the the transmitter and said: "309 to Hague and Dunlap . . . 4:05." He swung the car toward the scene of the accident. A little girl lay beside the curb, and her weeping mother was wiping blood from her daughter's face with a cloth. The child had darted from the curb into the path of an automobile. There had been a screech of brakes and the girl had been hurled to the curb, unconscious.

As Dolan recalled the scene later in talking to me: "Schwartz, as big as he was, was out of the car ahead of me. He went straight to the little girl and her mother and I never would have believed those big hands could be so gentle. He soothed the mother with a few words, and when he saw the girl wasn't seriously hurt, he picked her up in his arms and carried her into her home as though she were his own daughter."

Then Dolan added, "I was very proud of Schwartz that day and of being his partner in Car 309."

Twelve years after receiving the kick in the pants from Schwartz, Dolan was among the students selected to attend the Treasury Department's Law Enforcement School at 711 12th Street in downtown Washington, D. C. He finally had decided to become a Secret Service agent, and now he was receiving basic training with rookie agents from the Customs Bureau, the Narcotics Bureau, the Secret Service, the Coast Guard, and units of the Internal Revenue Service.

Watching these young men in training, you wondered what it was that moved each of them to choose Federal law enforcement as a career. The work is difficult and demanding, calling for stern self-discipline. The hours are long, irregular and often filled with danger. No agent ever knows when he may be called from his home on an emergency assignment which may last for weeks. The pay, ranging from $5,355 per year for a rookie to a high of $10,255 for a veteran agent (only the supervising agents receive higher pay) is not exactly an economic bonanza for a college graduate. Salary is not the primary inducement; many of the youths have wanted to be in law enforcement since childhood.

One youth told me, "My father was shot and killed by a bootlegger when I was just a boy. I grew up in a tough neighborhood. I've always wanted to be in law enforcement to help fight crime."

"I like the excitement of the work," another said, "never knowing from one day to the next what the problem will be or how it will be solved."

"I didn't have much chance for advancement as a city policeman, but it's different as a Federal agent."

"There's no politics in Federal law enforcement—not like you find in local law enforcement. You don't have to worry about the politicians."

A good many of the rookie agents who come to the school studied police administration in college and then worked on city police forces before taking the Civil Service examination required of candidates for Federal law enforcement jobs.

When an applicant passes the examination, his name goes on the Federal Registry, and it is from this registry that most of the new agents are chosen. Regional boards composed of representatives from the various Treasury divisions interview the applicants as openings occur from time to time in the agents' ranks. Customs may need a Spanish-speaking agent for duty on the Mexican border. Narcotics may be looking for a man of Italian ancestry who speaks Sicilian fluently. Or Revenue may be searching for an investigator with a knowledge of accounting.

If an applicant wins approval on the regional board, his background is investigated and he is given a physical examination. If all goes well, he is sworn into the service of his choice.

The rookie agents spend their first months in service receiving on-the-job training by working with experienced officers. Then they are sent to the Treasury's Law Enforcement School for six weeks of study in basic courses such as how to make searches and seizures, how to conduct a surveillance, how to plan a raid, how to photograph the scene of a crime, how to take latent fingerprints, how to interview witnesses and interrogate suspects, and how to conduct themselves in a courtroom under cross-examination.

The Treasury school was established permanently in Washington in 1951 and has now graduated more than 15,000 agents. It is headed by Director Patrick O'Carroll, a forty-two-year-old former Narcotics agent who was reared in New York City. O'Carroll was graduated from Fordham University in 1944, where he majored in psychology. Dark-haired, handsome Pat O'Carroll guides a staff of fifty instructors, who give the basic training to rookies and also instruct veteran agents in specialized courses involving administrative duties. At present the school is conducting six 6-week courses a year for rookies, with an average of eighty students in each class. There also are a scattering of foreign students, sent by their governments to study American police methods.

O'Carroll and his aides strive to make the instruction as realistic as possible by providing problems which simulate actual situations the young agents will face in their everyday work. In the 9 A.M. to 5 P.M. classes, held five days a week, the men spend about half their time working on practical law enforcement problems. The other half is spent in listening to lectures by agents, police administrators, college professors and attorneys. The lectures cover such subjects as constitutional law, civil rights and rules of criminal law procedure.

Toward the end of the course, the students are divided into squads of five men and given the problem of arresting a suspected criminal, searching his apartment for evidence, preparing the case for presentation to a grand jury, and appearing in court as witnesses.

On the fourth floor of the school building is a furnished room in which have been hidden narcotics, counterfeit money, betting slips, jewels and other incriminating evidence. The room is occupied by a veteran agent posing as "Richard Roe," the suspected criminal.

Roe gives them a rough time. He complains of a serious heart condition and asks to be given medicine from a bottle on a table. He accuses the agents of stealing money and a diamond ring from a desk drawer. He continually demands to see his lawyer. A postman delivers a registered letter and Roe challenges the right of the agents to open the letter after he has signed for it. He tries everything short of violence to impede the search.

Sometimes the young agents refuse to give Roe his medicine. They ignore his accusations of theft. Or they accept his argument that they have no right to seize the registered letter.

If the searching party fails to find at least 80 per cent of the items concealed in the room, they do not obtain a "conviction." Then experienced agents carefully explain where they made mistakes in the handling of the suspect.

When Roe claimed he was ill, the agents should have called his doctor to determine the truth. Upon their entering the room, Roe should have been advised to collect any valuables so that an inventory could have been made on the spot to be signed by him. When Roe signed for the registered letter, then it legally could be seized with no invasion of his privacy. Roe's rights were not violated when his requests for an attorney were ignored during the search, prior to his arrest.

In a mock courtroom scene, an agent who formerly was a U.S. attorney acts as the defense counsel. He grills the rookies on every move made in Roe's apartment, seeking to confuse them while driving home the point that months of careful police work may be wasted by an inept or careless presentation of facts in court.

The school has proved to be such a success that it is now supported enthusiastically by all the Treasury agencies, which prorate the cost and make their best men available as instructors. But for many years a few men struggled to keep the school going in the face of apathy and even active opposition.

The man who perhaps contributed most to keeping alive the idea of a professionally directed school for Treasury agents was Harry M. Dengler, a retired Internal Revenue agent who now lives in Washington, D. C. A short, plump man of enormous energy, Dengler joined the Internal Revenue Service in 1918 after a dozen years of teaching in high schools in southeast Virginia and Montana. He was thirty-six at the time he was assigned to the IRS's Intelligence Division, working on internal police problems and on tax conspiracy cases.

The Treasury school stemmed from the fact that in 1927 the Bureau of Prohibition's enforcement of the Volstead Act was a mess. Part of the mess was due to the lack of trained enforcement officers. Illegal searches and seizures by Bureau agents aroused public indignation. Also, they created a serious problem in obtaining convictions of rumrunners and bootleggers.

L. C. Andrews, the Assistant Secretary of the Treasury, became so concerned over the situation that he persuaded Dengler to join the Bureau of Prohibition and to start an enforcement school for the Bureau's agents. Dengler had argued for years that Federal law enforcement officers should be schooled in their work to be effective and to deserve public confidence.

Dengler selected a few aides and they put together a course of instruction to be given to some 2,500 prohibition agents. Two men were chosen from each of the Treasury's eighteen districts throughout the country to come to Washington for four weeks of intensive schooling in proper law enforcement procedures.

The theory was that these thirty-six men would qualify themselves as instructors and then return to their home districts to teach what they had learned to other prohibition agents. But the system soon broke down because the district supervisors sabotaged the school.

"I know how to enforce the law without any help from Washington," one supervisor announced. He had the support of other supervisors.

The truth was that the supervisors were jealous of the men who had been brought to Washington for special training. They also were fearful that they would lose their jobs to the men with superior backgrounds in law enforcement. The result was that the schools were doomed even before they started. By the end of the year, the schools had been discontinued.

Dengler clung stubbornly to his belief that every Federal law enforcement officer should be trained for his job. He persuaded his superiors to let him organize a correspondence course, with the study to be voluntary. Hundreds of agents applied, convincing Dengler that the agents themselves were eager to know more about professional law enforcement.

The idea of a school was resurrected in 1930 by Amos W. W. Woodcock, when he became head of the Prohibition agency. Dengler again went to work to set up a course of study. But when Woodcock left office a few months later, his successor broke up the schools with the remark: "If a man is smart enough to get a job with us, he doesn't need any training."

Dengler confided to a friend later, "That was one of the low points of my life. These schools were badly needed by the government to improve the quality of Federal law enforcement. Hardly anyone seemed interested."

Indeed, for several years it seemed that no one was interested except Dengler and a few of his friends. But in 1937 Secretary of the Treasury Henry Morgenthau recognized that a major weakness in his department was the lack of organized training for new agents. He issued an order for all agencies within the Treasury to participate in a school program.

The first Dengler heard of the order was when Harold N. Graves, assistant to the Secretary, called him to his office. Graves said, "Harry, how long will it take you to get a course of instruction underway for our agents?"

"I can do it within sixty days," Dengler said.

Graves was dubious. "I don't think you can do it within that time," he said.

"I can do it," Dengler replied. "I've kept a group of instructors together. We've been giving some training to new men in our spare time. We've got a course of instruction already outlined. It won't take much work to bring it up to date."

Graves said, "Then get going. Bring your men in here this afternoon and we'll decide on the next move."

The decision was to open a pilot school in Boston. The first class met on March 15, 1937, and the course of instruction ran for four weeks. When it was ended, Graves was satisfied. He ordered a schedule of instruction for each of the Treasury districts. Attendance was not voluntary this time. Each man was required to attend classes, and to pass a written examination. Instructors were drawn from all the Treasury agencies.

In those early years, the instructors travelled from district to district to hold their classes. The classrooms were jury rooms, schoolrooms, banks, courthouses and Customs buildings.

Dengler argued that the school should be located permanently in Washington. Instead of having instructors moving from place to place, he insisted it would be far better to have the students come to Washington to get their training at a school housed in its own building and having the proper equipment.

Dengler's persistence won. In 1950, Treasury officials decided to see how his plan would work. It worked so well that when Dengler retired in December, 1952, the Treasury Law Enforcement School was an established institution receiving all-out support from all the Treasury agencies.

The Treasury school, however, is only a phase of instruction in law enforcement for the young Customs agents (as it is for all Treasury agents). The intensive training comes when the men are assigned to work regularly with older agents.

The turnover among Customs agents is surprisingly small and is among the lowest within the government. Few of them leave the Service voluntarily once they have launched into their careers. The reason for this stability was summed up by one veteran agent in this manner: "Every man likes to feel he is doing something worthwhile—and you get that kind of satisfaction from this work. That's why I'll never leave it."

8

TEST TUBE DETECTIVES

Shortly before World War II, a rusted old freighter slid into its berth at a Baltimore pier, completing its long voyage from the Orient. Customs officers boarded the vessel to check the manifest, verify the cargo, and search for contraband. The search was the routine sort of thing that occurred every day at every major port in the United States.

An inspector hurried to the quarters of the crew members and began his rounds. He encountered nothing unusual until he reached one crewman's cabin and found the door locked. He knocked on the door and a muffled voice said, "Who is it?"

"This is the Customs inspector," the officer said. "Open up."

The door opened and a seaman said gruffly, "There's nothing in here. You'll find everything on my declaration." He was a slender, middle-aged man with thinning hair and tattoos on his forearms.

"It's a routine check," the inspector said. "You've got nothing to worry about."

The seaman made no move to stand aside. "I told you there's nothing in here," he insisted.

"Look, Mac," the inspector snapped, "you've been through this sort of thing before and you know it's got to be done. So let me get at it." He pushed his way into the cabin.

On a table he saw a hypodermic needle. He picked it up and turned to the seaman. "Are you a junkie?" he asked. "Have you got any narcotics?"

The seaman's face reddened with anger. "Hell, no! I wouldn't touch the stuff."

The inspector wasn't impressed with the denial. That's what they all said until you found their supply of narcotics.

When he started to open a locker, the crewman said, "It's empty. I've already taken everything out."

The inspector looked at the man's hands shake as he lit a cigarette. "Why don't you sit down and take it easy, mister?" he said. "I've just decided to take a good look around."

Slowly he went over the cabin. At last he pulled the locker away from the bulkhead and saw a small cotton bag taped to the back of the locker. He yanked it loose and held it out toward the seaman. "What is this?"

The seaman made a grab for the bag. "Give that to me!" he said. "It's nothing that interests you."

The inspector opened the bag and saw that it contained a white powder which looked suspiciously like heroin. He said, "Mister, if this is heroin, you are in trouble."

"It's not heroin," the seaman said sullenly.

"If it isn't heroin," the inspector said, "then what is it? Why did you hide it behind the locker? What are you trying to hide?" But the seaman remained silent.

The inspector said, "You are not to leave this ship until I have an analysis made of this powder. Do you understand?"

The seaman nodded. The inspector left the cabin and went to

the captain to explain the situation. He requested the seaman be detained on the freighter pending a chemical test of the powder.

"It looks like heroin," the inspector said. "If it is, we'll have to take him into custody."

"How long will it take to make the test?" the skipper asked. "We're sailing tomorrow afternoon. If this man is in trouble, I'll have to take on another seaman."

"We should know the results before you sail," the inspector said. "I'll be in touch with you."

The sack of powder was sent to the Baltimore Customs laboratory with an urgent request for a quick test. It was turned over to tall, lanky Edward Kenney, who had received his training as a chemist at the University of Maine, Massachusetts Institute of Technology and Johns Hopkins University. Kenney was among the small group of men and women who had found the Customs laboratories to be a daily adventure in solving riddles posed by the legal necessity of identifying and classifying a bewildering variety of imports which poured into the United States daily from all parts of the world.

The analysis of the powder taken from the seaman was one of the routine chores which posed no problem for Kenney. The test for heroin was negative—and he sent his findings to the chief chemist to be relayed to the inspector on the case.

A few minutes later, Kenney received a telephone call from the inspector. "Mr. Kenney," he said, "I just can't believe that report you made on the powder I seized from the seaman. If ever I saw a guilty man, this one is guilty. Would you mind running another test?"

"I'm sure the report was correct," Kenney said, "but if it will make you feel better, I'll make another test. Would you like to come over and watch?"

"I certainly would," the inspector said.

When the inspector arrived at the laboratory, Kenney took a sampling from the powder and placed it in a glass container. Then he picked up a bottle of liquid from a cabinet.

"This liquid is a mixture of sulphuric acid and formaldehyde," he explained. "I'm going to make a Marquis test. It's named after the man who invented it long before either you or I were born. Nobody seems to know much about Marquis, but he knew what he was doing. He found that when you add this liquid to an opium narcotic powder, the powder will show purple discoloration. Now watch."

Kenney poured a few drops of the liquid onto the powder to dissolve it. But there was no indication of a purple color.

"Is that test conclusive?" the inspector asked.

"No, not necessarily," Kenney said. "There are some impurities which could produce a purple discoloration. Let's see if we can isolate any opium with another test." But when an effort was made to extract opium from the powder with an infallible procedure, the result was negative. The powder beyond doubt did not contain narcotics.

"Well," Kenney said, "that's it. Your seamen wasn't smuggling narcotics."

The inspector said, "I know you're right but I was certain I had grabbed a sack of heroin. What is the stuff in the sack?"

Kenney said, "I don't know, but I've got a pretty good hunch. I'll run another test and let you know the results."

When Kenney completed his testing the following morning, he called the inspector. "Your man was carrying saccharine," he said.

The inspector returned to the ship to have the seaman freed from detention and to question him further. "The powder wasn't heroin," he said. "It was saccharine. I'd like to know one thing. Why did you make such a big mystery of it?"

The seaman at last disclosed that he was a diabetic—and that for months he had kept this fact from his shipmates and from the ship's officers. He gave himself insulin shots secretly and used saccharine instead of sugar in his coffee. He had been fearful that if anyone aboard the ship learned he was a diabetic, he would be barred from going to sea—a fear which he was to learn was entirely groundless.

When the inspector met Kenney later, he said, "I'm sorry I put you to so much trouble for nothing. The whole thing was a waste of time."

Kenney shook his head in disagreement. "I don't think it was a waste of time at all," he said. "We proved the seaman was innocent of smuggling narcotics and we helped him get rid of an unreasonable fear. As I see it, the results were pretty good."

The case of the diabetic seaman is only one of many strange cases which find their way to the Customs Bureau's laboratories located in New York, Boston, Baltimore, Philadelphia, Savannah, New Orleans, Los Angeles, San Francisco, Chicago, and San Juan, Puerto Rico. Thousands of items, from yak hair to heroin, come to the chemists to be sampled, tested and identified.

In the course of a day, a laboratory may be called on to identify and determine the amount of grease and dirt that is in a shipment of Australian wool; report the percentage of tungsten in a shipment of ore; determine the antiquity of a diamond-studded tiara; test the alcoholic content of Scotch whiskey; examine a rosary case made in Japan, in order to establish its chief component; and analyze a sample of powdered milk from Holland to measure its butter fat.

Or the laboratory may be called on to analyze a shipment of mica to determine whether the mica splittings measure more or less than .0012 inches in thickness. The measurement of the mica has a dollars-and-cents importance to the shipper, the importer and the government because the duty is based on the thickness of the mica splittings, which in turn affects the market value of the import.

No laboratories in all the world have a more varied job to do than those of Customs. Every article that is known to commerce reaches these laboratories at one time or another. The examinations are necessary because only by a precise determination of the contents of many shipments are the appraiser and the collector able to establish value and thus determine the rate of duty which is to be paid into the Treasury of the United States.

The scientists never know when one of their analyses will touch off a court battle which will involve an entire industry and which may mean a difference of millions of dollars to businessmen.

Such a case occurred several years ago when one of the Bureau's laboratories received for analysis a sample of a product imported from Canada under the trade name "Lioxin." This product had a great many industrial uses and was competitive with vanillin, which is derived from the vanilla bean and also from coal tar. The imported product was being offered on the market at a price considerably below that of the competing vanillin product—at a price so low, in fact, that it threatened to upset the entire vanillin trade.

The discovery of Lioxin had been one of those accidents of science in which a waste product is found to be extremely valuable. A wood pulp company was dumping waste matter into a nearby stream, and sportsmen complained that it was killing all the fish. The complaints became so numerous that the company called in a scientist to see what could be done about correcting the situation. The scientist found while experimenting with certain chemical compounds that he could convert the waste matter into a substance that was 96 to 97 per cent vanillin. And it could be done much more cheaply than extracting vanillin from the vanilla bean or from coal tar.

When Customs chemists analyzed the product, they found that it contained impurities—but the impurities could be removed quite easily and cheaply. The end product was almost pure vanillin, meeting all the rigid standards set up by the U.S. Pharmacopoeia Act.

The result of the laboratory findings was a decision to classify Lioxin as vanillin, dutiable at $2.25 per pound based on the American selling price. The duty brought the price of the import into line with the competing American product.

The Bureau's decision was protested by the importer. The claim was made that the compound was not vanillin under the terms of the Tariff Act. It was argued that when Congress passed the law setting the duty on vanillin, the lawmakers had in mind the vanillin which came from the vanilla bean and from coal tar.

However, the courts held that the import was only "one step short of the finished product" and that when the impurities were removed in a very simple process, then the end product was a vanillin conforming to the standards of the U.S.P. As such, it was held to be subject to the same tariff payment as other vanillin imports.

The case of the synthetic vanillin explains in a large measure why the turnover among scientists and technicians in the Customs laboratories is among the lowest in the entire Federal government. A day rarely passes in which they are not presented with a new and challenging problem—not unlike the solving of a mystery. There simply is no time to become bored.

Frequently these men must devise their own methods of examination and establish their own standards for a product simply because there is nothing in the book which they can use as a guide. Many new products have come into the markets in the past few years—particularly in the field of chemicals—which are not provided for in the law except in a vague, catch-all phrase "and not specially provided for."

The laboratories never know what to expect next. This was the case when the New York laboratory received a sample of a shipment of artificial Christmas trees resembling small pine trees. The examiners at the pier who first inspected the trees were baffled as to how they should be classified and what the rate of duty on them should be. The trees were made from materials which the examiners could not identify. And identification had to be made before a rate of duty could be fixed.

One of the trees was sent to the Customs laboratory on Varick Street, where it was taken apart piece by piece. It was found that the base was made from pasteboard. The trunk was fashioned of wire and the bark from paper. But the artificial pine needles were discovered to be dyed goose feathers. Since the law holds that the duty must be paid on the "component material of chief value" —then the Christmas tree's actual chief value was in the dyed goose feathers. Dyed goose feathers called for a duty of 20 per cent of their value on the market.

Frequently the laboratory workers find themselves in the role of a Sherlock Holmes—using their test tubes and their spectrometers and their diffractometers as tools to help track down criminals.

One day an employee on the New York piers noticed that an automobile which was to be loaded aboard a ship for Europe seemed to be heavier in the rear than in the front. The car was setting too low on its rear springs, although there was nothing in the trunk of the car to put any undue weight on the springs.

This fact was called to the attention of Customs officers, and they decided to examine the car. They went over it carefully and finally discovered a section behind the rear seat which appeared to have been tampered with. There were scratches on the metal which seemed to have been made only recently. A further examination disclosed a secret compartment built into the car, and when this was pried open, it was found to contain about $30,000 worth of gold bars. They were being smuggled out of the country.

The bars were taken to the New York laboratory for examination. There seemed to be no way to identify them because the serial numbers—which are stamped into each bar of gold and recorded by the government—had been hacked and gouged from the soft metal. But the laboratory discovered a method—still secret—by which they were able to read the numbers on each of the bars. This information was turned over to the Secret Service, and Secret Service agents were able to track down the man who had made the original purchase of the bars.

Part of the laboratories' job is to watch for improper classification of imports by shippers who hope to slip them into the country under a lower rate of duty than the Tariff Act provides for. As aids in this work the chemists have spectrographs (used for the most part in analyzing metals), X-ray diffractometers, electrolytic machines and other instruments enabling them to break down and identify the component parts of materials brought into the country.

By use of the diffractometer and X-ray, the laboratories have been able to determine in innumerable cases that shipments have been improperly classified by the shippers either intentionally or unintentionally. At any rate, the shipments have been uniformly reclassified at higher rates of duty, saving the U.S. Treasury many thousands of dollars.

There is one case on record in which a diffractometer was credited with reversing a court decision. Before the diffractometer was installed in the New York laboratory, an importer brought into the country a shipment of material which he listed as duty-free zirconium oxide. A chemical analysis, while not very convincing, showed that the material was not zirconium oxide. But the method of testing was such that the importer successfully challenged the Customs finding and the Customs court ruled that the material should be admitted as zirconium oxide, free of duty.

However, the laboratory was not finished with this case. Soon after this decision a diffractometer was installed in the laboratory. Another analysis of the material was made. And the diffractometer revealed beyond the shadow of doubt that the material was not what the importer claimed. The crystals in the material showed that it was stabilized zirconium oxide, dutiable at 15 per cent of its value, rather than ordinary zirconium oxide, free of any duty. The result was that the diffractometer's findings were accepted by the court and the original ruling in favor of the importer was reversed.

Sometimes the secretiveness of shippers poses an unusual problem. Such was the case when a Swedish manufacturer of homogenized ham-and-cheese spread decided to send his product into the American market. He would not disclose to Customs the recipe for this spread—obviously feeling that his trade secret might fall into the hands of a competitor.

Customs chemists were given the job of determining which of the materials in the spread was the major dutiable material. It was a tricky problem because both ham and cheese are of animal origin and consist of protein and fats. After two weeks the laboratory was able to report that the Swedish manufacturer's product was primarily ham. Then there was no problem in fixing the tariff rate.

New York is the largest of the laboratories and tests about one-fourth of more than 120,000 samples which are examined each year. Boston is the next largest, and then comes New Orleans. Over the years each laboratory has become a specialist in certain examinations. Most of the wool entering the United States is examined in Boston. Chicago leads in the examinations of samples of ore, grain, and metals. New York does the great majority of testing of dyestuffs; and New Orleans has become a major center in the examination of narcotics, because of its geographic location near the Mexican border.

The laboratories are constantly seeking new and better ways of testing materials. A notable achievement in this field was made by Melvin Lerner, now the chief chemist in the Baltimore laboratory, when he developed an entirely new method for determining, easily and accurately, the opium content of any materials, in addition to identifying prohibited synthetic narcotics.

The process involves dissolving a small amount of the suspected powder in a mixture of trichloroethane, chloroform, nitric acid and phosphoric acid. If no heroin is present, the liquid will be colorless or have an apple-green hue. But if heroin is present, the liquid will range in color from light yellow to yellowish brown —the darker color indicating the powder is almost 100 per cent pure heroin. Distinctive coloring is produced also by the synthetics.

The Lerner test for identifying prohibited synthetic narcotics has created world-wide interest. Virtually every country in the world has written to the Customs Bureau requesting information on this process and asking for one of the small field kits with which the tests can be made.

Frequently the laboratories are able to give invaluable help to importers in protecting them from fraud and sometimes saving them from embarrassment. There was one case in which a curator of a museum vouched for the antiquity of a tapestry which he had imported for the museum from Europe. As an antiquity—that is, an article made before 1830—it would not have been subject to any tariff duty. The curator was quite insistent about the age of the tapestry. But laboratory experts discovered that the tapestry's threads had been stained with coal tar dyes. Since coal tar dyes were not used before 1857, the tapestry obviously was not an antiquity. The curator was embarrassed over being proved wrong, but nevertheless he was grateful that the discovery had been made before the tapestry was hung in the museum.

In another case the laboratory experts were able to set at ease the mind of an importer of an extremely valuable gold, diamond, and ruby tiara which had been purchased as a museum piece. Even though the tiara was known to be very old, it was suspected that the piece had undergone major repairs. If this were true, it meant that duty would have to be paid on any substantial repairs to the import.

The tiara was taken to the New York laboratory. A chemist rubbed the tiara lightly with a very fine sandpaper to remove a few flecks of gold. These flecks were then analyzed by a spectrograph, which revealed that the gold contained the impurities commonly found in gold refined by antique methods. There was no need for the payment of any duty on the tiara.

The laboratory experts work in close cooperation with the Bureau's enforcement division, and they never know when they may be called upon to don their detective hats. There was one case in which it was suspected that cattle were being smuggled from Canada into upper New York State. The laboratory supplied agents with a certain chemical which they took into Canada and, with the cooperation of Canadian law enforcement officers, secretly smeared on herds of cattle in the area where the smuggling had been taking place. When the chemical dried on the cattle, it left no visible trace.

Later the agents smeared a second chemical on cattle which were suspected of having been smuggled into New York State. No sooner was this done than large red blotches appeared on the cattle—irrefutable evidence that these animals had been smuggled in from Canada. This may have been the first time that science got into the business of combatting cattle rustling.

The Customs laboratories trace their beginning to 1848, when Congress wrote into law a requirement that Customs should examine all drugs, medicines, medicinal preparations, and chemical preparations used as medicine to determine their quality and purity. Standards of strength and purity were established. The analyzing was farmed out to chemists in commercial firms or to pharmacists and physicians.

Although this law was passed in 1848, it was not until 1880 that the Customs Bureau was authorized to employ its own chemist. By this time there was imperative need for more laboratory work to aid the Customs appraisers.

In the early 1880s the Bureau first began using instruments such as the polariscope to determine the actual strength of sugar being imported.

Old records show that chemists were added to the Customs staff at New York and San Francisco between 1880 and 1890. A Customs laboratory was established in Philadelphia in 1892 and in San Francisco in 1899. Despite the obvious value of their work, the chemists were not regarded very highly in the government service, and until 1910 their salaries were $1,200 a year—the same as that received by an ordinary clerk.

As the tariff laws became more complex, the work in the laboratories increased correspondingly. For example, the Tariff Act of 1922 fixed duties on the components of certain imports, such as the amount of calcium fluoride in fluorspar and the amount of silica in glass sand and ferro alloys. Congress also defined in the Tariff Act items such as vinegar, cellulose compounds, hardened and vegetable oils, molasses and sirups. Other laws called for duties on copper, fatty acids, soaps and petroleum. The passage of the laws required scientific analyses of shipments to obtain a precise determination of their dutiable contents.

Until 1936 the laboratories throughout the country operated more or less independently of each other with only a loose system of cooperation between them. But in 1936 a Division of Laboratories was established within the Bureau to direct operations and to fix uniform procedures throughout the service.

In 1953, the then Commissioner of Customs, Ralph Kelly, expanded the duties of the Division of Laboratories and changed its name to the Division of Technical Services. The Division, now located at the Customs Bureau headquarters in Washington, directs the operations of Customs laboratories; furnishes to the Commissioner information on engineering, chemical, statistical, and other scientific and technical developments; plans and standardizes sampling, weighing, and testing standards and procedures; inspects the laboratories; and furnishes any needed engineering services.

This division, under the direction of Dr. George Vlasses, is the smallest of the seven administrative divisions in the Customs Bureau, with only seven employees. In all, the laboratories have a total of 136 employees, of which 76 are chemists. The balance are physical science aides, laboratory helpers, and administrative and clerical employees.

Even though these men and women cannot take people's motives apart and test them, the relative purity of their motives often is revealed quite clearly to these test-tube detectives.

9

THE INFORMERS

The giant luxury liner, the SS *Ile de France,* slid by the Statue of Liberty in New York harbor on October 7, 1938, with her passengers crowding the rail for a view of the skyline of New York. It was a gay crowd, most of them returning from European vacations. But among them were those to whom the arrival meant more than gaiety—it meant life itself. These were the refugees from Hitler's Germany.

As the tugs shouldered the liner into its berth on Manhattan Island, there was confusion ashore. Scores of people had gathered to greet returning friends and relatives. Customs officers were busy preparing for the rush of passengers to the pier, the inspection of baggage and all the little details that are required when a ship brings its cargo from across the sea.

Among those who came ashore on this day was a dark-haired man of medium build, about 5 feet 7 inches tall and hardly looking his forty-five years of age. He was accompanied by a handsome, beautifully groomed woman wearing a smartly tailored suit. These two obviously were experienced travellers. They waited patiently under the huge sign marked with the letter "C" until their baggage arrived from the ship, and then they sought a Customs inspector to present their baggage declaration.

The Customs inspector took the declaration and glanced at it. He said, "Mr. and Mrs. Nathaniel Chaperau?"

"That is correct," replied the dark-haired man. "I believe all of our baggage is in this group."

The inspector read the declaration and noted that Mr. Chaperau had signed it as a commercial attaché for the Nicaraguan government—which meant that he and his wife were entitled to pass through customs without the formality of a baggage inspection. Mr. Chaperau handed the inspector Nicaraguan passports and a letter signed by the Consul General of Nicaragua in New York authenticating the endorsement on the customs declaration.

"Everything seems to be in order, Mr. Chaperau," the Customs inspector said, handing back the letter. He quickly placed stamps on the luggage, indicating that the baggage had been cleared to be taken from the pier. The formalities at the pier required only a few minutes. Then the Chaperaus had their luggage loaded into a taxi and they were driven to the Hotel Pierre at the corner of 63rd Street and Fifth Avenue, where they made their home.

The following day Chaperau left the hotel carrying a black suitcase and a hat box. He took a cab to 570 Park Avenue, entered the building, and rang the bell of the apartment occupied by New York State Supreme Court Justice and Mrs. Edward J. Lauer. A maid admitted Chaperau to the apartment and he said, "Please tell Mrs. Lauer that Mr. Chaperau is here. She is expecting me."

Mrs. Lauer greeted her visitor warmly and exclaimed, "Nat, it is wonderful to see you! Please do come in." And then Mrs. Lauer turned to the maid and said, "Rosa, take this suitcase and hat box to my room, please. There are some of my things from Paris I told you I was expecting."

The maid, Rosa Weber, carried the bag and box to Mrs. Lauer's bedroom. She knew they contained purchases which her employer had made when she and the Judge were in Europe during the summer. They had returned to New York aboard the SS *Normandie* on September 12, and Rosa remembered the beautiful clothing Mrs. Lauer brought with her. Rosa had helped her unpack, exclaiming over the beauty of the new styles. And Rosa remembered Mrs. Lauer saying, "That's not all, Rosa. Some lovely things are coming later. They weren't finished when I left Paris." Mrs. Lauer also left Rosa with the definite impression that one of the nicest things of all was that she had brought back gowns, hats, and jewelry without paying duty to Customs.

A few days after Chaperau's visit to the apartment, both Mr. and Mrs. Chaperau were guests of the Lauers at a cocktail party. Among other guests was the famous international financier and playboy—somewhat of a mystery man about New York—Serge Rubenstein.

And then on October 21 Rosa helped Mrs. Lauer prepare for a dinner party in the apartment. Rosa brought her sister along to help with the affair, and again the Chaperaus were among the guests. It was a gay gathering, and after drinks the guests were seated in the dining room.

Rosa could not help but hear everything said by the guests as she served the table. And there was much for them to talk about. At this time war clouds were gathering in Europe.

As the conversation grew more animated, there were loud and bitter denunciations of Adolph Hitler and his treatment of the Jews.

Rosa Weber listened to the denunciations of Hitler with mounting fury. No one noticed that her face was flushed with anger until she crashed a plate of meat onto the table. The guests looked at the maid in open-mouthed astonishment. Into this silence Rosa Weber shouted: "Ladies and gentlemen, I am a real German! If you don't stop talking about Herr Hitler while I am in this house, I am through here!" And then the maid glared at Mrs. Lauer and said, "Madam, it is up to you."

For a full thirty seconds there was no sound, and then a babble of protest broke out. Judge and Mrs. Lauer were on their feet shouting. Rosa Weber stalked into the pantry followed by Judge Lauer, who demanded, "Get out of this house immediately!"

Rosa said to the Judge, "All right, Judge, I'll go." And she went to her room with her sister to pack her belongings. Chaperau and another guest followed the maid to her room and stood at the door while she was packing. Chaperau snapped, "Hurry up; how long does it take you?"

Judge Lauer came to the room, and Chaperau said to the Judge, "You had better watch when she goes. She might take some of your valuables with her." With this insult sounding in her ears, the maid hurried from the apartment and slammed the door behind her.

Four days after the dinner party on Park Avenue, a woman entered the Customs building at 21 Varick Street in New York and asked to see the Supervising Customs Agent. She was shown into his office. And it was there that Rosa Weber, in the role of informer, got her revenge. She told what had happened at the dinner. She accused Mrs. Lauer of smuggling Paris gowns and other finery into the United States without paying customs duties. She told agents of the conversation she had overheard between Mrs. Lauer and Chaperau, of remarks that had been made by Mrs. Lauer. She described how she had helped Mrs. Lauer unpack the dresses, and of Chaperau's visit to the apartment with the black suitcase and the hat box.

While she was packing to leave the Lauer apartment, she said, Chaperau had cursed her and said, "I'm just thinking it over—whether I should arrest you, because I'm from the police department." She added, "They threatened to have me deported to Germany, and also said that there was no concentration camp here but that I would be put in jail."

When the maid left the Customs agent's office that day, agents began a routine check on Nathaniel Chaperau. Rosa Weber was an angry, vindictive woman whose story might have been motivated solely by spite as far as the Customs agents knew. But all such stories were checked, even if the source were a pro-Hitler maid. Each report of a customs violation was handled in the same manner, regardless of the prominence of the accused, when an informant gave such minute details of smuggling as did Rosa Weber.

Agents quickly found that Chaperau conducted a film business from an office at 30 Rockefeller Plaza with the cable address "Chapfilm." He had prominent connections in the movie world in New York and Hollywood and he boasted of his close friendship with several stars of the entertainment world. On the surface, his business looked legitimate. There was no record that he had ever been engaged in smuggling.

But in checking into Chaperau's travels outside the country, the agents were curious as to why Chaperau had used a Nicaraguan passport on his return from Europe early in October. A visit to the Nicaraguan Consulate turned up some interesting information. The Consul General disclosed that he had given a letter to Chaperau intended only as an aid to Chaperau in making a film in Nicaragua. Chaperau had called on the Consul General and told him that he hoped he could go to Nicaragua and take pictures of the country's beautiful lakes and other natural scenery for advertising purposes—without expense to the Nicaraguan government.

The idea appealed to the Consul General. Chaperau's credentials appeared to be excellent, his business address implied a firm of financial integrity, and Chaperau obviously was well-connected in the film world.

It seemed like an attractive proposition to the consular chief and, quite naturally, he had asked what aid he could give in the project. Chaperau had said it would be helpful if he carried a letter from the Consul General explaining his mission in Nicaragua and stating that the commercial enterprise had the approval of the Consul General.

The diplomat had furnished Chaperau with the letter and, to be helpful further, with Nicaraguan passports. However, the Consul General insisted to the agents that the documents were intended for use solely in connection with the movie-making trip to Nicaragua. Under no circumstances had they been intended for use in connection with trips to any other country. He added that the letter had not been given with any authorization from his government and that no diplomatic privileges had been extended with these documents.

A query was sent to the State Department in Washington asking if Chaperau had ever been registered as the representative of the Nicaraguan government. The State Department reported promptly that there was no record of his being attached to the Nicaraguan diplomatic service—or to any other agency registered with the State Department. In short, he had not been entitled to the diplomatic courtesies extended by Customs.

After these disclosures, the agents discovered that Nathaniel Chaperau had a truly interesting background. An inquiry sent to the FBI uncovered a criminal record. Chaperau had several aliases, among them Albert Chaperau, Albert Chippero, Harry Schwarz, and Nathan Wise. As Nathan Wise he had been sent to the New York City Reformatory on a petty larceny charge. He also had been involved in a mail fraud case in Wisconsin and had been sentenced to the Federal penitentiary at Leavenworth to serve a year and six months.

But Chaperau had not confined his activities to the United States. Reports came from France, Belgium and England. In 1927, Chaperau had been refused admittance to England, and his passport had been cancelled. Later, Scotland Yard reported Chaperau had a long criminal record and was wanted by them under the name of "White" in connection with a swindling transaction in May, 1935. The report from Scotland Yard said Albert Nathaniel Chaperau, alias R. L. Werner, was wanted by London police for conspiracy and fraudulent conversion of worthless shares of stock, that he was internationally known and that he had been connected "with large-scale fraudulent activities in England and on the continent." The French police record showed that Chaperau had been involved in passing bad checks and in something irregular which the French called *abus de confiance*.

Armed with this information, Customs decided the smuggling story told by Rosa Weber was more than the spiteful babbling of an angry woman. Search warrants were obtained. One agent called at the apartment of Justice and Mrs. Lauer. When he knocked on the door, the Justice himself opened the door to inquire sternly what it was the caller wanted. The agent identified himself, showed the Justice the search warrant, and said, "I don't have to explain to you, Mr. Justice, that you can do this one of two ways. You can do this the easy way, or we can do it the hard way."

Then the agent couldn't resist a sudden impulse. He added, "I would suggest that you cough up the loot." The language was inelegant, but the Justice got the point. He invited the agent in and closed the door behind him.

At this moment, other agents were entering the apartment of the Chaperaus in the Hotel Pierre. One article in the apartment which caught their attention was a photograph of the radio team of George Burns and Gracie Allen inscribed to "June, Nat, and Paula, you charming people, sincerely, George and Gracie."

Papers in the apartment indicated that on his trip to Europe ending October 7, Chaperau had brought back with him jewelry for George Burns. And there was a letter, written in friendly terms, in which Burns thanked Chaperau for bringing the jewelry over from France. Further search disclosed correspondence and documents which also indicated Chaperau had brought back jewelry for comedian Jack Benny. There was no Customs record that such jewelry had been declared or that duty had been paid.

The information obtained in New York was sent to Customs agents in Los Angeles. As a result Burns handed over to agents a ring and bracelet valued at approximately $30,000. Jewelry was also obtained by the agents from Jack Benny. The case was a minor sensation in the daily press and particularly in the Hollywood community.

Nathaniel Chaperau hoodwinked many of the stars in the film colony with his front of the affable, worldly-wise man ready any time to do a favor for a friend. He met most of them in Paris. He and his wife were attractive and interesting people who seemed to have good connections because they could buy almost anything at wholesale prices. Chaperau let his friends know that he not only could help them buy at wholesale prices, but that he would be glad to do them a favor and bring the purchases through Customs himself.

George Burns and Jack Benny protested any intent of wrongdoing. But they were charged with smuggling and both pleaded guilty when brought into court. Burns was sentenced to a year and a day on each of nine counts and fined $8,000. However, the execution of the sentence was suspended and he was placed on probation for a year and a day. Jack Benny was also sentenced to a year and a day in prison, his sentence was suspended, and he was placed on probation for a year. He was required to pay fines totalling $10,000.

The tattling of Rosa Weber brought tragedy to the Lauers. Justice Lauer resigned from the court in the uproar which followed the smuggling exposé. Mrs. Lauer was sentenced to three months in prison.

The dapper Chaperau confessed to the smuggling. He was fined $5,000 and sentenced to five years in prison, but because of his cooperation in the case, President Roosevelt ordered his release from prison in April, 1940.

The story of Rosa Weber is not a new one to Customs officers or, for that matter, to any of the Federal and local police agencies, because the informer has always played an important role in law enforcement's never-ending battle against the criminal world.

In 1955, FBI Director J. Edgar Hoover wrote in the *FBI Law Enforcement Bulletin:*

The objective of the investigator must be to ferret out the truth. It is fundamental that the search include the most logical source of information—those persons with immediate access to necessary facts who are willing to cooperate in the interest of the common good. Their services contribute greatly to the ultimate goal of justice— convicting the guilty and clearing the innocent. Necessarily unheralded in their daily efforts, they not only uncover crimes but also furnish the intelligence data so vital in preventing serious violations of law and national security.

The Customs Bureau—along with other enforcement agencies —has developed a network of informers who aid in combatting smuggling and other violations of the tariff laws. Information comes from maids, disgruntled employees, ship's officers and stewards, shop girls, bartenders, narcotics addicts, businessmen, racketeers, and jealous mistresses—each with his own motive for passing information to the agents.

Some informers are motivated by a momentary fit of anger— as was Rosa Weber. Some report smuggling activities to settle an old grudge against an enemy. Some inform through fear of the law—fear of deportation, fear of a severe prison sentence, or fear that unless they get the law on their side, their underworld enemies will destroy them. Then there is the information which comes from citizens who have no other motive than the desire to see the law upheld.

There are petty criminals who turn informer because it gives them a feeling of holding the whip-hand over the "big shots" of the underworld. Others inform because of a sincere desire to break with their criminal past and to start a new life with a clean slate.

But a sizable number of Customs informers are those who seek a money reward. Among these are professional informers, who make a regular business of checking on the sales of jewelry, clothing and other merchandise in Europe, and learning whether the buyers intend to declare their purchases to customs on arrival in the United States.

Most of the large seizures of heroin, diamonds, gold and other contraband have been discovered because some one gave advance information. Customs agents readily concede that most smuggling rings are broken up because of the tips that come from informers who often play a deadly and dangerous game.

Federal agents are taught the art of developing contacts with informers—and the absolute necessity for acquiring information from those with first-hand knowledge of a criminal operation.

The agents cannot often disclose the full story of how an informer was enlisted, and how he aided them in breaking up a criminal combine, because the disclosure could be fatal to the informer. But the story of how Narcotics Agent Pat O'Carroll, a handsome, black-haired Irishman, recruited one informer can now be told.

Shortly after World War II, O'Carroll was assigned to the Bureau of Narcotics' International Squad in New York City to help with the investigations being made into the narcotics traffic. Two of the squad's prime targets were Benny Bellanca, who lived in Jersey City, and Pietro Beddia, who resided in Westchester.

Both men were suspected of being involved deeply in the international narcotics traffic—with connections in France and Italy —but agents were unable to make a case against them and they remained untouchable. Perhaps they would have continued their operations for years, except that O'Carroll played a hunch.

The case began to take shape when Agent Angelo Zurlo, tailing a suspected narcotics pusher on New York's Lower East Side, saw his man enter a small olive oil and cheese shop on Christie Street near Delancey. He noted the name and address of the shop in his notebook and later made a memorandum of the incident which went into the Bureau's cross-indexed file. Some months later, Narcotics agents following another suspect saw him enter the olive oil and cheese shop on Christie Street. They made a memorandum, also, which went into the files.

In the summer of 1952, O'Carroll was checking the files when he noted the two memos mentioning the small shop on Christie. Further investigation revealed it had been owned by Alphonse Attardi before he was sentenced to serve an eight-year prison term for a narcotics violation in Galveston, Texas, in the early 1940s. Attardi had completed the sentence, but Immigration authorities were studying the possibility of extradition proceedings, inasmuch as Attardi was Italian by birth.

Attardi at this time was sixty years old, 5 feet 3, and weighed about 140 pounds. He had the appearance of a meek and humble little shoemaker, and he scarcely fitted the part of an underworld character. He had an engaging, warm personality, and he was known in the Mafia as "The Peacemaker" because of his knack for compromising disputes—but that was before he had served time in prison.

O'Carroll decided to pay a call on Attardi, who he learned was living in a cheap, transient rooming house on 16th Street just off Third Avenue. It was after midnight one warm night when he strolled down Third Avenue in the shadows of the old El to 16th Street. Even the softness of the night could not hide the shabbiness and the squalor of the area.

O'Carroll entered the rooming house and climbed two flights of stairs. He knocked on the door and then tried the doorknob. The door swung open, and at that moment the agent knew that Attardi was in a bad way financially. If he had had a bankroll, he wouldn't have left the door unbolted—not in this dive.

He saw Attardi sitting up in bed, a skinny gnome of a man wearing only undershirt and shorts.

"Who is it?" Attardi said. "What do you want?"

"Take it easy," O'Carroll said. "I'm a U.S. Treasury agent. I just want to talk to you."

Attardi switched on a light over the bed. "What do you want to see me about?" he said. "I'm clean."

"Have you got any narcotics in this room?" O'Carroll asked him.

Attardi shook his head. "No. You can search the room if you like. I'm out of the business."

O'Carroll pulled up a chair beside the bed and sat down. He began to talk about Attardi's connections with well-known underworld figures, asking him why it was that he had been convicted in Houston while others in the mob had gone free.

As they talked, bitterness began to creep into Attardi's voice. He had taken the rap in Houston—and then his pals had deserted him. They didn't even try to communicate with him while he was in prison. His wife had become ill and no one had come forward to help her. She had died. He had even lost the little olive oil and cheese shop on Christie Street.

"Now I have nothing," he said.

"Maybe we can help you," O'Carroll said. "I can't make any promises, but if you help us we may be able to help you when your deportation case comes up."

Attardi shook his head. "I can't do it. I'd be dead if I worked for you."

O'Carroll continued talking of the injustices done to Attardi by his old pals, insisting that he owed them nothing since they had deserted him. But Attardi continued to say no.

At last O'Carroll said, "Well, I'll leave my name and telephone number. If you ever need help—I'll be glad to talk to you." He wrote his name and telephone number on a slip of paper and handed it to Attardi.

For six months O'Carroll heard nothing from Attardi. He made no move to see the man again. He had planted the seed, and whether it took root depended on what went on in the mind of the skinny little ex-convict.

But in early December Attardi called the Narcotics Bureau office and Agent George O'Connor took the call. He explained that he wanted to talk to O'Carroll and he would be waiting for him on Delancey Street near Christie.

That afternoon O'Carroll and O'Connor drove to Delancey and parked near the street number mentioned by Attardi. A few min-

utes later the hoodlum walked from a doorway and ducked into
the car with them.

The agents had assumed that Attardi had made the call because
he was frightened over the prospect of being deported to Italy.
But it wasn't deportation that was on Attardi's mind. He had fallen in love. He had met a twenty-two-year-old waitress in one of
the mean little restaurants on the Lower East Side—and this girl
had become the most important thing in his life. They wanted to
get married, but he had no money.

Attardi said he was willing to put the agents onto some Puerto
Ricans living in Brooklyn who were dealing in narcotics. If the
price were right, Attardi would help knock off the gang.

The agents listened to Attardi's story and then O'Carroll shook
his head. "It's no deal," he said. "We want better cases than that.
We want to go to the top."

Attardi was frightened but he also was in love. And so he began
asking how the agents could protect him if he did agree to work
with them. He flatly refused to do any buying of narcotics himself.

At last it was agreed that Attardi would introduce an undercover agent to some of his friends who were in the peddling business. Then it would be up to the agent to handle the deals, Attardi's role being to vouch for the agent as "one of the boys."

Undercover Agent Joe Tremoglie, a big, curly-haired man, was
chosen to work with Attardi. Tremoglie's parents had come to the
United States from Sicily and Joe spoke fluent Italian. He knew
the underworld, its mannerisms, superstitions, and nuances. He
had about him a conspiratorial air that seemed to appeal to criminals and to disarm them.

Attardi's first assignment was to introduce Tremoglie to a cafe
cook on Newberry Street who was pushing narcotics on the side.
The agent made a small purchase and then let himself be seen in
the right places with Attardi—who began to introduce him as a
distant cousin.

As the weeks passed, Tremoglie met narcotics pushers and
wholesalers. He played poker with them. Slowly he moved up the
ladder until one day he was introduced to Benny Bellanca, who
took an immediate liking to him after Tremoglie had given the
right answers to all the questions. He liked him so well, in fact,

that they discussed the possibility of Tremoglie going to Europe as a courier to bring back a load of heroin.

He met Pietro Beddia, too, and an intensive surveillance by Narcotics agents disclosed a link between Bellanco and Beddia.

At the end of ten months of work by Tremoglie, the trap was set. Arrangements were made for Tremoglie to make a series of purchases during one afternoon and night on a timetable that was worked out to the minute. For twelve hours, Tremoglie raced from one meeting place to another, making the prearranged purchases of narcotics. And at 3 o'clock in the morning twenty of the leading narcotics dealers in the New York area—including Bellanca and Beddia—had been rounded up.

Alphonse Attardi wasn't around for the trials. He took his $5,000 reward money plus expenses—plus his bride—and faded from the scene. All he would tell agents was that he planned to buy a little place in the country and settle down to make an honest living.

The underworld finally figured out that it was Attardi who had sprung the trap on them, and defense counsel for the accused men demanded that he be produced by the government for questioning. But Narcotics agents could honestly say they knew nothing of Attardi's whereabouts. They didn't want to know.

Informers have given valuable aid to the Customs Service in its drive against smuggling, and there are many Alphonse Attardis —each with his own motive—who work with the agents.

Under the law, the Customs Service is permitted to pay up to $50,000 for information leading to the seizure of smuggled goods. The system provides that the informer may receive 25 per cent of the net recovery in any case in which he provides the original information leading to arrest and conviction for smuggling or fraud. Net recovery means the amount which goes into the Treasury of the United States as a result of a disclosure. For example, suppose Customs agents seize from a smuggler a diamond necklace that is worth $10,000, the appraisal being based on the American selling price. The necklace is forfeited and sold at public auction for $8,000. Assuming expenses of $400 involved in the case, then the net recovery is $7,600, of which the informant is entitled to $1,900.

The theory behind such payments is that the government has made a good bargain when it can pay an informer $1 and then have $3 left over for the Treasury—money which would have been lost without the cooperation of the informant.

There was one Customs informer working in Europe who received the top reward of $50,000 three times by uncovering the smuggling of huge shipments of diamonds into the United States. He refused to accept payment in Europe—but waited until he had $150,000 in credits with the U.S. Treasury. Then he came to the United States, received the money, and settled down to live the life of a country gentleman in the West.

And the rewards were tax free—as are all payments made to informers.

10

THE VIOLENT BORDER

Customs agents in the Laredo Tenth Customs Agency District—which includes the 2,000 miles of border and Gulf coastline from New Mexico into part of Louisiana—spend much of their time battling the smuggling of narcotics and marihuana from Mexico.

Federal officers estimate that the business of peddling narcotics to addicts grosses at least a half billion dollars a year for the underworld, and the total may be much more. No one actually knows the amount of narcotics which is smuggled successfully into the United States. Some Customs agents estimate that law enforcement officers seize less than 10 per cent of the total. One agent said, "If I thought that I was getting ten per cent of the total being smuggled, then I could sleep well at night."

Even though the size of the narcotics traffic is unknown, there is no doubt about the tremendous profits to be made from the illegal sale of drugs. Addicts will beg, borrow, steal and kill to obtain money with which to satisfy the terrible craving for narcotics once they are "hooked."

Unofficial estimates place the number of narcotic addicts in the United States at about 50,000. The average heroin addict requires something like ten grains per day to satisfy his needs. This means that over a period of a year the average heroin addict will use about 7.6 ounces of the drug—or a total for all addicts of about 380,000 ounces of heroin or a substitute drug. In their best years, Federal and state law enforcement officers have been able to seize only a fraction of this estimated total.

Several years ago the Mexican marihuana dealers took no responsibility for delivery into the United States; all arrangements for smuggling across the border had to be made by the purchasers who came from the States. But in recent years there has been a change, and the Mexican operators have been willing to make deliveries to New York, Chicago, Detroit and other cities. Jack Givens, Supervising Agent for the Laredo district, believes this change in delivery method is an indication that the supply of marihuana in Mexico has outgrown the demand. This has put the pressure on the Mexican operators to give their customers better service, resulting in the delivery system.

In recent years some of the United States marihuana operators have begun to bypass border operators. They have been driving to the interior of Mexico, making their own deals with the growers and bringing the stuff back into the United States themselves. Customs inspectors are always on guard against marihuana being smuggled in automobiles—hidden in upholstery, in luggage compartments, in door panels, or in secret compartments built into the cars.

Customs agents believe that most of the heroin and other narcotics smuggled into the United States come by way of Europe from the Middle East and Far East. But Mexico still is one of the favorite routes for the narcotics syndicates seeking to reach the American addicts. In addition, Mexico remains the major exporter of marihuana. The Mexican government has been cooperating with the United States in seeking to suppress the traffic, and there is a close working relationship between the American agents and the Mexican police. But the long and rugged boundary between the two countries makes it impossible to cover every smuggling point on the border.

Supervisor Givens has only thirty-nine agents and seventeen Customs enforcement officers assigned to him for the entire territory. The enforcement officers are a police force used primarily for guard duty and surveillance work under the agents' direction.

This small force, despite the geographic difficulties, has a high esprit de corps. Each man works many hours overtime each month with no expectation of compensation. The records show that the agents average approximately 120 hours of overtime each month in excess of the overtime required of them and for which they are paid. Often the men find themselves working overtime knowing that their extra effort will be rewarded with pay averaging 19 cents an hour.

Why do they do it? One agent explained it in this way: "There's more than money in this work once you become involved in it. Once you start working on a case, you simply cannot walk away from it at the end of eight hours. You have a feeling of achievement when you do break up a marihuana ring or pick up someone who is dealing in heroin."

Patrolling the Mexican border has been a major problem for Customs since the frontier days. In 1853 the Customs Mounted Patrol was organized, and horsemen rode across the deserts and through the mountains on lonely patrols to intercept cattle rustlers, smugglers and aliens trying to slip across the border. The mounted guard inevitably gave way to the automobile. But the horsemen rarely had more hair-raising experiences than those of the modern agents mounted on wheels. Such an incident occurred on August 7, 1960, in one of the wildest chases in the memory of Customs agents along the Texas-Mexico border.

It began when Agent Fred Rody, Jr., received a tip that an American was in the red-light district of Nuevo Laredo, trying to arrange for the purchase of 20 pounds of marihuana—obviously to be smuggled into the United States.

Further checking disclosed that the man was John Vaccaro, a known narcotics dealer working out of New Orleans. Vaccaro had been convicted of a marihuana violation in New Orleans and been placed under surveillance earlier in the year when he had visited Laredo. At that time agents had tried to intercept Vaccaro, suspected of smuggling marihuana, but in a wild chase on the highway Vaccaro pulled away from their car, even though their speedometer was registering 120 miles an hour. He also succeeded in eluding the police roadblocks which had been thrown up in front of him.

Agents kept a close watch on Vaccaro's car after Rody received his report. Finally they saw someone approach his automobile and place a suitcase in the front seat of his car. Then they saw Vaccaro, his wife, and their fourteen-year-old daughter enter the car.

When Vaccaro drove down San Bernardo Avenue and then onto U.S. Highway 59, he was followed by agents in three automobiles. When the Vaccaro car slowed in heavy traffic, the agents bracketed his car with one car in front, one behind, and the other alongside. Agent T. S. Simpson leaned out of his car and shouted, "Stop! We are Customs agents."

Vaccaro pulled his car to the side of the road and slowed down as though to stop. Suddenly he slammed his foot on the accelerator. His car leaped forward between two of the agents' vehicles and roared off on the left side of the highway, forcing terrified drivers to swerve into the ditch to avoid a collision. The agents gunned their cars in pursuit.

Simpson and Rody watched the speed indicator on their automobile reach 110 miles an hour, but Vaccaro's car still pulled away from them.

Agent Grady Grazner in a 1957 police interceptor-model Chevrolet moved past the Rody-Simpson car and slowly began gaining on the Vaccaro vehicle. His speedometer was reading 130 miles an hour when he moved up behind Vaccaro's automobile with his siren screaming. Grazner nudged Vaccaro's automobile with his bumper and signalled for Vaccaro to pull over and stop. The woman and girl in the car were looking out the rear window, screaming and motioning Grazner to pull away from their car.

For several miles the cars raced along at well over 100 miles an hour. Grazner fired four warning shots into the air trying to force Vaccaro to stop. He was afraid to fire directly into the vehicle because of the women inside.

Gradually Grazner's car moved up on the fleeing automobile.

As the front wheels of Grazner's car reached the left rear wheels of Vaccaro's car, the marihuana dealer suddenly swerved. The blow of his car knocked Grazner's vehicle to the side of the road. The car rolled over six times and bounced a distance of 471 feet. The only thing that saved Grazner's life was the fact that he was strapped into the seat by a safety belt.

Police had been alerted ahead by radio. In the little town of Ferret, Texas, Vaccaro saw the roadblock ahead. He tried to by-pass it by darting down a dirt road, but he was overtaken and brought to a halt.

Police found only fragments of marihuana in the Vaccaro car. When a search of the highway was later made by a helicopter, the pilot spotted a suitcase lying beside the road. Vaccaro had left his fingerprints on the suitcase when he tossed it out of his speeding automobile. It was stuffed with marihuana.

When Customs agents took Vaccaro into custody, Grazner said, "Why did you try to kill me? You might have killed your wife and little girl too."

Vaccaro spat on the agent and said insolently, "What in the hell are you talking about?"

Vaccaro was sentenced to twenty-five years in prison for this venture into violence.

The city of Laredo, Texas, dozed in the blazing noonday sun on an August day in 1957. Not many people were on the sun-baked streets at this hour, and even the Rio Grande had slowed to a lazy trickle. The only visible activity was at the Customs stations at the International Bridge spanning the river between Laredo and its twin city, Nuevo Laredo, on the Mexican bank of the river. The bridge was one of the major communications links between the United States and Mexico, but with the sun high in the heavens even the traffic across the bridge was moving at a listless pace.

At this hour, Dave Ellis, agent in charge, walked from his office in the old courthouse and sauntered to a battered automobile parked on a side street. He slipped behind the wheel and drove at a leisurely pace to the eastern edge of the city, where he turned off the street and parked beside the loading platform of a vacant warehouse. He switched off the engine, lit a cigarette and sat waiting.

When Ellis arrived at the office that morning he had found a cryptic note on his desk which said: "Meet me at the usual place." It was signed with the code name of one of the most reliable informers in all of northern Mexico.

Ellis hardly looked the part of an experienced Customs agent. He was nearing forty, but he looked ten years younger. The horn-rimmed spectacles he wore gave him an appearance of grave studiousness.

What few people knew was that Ellis' boyish face was deceiving. He had been toughened in a hard school of experience. He had survived a bullet through his chest leading a platoon into battle on Okinawa in World War II, and he had been with the first contingent going into Korea at the end of the war when no one was quite certain whether the Japanese were going to surrender or make a fight for it. He had returned home in 1946 to pick up his interrupted career as a Customs agent and had earned a reputation as one of the hardest-driving men in the field.

One lesson he had learned well was that no agent could operate successfully without reliable sources of information. That was why he waited patiently on this hot day to hear what it was that his tipster had on his mind. He had been at the rendezvous point only a few minutes when a car drove up beside his own and a Mexican got out, entered his car and began talking rapidly.

The Mexican was one of the key figures in a network of informers which the Customs agents had organized south of the border to help combat the smuggling of heroin and marihuana. The informers were a part, or on the fringe, of the Mexican underworld. They cooperated with the American agents for one reason only—U.S. dollars. If the information they provided resulted in the arrest and conviction of a smuggler, along with the seizure of the contraband, they were paid for the information from a special Customs contingency fund. In the case of marihuana, the payment was $5 for each pound of the weed, *cannabis sativa,* which was seized.

Ellis talked with his informant for perhaps thirty minutes. After the man returned to his car and drove away, Ellis headed back to the courthouse.

As he entered his office, an agent asked, "What was it all about?"

Ellis said, "My man tells me Muno Pena has a big marihuana

deal going—one of the biggest. He's getting ready to send a million dollars' worth of the weed across the border—and we've got to stop it."

The agent gave a low whistle. "So Muno Pena's at it again. I thought he had had enough."

"His kind never give up," Ellis said.

At the end of World War II, Pancho Trevino had been the kingpin in the Mexican marihuana and narcotics traffic, operating out of Nuevo Laredo. Muno Pena was a competitor but on a fairly small scale until, in 1952, the Mexican government got on Trevino's trail and threw him in jail. With Trevino behind bars, Muno Pena moved to the top. Pena remained on his home grounds in Mexico and never ventured north of the border. He had a highly organized syndicate and lieutenants who carried out his orders in the United States.

Ellis first ran into the Pena syndicate's operations in 1955 when he was transferred to Houston, Texas, and went to work to break up a marihuana smuggling ring which included a former Houston police officer. After weeks of collecting evidence during days and nights of tailing suspects and checking records of tourist courts, hotels and telephone calls, Ellis and his colleagues had pieced together a case against the smuggling ring. In a Christmas-night raid they seized 75 grams of heroin, and in two other raids seized 250 pounds of marihuana. Eleven men and women were arrested and convicted in this operation, which was one of the biggest roundups ever made by Customs officers in the Southwest.

The Houston raids had hurt Pena badly, but now he was back on the scene with a scheme to make a quick fortune—if the tipster who had called Ellis knew what he was talking about. Ellis was reasonably certain the information was correct.

According to the Mexican informant, Pena had gone to the farmers in the Monterey district south of Nuevo Laredo and purchased their entire crop of marihuana, a ton of the stuff. He had brought it to his ranch near Nuevo Laredo and processed it in one of the adobe sheds on the place.

Trusted workers had placed armfuls of the dry weed on fine-mesh screens and rubbed it by hand. The fragments of leaves filtered through the screens onto sheets, leaving on the screens only the rough stems which later were burned. The fragmented leaves, as fine as cigarette tobacco, were carefully weighed into one-pound lots. Each lot was placed in a paper bag, which in turn was placed inside a plastic container and sealed with strips of adhesive tape. Then the plastic bags, in lots of thirty, were placed in cotton sugar sacks and stacked in a shed to await shipment. Now Pena was working on a deal to ship the entire lot to a distributor somewhere in the vicinity of Chicago. He had decided not to parcel out the processed marihuana in small amounts to buyers from the United States. Instead, he was going to bypass the middlemen and take the lion's share of the profits himself.

Ellis knew that a ton of "wheat" (the underworld term for marihuana) would produce about 1,000 pounds of the narcotic weed suitable for rolling into cigarettes. A pound of marihuana would make approximately 1,000 cigarettes. This meant that the retail value of Pena's shipment would run somewhere in the neighborhood of a million dollars. Never before had so bold a scheme been attempted in marihuana smuggling.

The important element missing in the informant's information was how and when Pena planned to move the marihuana. Ellis had sent his man back to Nuevo Laredo to get this information if possible. Without these facts, Pena held the upper hand. Ellis had only fifteen agents to cover the 400 miles of border in his district —and there were thousands of places where marihuana might be smuggled across the river.

This time the tipster ran into a blank wall. He learned that the sacks of marihuana were still stacked in the shed on Pena's ranch. But that was all he could learn, except that in the past Pena had smuggled shipments of marihuana across the Rio Grande at a bend in the river about five miles upstream from the little West Texas town of San Ygnacio. When the water was low, the carriers were able to walk across the stream. If the river rose from sudden rainfalls, the marihuana was floated across the river on inflated inner tubes or on inflated rubber boats. In each case, an automobile was waiting at a designated spot to receive the contraband.

Ellis ordered a continuous surveillance of the river bend. For more than three months agents kept watch in relays, hiding in the mesquite near a small roadside park on top of a hill overlooking the sweep of the river. But the watches were fruitless. Each time

Ellis inquired about the sacks of marihuana at Pena's ranch, he was told they were still there.

In December, Ellis was reading the routine reports from New York of marihuana seizures that had been made in the city. These reports were circulated periodically to all agents-in-charge throughout the United States. There seemed to be nothing unusual in this particular batch of reports until Ellis came across an account of the arrest of one Wilfredo Fernandez, who had been caught with 16 pounds of marihuana in his possession. The line which drew his attention said that the marihuana was packed in one-pound lots in paper sacks which had been enclosed in plastic and sealed with adhesive tape. Ellis sensed that, somehow, Muno Pena had outwitted him, and the very thought enraged him. He sent a message to New York for more information on the arrest of Fernandez and where he had obtained the marihuana.

Fernandez, it developed, had been arrested in November for possession of cocaine. When his apartment was searched, agents came across the packaged marihuana. Fernandez sullenly admitted that he had bought it in Chicago from a dealer he knew only as "The Lawyer." The Lawyer had taken him out on Lawrence Avenue, where they had met a man who appeared to be a Mexican, driving a stake truck with a green body. The Mexican had taken the marihuana from a large cotton sack—and then driven away. He had never seen the Mexican before and didn't know where he lived.

"He was a skinny fellow about five feet eight tall, and he had black hair and a pale complexion," Fernandez said. "That's all I know."

Ellis knew in his heart that this marihuana had come from Pena. And later he was to learn how cleverly Pena had outwitted him. Pena had stacked the sacks of processed marihuana in the shed on his ranch where any of the workers could see them as they passed by. But what the workers didn't know was that one night Pena had removed the marihuana to a hiding place known only to himself and substituted other sugar sacks which looked identical.

One night Pena had taken the sacks to the river, where he met a confederate. They had carried the sacks across the river to the highway where the confederate had hidden his automobile, to which was attached a U-Drive-It trailer. The marihuana was stacked in the trailer and then covered with a mattress, a set of bed springs and a few household articles. These were lashed down with a tarpaulin over them—and then the driver headed north. To all outward appearances, he was a worker moving with his household goods from one job to another.

Ellis asked Chicago Customs agents to check on long distance telephone calls made in November by The Lawyer. And within a few days he received a list of names ranging from barkeeps to uncles, aunts, and cousins, horse track bookies, and pool parlor operators.

Meanwhile, agents in Laredo had been checking on Pena's associates and on his family. They made a list of everyone known to have any connection, even casually, with Muno Pena.

It was when Ellis checked these two lists of names that he found there was one name which appeared on both lists. The name was Isuaro Garza. The agents' information was that Garza was married to Muno Pena's sister. Mrs. Garza and her three children lived in Laredo and maintained a home there. But Garza, for some months, had been living on the outskirts of Kenosha, Wisconsin. Occasionally Mrs. Garza and the children would drive north to spend a few days with Garza. They never stayed for long and always returned to their Laredo home. No one seemed to know what Garza was doing in Kenosha.

Ellis thought he knew what Garza was doing there. He was certain that Garza was the man from whom The Lawyer had obtained the marihuana—and that Garza was Pena's man, making deliveries in Chicago from the 1,000 pounds of marihuana smuggled across the Rio Grande.

Ellis was so positive of this connection that he appealed to Washington for permission to take six agents from the Laredo office—men long accustomed to working on this type of case—for an investigation of Garza. But headquarters was in the midst of an economy wave. Ellis was told that funds were tight and that it would be impossible for him to take six men from Laredo on an uncertain mission. However, he was given authority to go to Kenosha himself and to take along one aide. If he could make a case against Garza within ten days, well and good. But at the end of ten days he must return at once to his post in Laredo.

Ellis chose Agent G. L. Latimer to accompany him. The two set out for Kenosha, driving day and night, through a snow storm which was sweeping the Middle West. They located Garza's home. He was living in a small white frame house just outside the northern edge of the town.

"There were two or three feet of snow on the ground," Ellis recalls, "and it looked like we were going to have to stake out the place by living in sleeping bags. But there was a motel nearby which was closed for the winter. We got permission from the owner to slip into the court from which we could see Garza's house. We were sure he was our man—but we wanted to know who was calling for the marihuana and where it was hidden. We wanted to catch the whole apparatus if possible. So day and night we watched Garza's house."

Occasionally Garza would leave the house for a trip to the grocery store, to go to a movie, or to visit in the city. The agents were unable to detect him making any deliveries. But on the tenth day—the last day of grace for Ellis and Latimer to be away from their Laredo posts—a car drove up to the white frame house. A man entered and shortly came out carrying a package which he stowed in his automobile. When he had driven a short distance from Garza's home, he was halted. Ellis found the package filled with marihuana. It was in a paper sack enclosed in plastic and taped with adhesive.

With this evidence, a search warrant was obtained and the agents advanced on Garza's house. It was nearing midnight when Ellis knocked at the door. A light came on and then the door was opened and a voice said, "Who is it? What do you want?"

Ellis shoved the door open, revealing a skinny Mexican standing in his long-handled underwear, shivering from the cold.

"We are U.S. Customs agents," Ellis said. "We have a warrant to search this place."

Isauro Garza submitted meekly. A loaded pistol lay on a table near his bed, but he gave no resistance. The agents found 720 one-pound sacks of marihuana hidden in closets and in the attic —the largest haul of marihuana ever to be made in the United States. Its retail value was $720,000.

Garza feigned surprise over the discovery of the marihuana. He told officers he "had no idea what was in the sacks." He said a

man named Tony called at his home one day and left a truckload
of sacks. Tony asked him to keep them for him. Another fellow
named Pepe came from Chicago three or four times. "He picked
up some of the stuff and gave me $600 for rent and expenses—but
I didn't know what it was all about," Garza said.

A jury thought otherwise. Garza was sent to prison for five
years. And Muno Pena? He had lost another round to Dave Ellis,
but he continued his operations on a smaller scale. Customs agents
are waiting for the day when he places one foot across the border
—and then he'll be out of circulation for quite a while.

11
A DIRTY BUSINESS

A cunning and ruthless hoodlum, two crooked Customs employees, two Greek narcotics peddlers in Shanghai and a supporting cast of killers, goons and dupes formed one of the greatest
narcotics syndicates the United States has ever known. Over a
span of less than two years in 1936–1937, this gang smuggled
into the country narcotics believed by Customs agents to have had
a retail value of at least $10 million. Their system was so simple
that it was almost foolproof. Almost . . . but not quite.

The prime mover in this profitable operation was Louis "Lepke"
Buchalter—a name which perhaps doesn't mean much to the
younger generation. But in the prohibition era and the years of
the depression, Lepke built a fantastic financial empire on a
foundation of terror, violence and murder combined with a genius
for organizing. He was, in many respects, more powerful and
more successful than "Scarface" Al Capone and dozens of other
hoodlums of the times who were more publicized in the nation's
press.

Louis Lepke Buchalter rose to power in the shadow of the Jazz Age, the era which evokes sentimental memories for so many Americans. But Lepke's world was about as sentimental as a tommygun.

He was a small, slender man—5 feet 7—with a dark complexion and black hair which he parted on the side. He was soft-spoken and seemingly humble in manner. He had large brown eyes that appeared as soft and gentle as the eyes of a fawn. But his eyes only masked the evil in this man who schemed and killed until he ranked at the top of the list of U.S. criminals.

By all odds, Lepke was the most brilliant—and the most dangerous—of the criminals. It was Lepke who showed the underworld how to infiltrate and take over control of labor unions, and how to become silent partners in the management of industries. It was Lepke who put murder on a wholesale basis with an organization that became known as Murder, Inc. It was Lepke who found the chink in the U.S. Customs Bureau's defenses against narcotics smuggling—and who made narcotics smuggling almost a pleasant pastime.

Lepke is worth at least a footnote in any history of our times because he symbolized an era of graft, corruption and violence the likes of which the nation had never known before. He was born on February 6, 1897, in Manhattan's Lower East Side, one of a family of eleven children. The family lived in shattering confusion in a small, crowded apartment over the hardware store owned by the father, Barnet Buchalter.

Lepke's mother called him "Lepkeleh," the Jewish diminutive for "Little Louis," and his friends shortened the nickname to Lepke. He was not a bad student in grade school. But he quit school after finishing the eighth grade and for a time worked as a delivery boy at $3 a week.

His father died when he was thirteen. The family broke up and scattered. The other ten children went on to become respectable, useful citizens. But not "Little Louis." He rented a furnished room on the East Side and turned to crime. He organized raids on pushcart peddlers, stole from lofts, picked pockets, and lived by his wits. He was sent to the reformatory and to prison for short terms for larceny, but he always returned to the old life. He had ambitions to become a big shot in New York's underworld.

In the early 1920s, Lepke joined an East Side mob headed by "Little Augie" Orgen. But while most of the underworld scrambled to satisfy the country's unquenchable thirst for bootleg whiskey, Lepke convinced Little Augie that it was safer, smarter and more profitable to specialize in labor racketeering and in selling "protection" to businessmen.

If an employer was having trouble with strikers, Lepke would see to it that the recalcitrant workers were beaten up by his goons and that peace was restored at no increase in wages. If union leaders were having trouble with rank-and-file members, Lepke's strong-arm squad would bring the rebels back into line with beatings and threats against the men's families.

Other mobs sold such services on a flat-fee basis. But not Lepke. When his men were hired to put down a union revolt, they remained as members and then slowly muscled their way into the management of the union. The members' dues were increased to pay for the services rendered.

Businessmen who hired Lepke's strike-breaking services were ordered to buy the protection on a continuing basis. If they refused, a bomb would be hurled through a window to wreck a plant or a shop. Acid would be thrown onto merchandise, or someone's face would be splashed with acid as he walked from his place of business to his home.

Those who capitulated—and most of them did—soon found Lepke's men demanding a voice in management, even to the dictation of contracts (from which they received a kickback) and the placement of a man in the business office to keep a check on the money.

Little Augie was pleased with Lepke's organizing brilliance and the profits that were rolling in. But the word got around that he didn't like Lepke's growing strength in the organization, where he was known as "The Judge" and "Judge Louis."

Little Augie's irritation was short-lived. On October 16, 1927, as he stood in a doorway at 103 Norfolk Street talking with his young bodyguard, a sedan suddenly swerved to the curb. A voice called, "Hey, Little Augie!" As the gang chief turned, a burst of machinegun fire cut him down. His wounded bodyguard was identified by police as John Diamond—later to become better known as Jack "Legs" Diamond.

The underworld hummed with the story that Little Augie had fallen victim to Lepke's ambition. On the basis of an informer's tip, police picked up Lepke, "Gurrah Jake" Shapiro and "Little Hymie" Holtz and charged them with murder. But no one could prove anything and the case soon was dropped.

With Little Augie out of the way, Lepke set to work to consolidate his empire. He moved more solidly into the leather, baking, garment, fur and transportation industries. At the peak of his power, Lepke personally directed some 250 criminal operations. He rode about New York in a limousine with a liveried chauffeur. He had a staff of 300 men looking after his affairs, plus an assortment of accountants, bookkeepers, gunmen, strong-arm men, and experts in such matters as acid-throwing.

He also put murder on a cash-and-carry basis. If a member of the mob became careless or talked too much, he was executed summarily. Dangerous witnesses were ordered to leave the state under the threat of death—and if they refused to obey, they were killed.

Oddly enough, even at the height of his power, Lepke was virtually an unknown in New York and throughout the country. While other hoodlums gained the headlines, Lepke remained in the shadows with few people realizing the extent of his empire, whose earnings have been estimated at more than $50 million a year. Nor was it known for twelve years—1927 until 1939—that Lepke alone had ordered the deaths of from sixty to eighty men whom he considered a threat to his own safety and prosperity.

By 1933, however, the operations of Lepke and other racketeers had aroused such popular indignation that the U.S. government moved against them. In November of that year a Federal grand jury indicted Lepke on two counts of violating the antitrust laws through his domination of the rabbit-fur-dressing industry. He was arrested and released on bail. He returned home to his wife and adopted son to continue operations as usual while the wheels of justice turned slowly.

It was during this period that another opportunity came to Lepke quite unexpectedly. Three hoodlums—Jack Katzenberg, Jake Lvovsky, and Sam Gross—were allied with other gangsters in the operation of an illicit chemical plant in Newark, New Jersey.

The gang was smuggling opium into the country, taking it to the plant and extracting morphine from the opium, to be sold at wholesale across the country. This business was wiped out on February 25, 1935, when an explosion destroyed the chemical plant.

Katzenberg, Lvovsky, and Gross had found the narcotics business too profitable to give up. They began looking around for other ways to get back into the business, and they decided to talk the problem over with Lepke. A mutual friend brought them together in his apartment, where they discussed setting up an international organization which would obtain narcotics in Shanghai and smuggle them into the United States. The sale of narcotics was to be put on the same efficient basis as the sale of murder.

The major stumbling block to the plan was the U.S. Customs. It would be relatively simple to obtain heroin in Shanghai and to bring it as far as the port of New York. The problem was how to smuggle it past the Customs inspectors on a continuing basis that would guarantee a steady supply with a minimum risk.

Lepke was a firm believer in the adage that every man has his price—and he was certain he would have no difficulty in finding someone whose price was reasonable and who would cooperate with the syndicate. This direct approach had always worked in the past and Lepke had no reason to change tactics now.

One of Lepke's first moves was to investigate the Customs procedures at the New York pier. He found that when vessels arrived at the Port of New York, the passengers' baggage and trunks were brought to the pier for examination. And when they had been examined, a Customs inspector affixed a colored stamp on each piece of luggage. Once the stamps were affixed, the luggage could be removed from the pier and placed in a taxi or in a truck to be carted away.

Lepke saw that the stamps were the key to his problem. If he could find a Customs employee who would furnish him with the colored stickers, then a sticker could be affixed to a trunk or a suitcase containing narcotics and it would pass through Customs without an actual inspection.

Carefully, Lepke's lieutenants made inquiries along the waterfront. At last they found their men, two guards who were willing

—for a price of $1,000 a trip—to furnish Lepke and his men with the necessary stickers on the day that the narcotics carriers arrived. The price was cheaper than Lepke had expected.

With easy entry for the narcotics assured, Lepke arranged to obtain heroin from two Greek dealers in Shanghai.

This was the state of affairs when Jack Katzenberg made a trip to Brooklyn for a visit with his brother-in-law, Ben Schisoff, a balding, sad-eyed man with the face of a ferret. Ben and his wife Bella operated a Coney Island hot dog concession. They cleared about $1,500 to $2,000 in profit each season, enough to live on through the winter and to take care of the concession rental for the next season.

Katzenberg generously offered to send Ben on an all-expenses-paid trip around the world by luxury liner. All he asked in return was that Schisoff bring back two trunks from Shanghai. "You won't even have to bother about looking after the trunks," Katzenberg said, "because there'll be somebody to do that for you. And when you get back I'll have some money for you."

Schisoff was confused. (At least that was the story he would tell Customs agents later.) Why would his brother-in-law suddenly wish to send him around the world with all expenses paid —and then give him money at the end of the trip? He knew his brother-in-law was in the rackets. He knew his reputation as a hoodlum. He also had heard all the rumors that Katzenberg was connected with the narcotics traffic even though he had managed to elude Federal officers. Schisoff told Katzenberg to give him a few days to think it over.

Schisoff finally sat down with his wife and said, "Listen, Bella, I want to go on a trip by myself. You go to Miami. You've worked hard and now you are entitled to share the money we have. I want to go alone. You know I am a nervous type of man and I want to go for a couple of months to recuperate. You can stay home or you can go to Miami or do whatever you please. How about it?"

But Bella was having none of this business of her husband taking a vacation alone. She loudly insisted that if he were going on a trip, then she was going with him. She wasn't going to let him go gallivanting off by himself to get into God knows what sort of trouble. Her answer was "no!"

Schisoff reluctantly told Katzenberg that his sister insisted on going along. He expected his brother-in-law to call off the deal. But instead Katzenberg amiably agreed that both of them could go and that he would pay their expenses. And so on November 15, 1935, the couple boarded the SS *President Lincoln* in San Francisco and set sail that day on their voyage around the world by way of Shanghai.

When the *President Lincoln* arrived in Shanghai, Sam Gross was waiting at the pier to meet them. He introduced them to his two Greek companions and then took them to the Metropole Hotel, where he had made reservations for them. Sam said, "Now you two get a good rest. Everything is going all right."

As Schisoff told the story later: "A few days later, Sam Gross tells me that he is going away for a week. He said to us, 'Don't walk too often in the street because it is not so good.' I said, 'All right. But what will I do if anything happens? Maybe I'll get sick. I don't know anybody around here.' So he gave me an address. In case anything went wrong I should call that telephone number. I don't remember the address and the number. It was a Greek fellow, named Jay, and his wife. Finally Sammy Gross puts a scare into me and tells me not to go into the streets.

"And so we stayed in the hotel until we got blue in the face. And so my wife finally says, 'We have money. Why sit in the hotel? I want to do some shopping. Everything is so cheap here.'

"So we were sitting there about three days and then I called that number that Sam gives me and the wife answered. I told her about us. She answered, 'All right, I'm going to send my chauffeur to bring you over. . . .' She treated us to a meal and we spent the afternoon there and then went home.

"Gross finally returned and said, 'Listen, the ship is going to be here in a day or two. I'll have two trunks for you to take with you. You don't have to do anything. We will put the trunks on board for you and I will show you what to do when you are on the boat. You forget about the trunks. When you are about three days out of Marseilles, go to the purser and say that you want to have the trunks shipped across France to Cherbourg in transit. Then when you get to Marseilles, there'll be somebody waiting for you to take care of everything. That way they don't have to open the trunks when they go through France.' "

The Schisoffs had a gay Christmas party at the home of the

Greeks, and four days later they boarded their ship and sailed from Shanghai. They were met in Marseilles by one of Lepke's henchmen, who handled the trans-shipment of the trunks. Then the Schisoffs left the ship at Marseilles and went by train to Cherbourg to catch the SS *Majestic* for New York.

Lepke's man told them, "Don't put those two trunks on your baggage declaration."

Schisoff said, "How am I going to do it then?"

The hoodlum said, "You've got eight pieces of luggage of your own. You put down everything on the declaration that you bought but leave these two trunks out. They will be taken care of. Don't you worry about that."

Schisoff replied, "All right. Whatever you say is all right with me."

On the night of February 4, 1936, the night before the *Majestic* was to dock in New York, Jake Lvovsky and Jack Katzenberg registered at the Luxor Hotel in New York. A short time after they went to their rooms they were joined by two Customs guards, John McAdams and Al Hoffman. It was agreed that Lvovsky would meet McAdams and Hoffman at the pier the next morning before the *Majestic* docked and they would turn over to him the stickers to be placed on the trunks brought in by the Schisoffs. The stickers were issued to the guards each morning and a new color was used each day. For that reason the delivery of the stickers had to be made at the pier.

Lvovsky arrived at the pier as the *Majestic* was docking. He stopped and chatted casually with McAdams, who slipped him the stickers. When the baggage was unloaded, the Schisoffs' trunks were sent to the section marked with the initial "S." Schisoff pointed out the two trunks to Lvovsky, who walked over casually and sat down on a trunk to smoke a cigarette, as though waiting for an inspector to check the luggage. Unobtrusively he took one of the stickers and pasted it to the trunk. He moved to the other trunk, sat down, and pasted a sticker on that trunk. And then he strolled away.

A Customs inspector examined the Schisoffs' suitcases, but he noted the trunks already had the inspection stickers on them so he permitted them to be carted off. They were loaded into taxis by

Lvovsky and Katzenberg and hustled off to an unknown destination.

The system worked like a charm. Each time that Lvovsky notified the two Customs guards of an arrival of a "world traveller" the guards would arrange to be on duty at those hours so that they could obtain stickers and pass them on to Lvovsky. Six times the confederates of the gang made the trip safely from Shanghai without any inspection of the heroin-loaded trunks.

But Treasury agents were closing in on the gang. Narcotics agents, with aid from Customs agents, had opened an investigation of Lepke's narcotics smuggling ring after an informant had squealed to Narcotics Commissioner Harry Anslinger. The informant—whose name has never been disclosed—was a woman with revenge in her heart. Her boy friend—one of the Lepke mob —had been playing around with another woman and she wanted to get even with him for his infidelity. She gave Anslinger enough information, with facts that could be verified, to start the ball rolling. Bit by bit, the agents closed in on the gangsters. And they discovered by a close check of the stickers issued to all pier personnel that there was an irregularity in the stickers which had been issued to the guards McAdams and Hoffman.

As the agents began to put on the heat, underworld characters started to talk. Those "world travellers" who had helped bring narcotics into the country began to confess. Evidence mounted against the gang, and when the crackdown finally came, a total of thirty-one persons were involved. Lepke was indicted on ten counts of a conspiracy to smuggle narcotics into the United States.

At this time—December, 1937—Lepke was a fugitive. A little more than a year earlier he and Gurrah Jake Shapiro had been convicted on the antitrust charges brought against them four years earlier. They had been sentenced to two years in prison and fined $10,000. But Lepke appealed. He was released under $3,000 bail and immediately went into hiding.

For almost two years Lepke's pals hid him from the law. He lived for a time in the old Oriental Dance Hall on Coney Island. Then, twenty pounds heavier and wearing a mustache, he moved to a flat in Brooklyn. Later he occupied a house in Flatbush, posing as the paralyzed husband of a Mrs. Walker. All this time he continued directing the affairs of his criminal organization.

But now, in 1939, the search for Lepke had become the most intense manhunt the country had seen in years. The Federal government wanted him on the narcotics charges growing out of his syndicate operations. And he was the No. 1 man on the most-wanted list of New York's District Attorney Thomas E. Dewey, who then was opening his first bid for the Republican Presidential nomination. Among other things, Dewey was certain he could pin a murder charge on Lepke—who now had "dead or alive" rewards on his head totalling $50,000.

As the pressures mounted, the hunted man became desperate. And desperately he tried to wreck the cases against him by sending witnesses out of the state, by intimidation, and by murder. The heat was on the underworld as it had never been before. The rumor spread that if Lepke did not surrender to the authorities, he would be killed by one of his own kind. Lepke had at last become too much of a liability even to his old pals.

Hunted and frightened, with every day holding the threat of sudden death, Lepke began negotiations to surrender to New York Columnist Walter Winchell—on the condition that he would be turned over to the FBI rather than New York State authorities.

During the evening of August 5, Winchell received a telephone call from a man who refused to identify himself. "Lepke wants to come in," he said. "But he's heard so many different stories about what will happen to him. He can't trust anybody, he says. If he can find someone he can trust, he will give himself up to that person. The talk around town is that Lepke would be shot while supposedly escaping."

Winchell called FBI Director John Edgar Hoover in Washington and told him of the mysterious call and Lepke's willingness to surrender if he could be assured of protection.

Hoover told Winchell: "You are authorized to state that the FBI will guarantee it."

For almost three weeks the dickering continued between Winchell and his mysterious callers until Hoover finally said, "This is a lot of bunk, Walter. You are being made a fool of, and so are we. If you contact those people again, tell them the time limit is up!

Winchell relayed this information to the intermediary. Then it was that arrangements were made for Hoover to be waiting in his automobile on 28th Street near Fifth Avenue at 10:15 on the evening of August 24.

Winchell was parked in his car at Madison Square when Lepke came out of the shadows and stepped into the car beside him. "Hello," Lepke said. "Thanks very much."

Quickly, the columnist drove to 28th Street, where he pulled up behind Hoover's car. Lepke quickly moved into the automobile beside Hoover.

Winchell said, "Mr. Hoover, this is Lepke."

"How do you do," Lepke replied. "Let's go."

And so ended one of the greatest manhunts in American criminal history.

Four months later, Lepke went on trial in the Federal district court in New York City. He sat in silence, his brown eyes expressionless, as his former henchmen paraded to the stand to tell the details of their narcotics smuggling.

Among the government witnesses, many of them pale from sunless days in prison, were Jack Katzenberg, Ben Schisoff and John McAdams, the Customs employee. No longer were they afraid of the little man who sat there staring at them.

The trial dragged through fifteen days, but in the end Lepke was convicted. He was sentenced to serve fourteen years in prison and was fined $2,500 on ten narcotics charges. Two weeks later in General Sessions Court, Lepke was convicted on thirty-six counts of extortion and sentenced to an additional thirty years in prison.

Among the others involved in the smuggling ring, Lvovsky received seven years in prison and was fined $15,000. Sam Gross was sentenced to six years and fined $15,000, while Katzenberg was given ten years and a $10,000 fine. Both the Customs employees, McAdams and Hoffman, also received prison sentences.

But the final ordeal for Lepke was yet to come. In October, 1941, Lepke was taken from prison and returned to New York to stand trial for his role as mastermind in the operations of Murder, Inc. Specifically, he was charged with ordering the murder of a former garment industry truck driver, Joseph Rosen, who had ignored his warnings to get out of town and out of reach of questioning by District Attorney Dewey at the time Dewey was investigating the rackets in New York.

Manuel "Mendy" Weiss was named by the state as the actual triggerman in the slaying, and a small-time hood named Louis Capone (no kin to Al Capone) was accused of being the man who assisted Weiss in his getaway. Rosen had been found shot to death on the morning of September 13, 1936, lying on the floor of his small candy shop in Brooklyn.

One of the witnesses against Lepke was Max Ruben, whose death Lepke had ordered when Ruben refused to stay out of New York. One of Lepke's henchmen had shot Ruben through the neck and left him lying near death. But he had recovered to tell his story to Prosecutor Burton Turkus.

Ruben testified that Lepke—two days before Rosen was killed —told him: "That bastard Rosen is going around Brownsville shooting his mouth off that he's going downtown. He and nobody else are going down anyplace or do any more talking . . . or any talking at all."

Allie Tannenbaum, another of Lepke's triggermen, supported Ruben's testimony. He said he had heard Lepke say of Rosen: "There's one son-of-a-bitch who'll never go downtown." By downtown, Lepke meant the office of the district attorney.

Tannenbaum also told of hearing Mendy Weiss describe how he had shot Rosen—after which his pal, "Pittsburgh Phil" Strauss, had pumped bullets into the body just for kicks.

When Lepke was advised that Rosen was dead, Tannenbaum said his boss replied, "What's the difference as long as everyone is clean and got away all right."

A battery of nine attorneys defended Lepke. But this time the king of the underworld couldn't squeeze out of the trap. Too many of his old gang had decided to talk. They had lived too long in fear that Lepke would order their own deaths in his effort to remove anyone who might be dangerous to him. Now they wanted Lepke out of the way.

Lepke, Weiss and Capone were convicted of murder and sentenced to die in the electric chair. They went to their deaths in March, 1944.

Control of the narcotics traffic in the United States is primarily the responsibility of the Narcotics Bureau. But Customs agents also have a direct responsibility in the government's efforts to throttle the illicit trade. For this reason Customs agents frequently are teamed with Narcotics agents in investigations which often are international in scope.

It is not unusual for Customs agents to work for as much as two years in tracking down a single narcotics smuggler and removing him from circulation. These cases require endless hours of surveillance and hunting for the one bit of information which will trap the quarry.

Such a case was dropped in the laps of Customs agents in San Francisco and Seattle on August 2, 1954, when an informant tipped Customs agents at Seattle that $30,000 worth of heroin was to be smuggled into the United States aboard the SS *M. N. Patrick* by a Negro seaman named Robert King. He described King as tall, jug-eared and middle-aged, with a taste for conservative clothes and gaudy night spots. The tipster said King planned to take the heroin ashore in San Francisco when the *Patrick* completed her run from Hong Kong.

Seattle forwarded a teletype message to San Francisco saying: "Information considered to be very reliable received today that ship *M.N. Patrick* arriving San Francisco between August 4 and August 8 from India via Hong Kong has heroin valued at about $30,000 on board. Vessel supposed to be in Seattle today but not verified. The suspect, Robert King, in steward's department, is owner and will try to bring ashore at San Francisco."

Alerted by this message, San Francisco agents began checking on the probable arrival time of the *Patrick* only to discover that the ship had changed its sailing schedule and would not touch San Francisco on that trip. A message was forwarded to Seattle saying: "We have just checked here and find that *Patrick* is not coming to San Francisco this trip. She is due in Seattle today (August 6) and will make two trips from Seattle to Alaska and then back to Far East. Under circumstances consider probable that King will try to unload at Seattle. . . ."

The *Patrick* had already docked in Seattle when this message was received. Agents rushed to the waterfront. But as the agents were walking aboard the ship, King was walking off undetected, apparently carrying the heroin with him.

A few hours later it was learned that King had contacted a known narcotics peddler in Los Angeles and had arranged for a

$30,000 "loan." It was suspected by agents that King had made his contact successfully and disposed of the narcotics before agents could get on his trail.

Agents began checking on King's background and on his movements as far as possible in previous years. They discovered that while he had no known source of income, he owned an apartment building in San Francisco valued at $135,000. He maintained a bank account which showed heavy deposits and withdrawals. It was discovered also that in past years he had made frequent trips to Hong Kong and Japan. On occasions he had shipped as a seaman, and at other times he had gone abroad as a tourist.

Treasury agents in Japan found that King often frequented the Port Hole Bar in Yokohama, which was a known meeting place of narcotics peddlers when they were trying to contact seamen to use as carriers.

For more than a year and a half agents kept a periodic check on King's movements in an effort to trap him in an act of smuggling or trafficking in narcotics. They had no success until a seemingly unrelated incident occurred in Japan.

On February 9, 1956, Japanese postal inspectors at Yokohama seized a shipment of narcotics which proved to be of special interest to Customs agents in San Francisco and Seattle. While making a routine examination of a package mailed by international air mail, they found 167 grams of heroin and 217 capsules of cocaine hidden in the folds of a pair of woman's pajamas and slippers. The package was addressed to a Mrs. Hazel Scott in Seattle, Washington. The Customs declaration tag gave the name of the sender as W. M. Scott and listed an address in Yokohama. The addresses were written by typewriter. The narcotics were in a manila envelope bearing the words "For Walker." The Japanese turned this information over to the U.S. Embassy.

During the years of the Allied Occupation of Japan after World War II, American and Japanese authorities had achieved close cooperation in combatting the traffic in narcotics and other contraband. This cooperation was continued after the signing of the Peace Treaty in 1952 formally ending the occupation.

The United Nations made the control of narcotics traffic one of its important objectives soon after its formation, resulting in a combined effort by many nations to strangle the illicit trade by joint efforts which were unknown in the years prior to the war.

Treasury agents were stationed in Tokyo as liaison officers to work with Japanese authorities on any cases involving American interests. And it was a routine matter for the Japanese police to give Treasury agents the information on the seizure of the package addressed to Mrs. Scott. This information was relayed from the U.S. Embassy to Customs agents in San Francisco.

The agents found there had been a seaman named Walter Scott aboard an American naval vessel in Yokohama at the time the package was sent—but Scott had not mailed a package while his ship was in Yokohama. Obviously whoever had sent the package containing narcotics had used Scott's name without his knowledge. As for the envelope marked "For Walker," agents suspected that it was probably intended for a known narcotics dealer named Roosevelt Walker, who first came to the attention of Customs in 1940 when he was arrested in Nogales, Arizona, and was charged with smuggling a quantity of marihuana into the country.

And agents found another interesting fact: Walker was a companion of Robert L. King. King had been in Tokyo at the time the package was mailed, but there apparently was no way to link him with this smuggling effort.

And so the surveillance of King was continued. On July 16, 1956, agents trailed King to the International Airport at San Francisco. He had booked passage on Pan American Flight 831 for Tokyo by way of Honolulu and Manila. King was nattily dressed in a brown business suit and he wore a rakish straw hat as he boarded the plane. The agents watched his plane leave San Francisco at 10 A.M., making no effort to stop him. Honolulu and Tokyo were alerted to the fact that King was aboard the plane and that his movements should be watched.

King was permitted to enter Japan unmolested. He also was allowed to leave Japan for a trip to Hong Kong, where he spent several days shopping before returning to Tokyo.

The return to Tokyo was a mistake for King. For months Japanese police had been trying to trace the typewriter which had written the addresses on the package containing the narcotics. They found that King, at the time the package was mailed, had been living in Yokohama at the Tomo Yei Hotel. They also found that King had rented a typewriter—two days before the parcel was mailed—from a Mr. Ono who ran a shop near the hotel. And then they matched a sample of typing from this machine with the typed address on the package containing narcotics. The comparison left no doubt that this was the machine which had been used by the would-be smuggler.

When King returned from Hong Kong on September 20, he was arrested by Japanese police at the Tokyo International Airport and lodged in jail at Yokohama, charged with narcotics smuggling. Unable to raise money for a bail bond, King remained in jail for six months while authorities in Japan and the United States investigated his case. But at last he obtained money from friends in the United States and made bond. He was released, pending a trial. The Japanese held on to his passport as insurance that he would not leave the country.

Passport or no passport, King was determined to get out of Japan before his trial. He went to the Yokohama waterfront and found an old friend who agreed to smuggle him aboard the military transport *General C. G. Morton*. The ship docked at Pier 5 at Oakland on April 14, 1957, and King slipped ashore.

Within a matter of hours, Customs agents were on his trail. The agents found a seaman who testified he had seen King aboard the *C. G. Morton*. The seaman told agents: "About two days before we got to San Francisco, a friend came to me and said, 'How would you like to make some money?' I asked him how and he said, 'Take a package off the ship for me in San Francisco.' He showed me the package and it contained ten rubbers filled with heroin. About two days after we got to San Francisco I took the narcotics off at Pier 5, Oakland Army Terminal. My friend walked off just ahead of me. I had the package of heroin under my coat. We got in my car and went to a motel somewhere in the Richmond district and registered. We stashed the package of heroin in our room. I don't know who picked up the heroin. The next night my friend gave me King's address and told me to go and see him. I went to the hotel and King gave me $500."

King denied that he had re-entered the United States illegally and claimed that he had returned on a Pan American flight from

Tokyo. But agents were able to prove that King had not been booked aboard the plane which he claimed he had been on. They broke down his alibis and at last King entered a plea of guilty to a charge of conspiracy to smuggle narcotics into the United States and to entering the United States without a passport. He was convicted, fined $13,000 and sent to prison for five years.

But it seems that whenever the Kings and the Lepkes are taken out of circulation, there is someone new to take their place. That is why there is a U.S. Customs force.

12

THE CASE OF THE CROOKED DIPLOMAT

The Case of the Crooked Diplomat had its beginning when an Arab informer whispered a warning to a U.S. Bureau of Narcotics agent in faraway Beirut, Lebanon. And before it was closed, agents of the Customs Bureau, the Bureau of Narcotics and the French Sûreté had teamed up in a cooperative drive to smash a ring of criminals attempting to smuggle $20 million worth of heroin into the United States.

They were an oddly assorted lot, the members of this ring. There were only four known members, but in early 1960 their operations had begun to stir alarm across the country among law enforcement agencies seeking the mysterious source of heroin which at intervals had begun to appear in large lots on the underworld market.

The quartet was composed of:

Mauricio Rosal, forty-seven, Guatemala's ambassador to Belgium and the Netherlands, and the son of a respected Central

American diplomat; a small, portly, balding man known favorably in many countries as a witty conversationalist and shrewd politician of seeming integrity; something of a dandy, he usually wore dark homburg hats, expensively tailored dark blue suits and maroon ties; he affected an air of aristocratic elegance both in dress and manners.

Etienne Tarditi, fifty-five, a short, heavy-jowled, paunchy, gross figure of the Parisian underworld with a cloudy background; addicted to trench coats, pork-pie hats and the notion that he resembled Alfred Hitchcock (which he did); a gambler who played for big stakes in narcotics, with connections in many countries; a manipulator who usually remained in the background.

Charles Bourbonnais, thirty-nine, a slender, dapper steward for Trans World Airways, who had an eye for a pretty girl when his wife was not looking; often seen in the company of Tarditi when in Paris, and a liberal spender for a salaried man; the messenger and fixer for the ring.

Nicholas Calamaris, forty-seven, a powerful man with a huge nose, jug ears, skull-like face and long arms which reached almost to his knees; employed as a New York longshoreman, but this job was merely the front for his nighttime operations as a big-time dealer in narcotics; a cautious, secretive man with few close friends.

In the winter and spring of 1960, Federal, state and city police agencies were at a loss to explain the source of heroin which was at times available in almost any quantity desired. Agents canvassed their underworld tipsters with little luck. The informers knew only that at intervals the word would spread that another large load of heroin had arrived in New York and was available. Where it came from and how it entered the country none could— or would—say.

It was not until June that Narcotics Agent Paul Knight picked up the first clue of substance in Beirut, which had become an important listening post for the Narcotics Bureau.

A tipster whispered to Knight that heroin processed in Beirut from a morphine base had been sent to a smuggling ring in Paris. The reputed leader of the ring was a man named Etienne Tarditi. He had, the tipster said, smuggled as much as 40 to 60 kilograms of heroin from Beirut to France, and, according to rumors, it had gone from France to the United States. The carrier was said to be a Spanish-speaking diplomat.

This was the first break. The information from Beirut was passed on to the French Sûreté Nationale with a request that the Narcotics Bureau be informed of Tarditi's movements and his associates.

In August, the Sûreté informed the Bureau that Tarditi had returned to Paris from a trip to New York. His plane companion on the trip, and on several previous trips, had been the Spanish-speaking Guatemalan ambassador, Mauricio Rosal. The Sûreté added that Tarditi also had been seen in Paris in the company of a TWA steward named Charles Bourbonnais.

From this time forward, Tarditi, Rosal and Bourbonnais were under almost constant police surveillance on the Continent. When Bourbonnais returned to the United States on August 24 he was placed under surveillance by Narcotics and Customs agents.

Bourbonnais, the agents found, was married to a TWA hostess. He lived on Long Island and in recent months had sold a residence for $40,000. He always seemed to have plenty of money, and he was something of a playboy when his wife was away from home or when he was in Paris.

Agents trailed Bourbonnais when he drove from the airport. He drove a devious route to an apartment house in Queens. He stood at the entrance of the building looking furtively about before entering.

"That guy is really jumpy," an agent remarked to another. "Do you think he knows we are on his tail?"

"I don't know," was the answer, "but we'd better drop the surveillance. He's suspicious of something. He could have spotted us."

The surveillance was called off temporarily. It wasn't until later that the agents learned that Bourbonnais' wariness had nothing to do with narcotics peddling. On this particular occasion he was on his way to a rendezvous with a girl friend—and he merely wanted to be certain that he wasn't being followed by private detectives hired by his wife.

As the same time, Customs agents began checking into the background of Mauricio Rosal, who they found had been a frequent visitor to the United States. Leafing through old files one day, Agent Mario Cozzi found a report showing that almost twenty years earlier Rosal had been under investigation for alleged smuggling, although nothing had ever been proved against him.

He had arrived in New York City aboard the SS *Nyassa* on August 9, 1941, carrying papers which identified him as a Guatemalan chargé d'affaires. He had claimed—and been granted—diplomatic courtesies when passing through Customs with his wife. His declaration showed that he was enroute from Lisbon to Mexico City on his way to Honduras.

The Rosals had remained in New York only a few days and then had departed with their seventeen pieces of luggage, none of which was subjected to Customs examination.

A few days after their departure, Customs agents were informed by a tipster that Rosal had carried essential oils worth $40,000 and diamonds worth $37,000 into the city. A diamond dealer was found who admitted that Rosal had brought the diamonds to him and offered to sell them.

"I refused to buy unless Rosal could produce receipts showing he had paid the customs duty," the dealer said. "When he could not show me a proper clearance from Customs, I turned down his offer."

Customs, however, had reason to believe that Rosal had disposed of the essential oils and the diamonds before he left the city. Months later, Customs Agent Salvador Pena had interviewed Rosal in Mexico City, inquiring about his reported failure to list the dutiable imports on his declaration.

Rosal blandly admitted he had carried the oils with him in a wooden box. "I brought them over from Vichy for a friend," he said, "and delivered them to his brother at the Waldorf-Astoria. I was assured the duty had been paid and I never dreamed, of course, there was anything irregular."

As for the diamonds, Rosal admitted he had approached a dealer and offered to sell him several diamonds. But he insisted that when no agreement was reached, he had taken the gems on to Venezuela, where he had disposed of them. Had he made the sale in New York, he added with a shrug, he would naturally have paid the required customs duty.

There was nothing further that Customs could do about the

matter and the case was closed. The report was filed away to gather dust until Rosal's name was linked with that of Tarditi.

On September 30, six weeks after Cozzi had found the old report, the Sûreté advised the Narcotics Bureau that Rosal and Tarditi had purchased tickets for a flight to New York and it was suspected they would be carrying narcotics. Tarditi was booked to arrive at Idlewild International Airport on October 1, and Rosal was due to arrive a day later. Bourbonnais was scheduled to leave Paris a short time after Tarditi as the steward aboard TWA's Flight 801.

As the original tip on the case had come to the Narcotics Bureau, the investigation was in the hands of District Director George H. Gaffney, a veteran agent, with Customs playing a supporting role.

Thus began one of the most remarkable cases of Federal agency cooperation in the war against smuggling. Gaffney laid his plans well, and when TWA's Flight 801 touched down at Idlewild at 5 P.M. on October 1, a squad of Narcotics and Customs agents was waiting to place Tarditi under surveillance. Customs inspectors had been alerted to signal an identification when Tarditi handed over his baggage declaration, and to make only a cursory examination of a single piece of his luggage.

Tarditi stepped from the plane wearing a trench coat and a pork-pie hat set jauntily at an angle. He seemed unconcerned when the inspector asked him to open the single bag he carried to the inspection station. The inspector noted on his declaration that his destination was the Sherry Netherlands Hotel.

And so it was that Tarditi passed through Customs with no hint given that several pairs of eyes were watching every move he made. A porter carried Tarditi's luggage to a waiting taxi while a radio message was flashed from Idlewild to a squad of agents in midtown Manhattan that the suspect was enroute to the Sherry Netherlands. Agents were instructed to keep him under surveillance when he reached the hotel.

The taxi driver stowed Tarditi's bag into the trunk of his cab and slid behind the wheel. He said, "Where to, sir?"

Tarditi replied, "To the Savoy Hilton."

The driver noted the destination on his trip sheet. He also scribbled the words "Savoy Hilton" on a piece of paper which he wadded into the palm of his left hand. The driver was Narcotics Agent Francis Waters.

As Waters drove from the loading platform, he placed his left hand carelessly on the doorframe and dropped the piece of paper from the car window. He noted with satisfaction in the rear-view mirror that the car behind him stopped suddenly and a man jumped out to pick up the note.

At the Savoy Hilton, Tarditi was given Room 1337. The guest in 1339 was a Narcotics Bureau agent.

Bourbonnais arrived on schedule about an hour after Tarditi.

The next afternoon, Sunday, agents were stationed at strategic points when Rosal walked from the Pan American jet and made his way to the Customs barrier where Inspector Pasquale Cammello had been assigned to weigh and clear his luggage.

Discreet inquiries at the State Department in Washington had disclosed that Rosal was not accredited in any way as a diplomat to the United States, and, further, that the Guatemalan embassy knew nothing of his trip to this country.

Under these circumstances, Rosal was travelling as a private citizen with no legitimate right to the courtesies usually accorded visiting diplomats. Nevertheless, he boldly claimed the privilege of immunity for the four suitcases which accompanied him and Inspector Cammello gave no hint that the claim was anything but routine.

Cammello noted that the bags weighed 19, 25, 50 and 52 pounds when he placed them on the scales. He chatted pleasantly with the diplomat and then waved Rosal on his way. A Pan American passenger representative was waiting to drive the Ambassador to the Plaza Hotel near the Savoy Hilton.

Rosal registered into Room 1205 at the Plaza, where agents had arranged to occupy an adjoining room. He had a leisurely dinner in the hotel dinning room and then he strolled to the nearby Savoy, where he met Tarditi in the lobby. The men kissed each other on the cheek and then sat in a secluded corner in animated conversation. It was almost midnight when they parted and went to their rooms.

The following morning, Tarditi left his hotel and took a cab to an apartment building on East 79th Street. He remained in the building only a few minutes, and when he emerged he was carrying a parcel wrapped in brown paper. He went directly back to his hotel.

About 11 A.M., Tarditi left the Savoy Hilton, carrying in his hand the brown parcel, and he walked to the Plaza Hotel.

Customs Agent Mario Cozzi was one of those watching Tarditi. Cozzi never knew what it was that drew his attention to a battered 1957 Ford station wagon parked at the northeast corner of Central Park South. Perhaps it was the driver. He was a huge man with a skull-like face and large ears who seemed to be interested in Tarditi, too. From long habit, Cozzi made a mental note of the license number, New York LK8935.

Tarditi went directly to Rosal's room, and left the brown parcel with the diplomat. Then he returned to his own hotel.

Narcotics Supervisor George Gaffney and Customs Agent-in-Charge Carl Esposita sat in a parked radio car near the Plaza Hotel entrance. They were reasonably certain that if heroin were being smuggled, then the contraband would be in Rosal's luggage, for which he had claimed diplomatic immunity. If their suspicions were correct, the question was: Where would the delivery take place and to whom?

A dozen agents were dispersed throughout the area in radio cars, receiving their orders by radio from Gaffney. At noon an alert was flashed when Rosal called for a bellman to take his bags from his room to a taxi. He checked out of the hotel and the bellman placed his four suitcases in the trunk of a taxi.

Only a few minutes earlier, Tarditi had left his hotel. Agents reported by radio that he had gone to the corner of 72nd Street and Lexington Avenue, where he was met by Charles Bourbonnais, the TWA steward, and by a tall, gangling man with a skull-like face. The three men were still standing on the corner talking when Rosal's taxi pulled away from the Plaza Hotel.

"This must be it," Gaffney said to Esposita. The command car followed a discreet distance behind Rosal's cab, which went directly across town to the corner of 72nd Street and Lexington Avenue. There the diplomat stepped from the taxi to be joined by Tarditi and Bourbonnais. Gaffney's radio car continued on down the street to a vacant parking space.

From the shadow of a doorway across the street, Mario Cozzi snapped a picture of Rosal, Tarditi and Bourbonnais as they stood talking beside the taxi. Then he noticed a familiar-looking Ford station wagon parked nearby. The man at the wheel was the jug-eared driver he had seen parked earlier in the day near the Plaza Hotel, watching Tarditi. The driver was Nicholas Calamaris.

Rosal spoke to the taxi driver, who opened the trunk of the car. The three men looked into the trunk and for a moment it appeared they were going to transfer the luggage from the cab to the station wagon. But Bourbonnais suddenly strode toward the station wagon, while Tarditi and Rosal entered the taxi after the driver had closed the lid of the trunk.

In that interval of a few seconds, a dozen agents were prepared to rush the men if the luggage had been transferred to the station wagon. When nothing happened, Gaffney withheld his order.

Bourbonnais slid into the seat beside Calamaris, who drove toward Third Avenue with Rosal and Tarditi following closely behind in the taxi. At Third Avenue the two cars swung north and still the occupants were totally unaware that their cars were bracketed by the automobiles carrying Narcotics and Customs agents.

At 75th Street, the taxi was halted by a stop light while the station wagon continued on. Gaffney made a sudden decision. "Let's not tail them any farther," he snapped into the microphone. "Let's get them now." The control car quickly shot forward and swerved in front of the cab. Other cars closed in to block the station wagon.

Mike Cozzi leaped from his car to the taxi, jerked open the door and flashed his agent's badge. "We're Treasury agents," he said. "Don't make a move."

"What is this?" Rosal exclaimed.

Tarditi protested, "Do you know who this man is? He is a diplomat! He is entitled to diplomatic immunity!"

The agents began firing questions at the two men.

"A diplomat to what country?"

"I am the Guatemalan ambassador to Brussels."

"Are you on a diplomatic mission to the United States?"

"No."

"Does your government know you are in the United States?"

"Well, no. . . ."

At the station wagon, Calamaris was protesting, too. "Why are you stopping us? What's going on?"

"Don't worry," an agent said, "just get moving. Drive off the Avenue onto 76th Street. Over there!"

"I don't know nothing. . . ."

"Get the car moving. You're blocking traffic."

Passersby gawked curiously as the four men were taken from the automobiles with a swarm of agents around them.

"What's in the trunk of the cab?" Rosal was asked.

"Four suitcases," he said. "One is mine but the other three don't belong to me."

"You brought them into the country, didn't you?"

"Yes, but they are not mine. . . ."

The cab driver, unable to comprehend what was taking place, was ordered to open the trunk of the taxi. An agent broke open one of the suitcases. It was packed with plastic bags containing a white powder which laboratory tests would later prove to be almost pure heroin.

Rosal himself opened the small case which he insisted was the only bag which belonged to him. Inside was a package wrapped in brown paper—the parcel which the agents had seen Tarditi carry into his room at the Plaza Hotel that morning. It contained $26,000 in U.S. currency.

The men were placed in the agents' cars along with the heroin-filled suitcases, and taken to the Narcotics Bureau headquarters for questioning.

Agent Frederick Cornetta said to Mike Cozzi, "I've got to drive the station wagon to headquarters. Why don't you ride with me?"

Mike climbed into the front seat of the station wagon beside Cornetta, who took the wheel.

As they moved down Third Avenue, Cozzi looked into the glove compartment and examined its contents. Then he ran his hand into the space beneath the seat and pulled out a paper sack.

"Hey!" he said to Cornetta, "I think I've got two more kilos of the stuff."

He looked inside and exclaimed, "Money! It's full of money."

The sack contained $41,949, which Calamaris and Bourbonnais intended to hand over to Tarditi.

At headquarters, Rosal talked freely. He claimed that he first met Tarditi in Paris in the summer of 1959 through a mutual friend. During one conversation, he had told Tarditi that his mother owed $35,000 on some property in Central America and was in danger of losing it if he could not raise the money.

A short time later, he continued, Tarditi had contacted him in Brussels and asked him to carry narcotics into the United States under a cloak of diplomatic immunity. Twice he had made deliveries successfully. The $26,000 found in his suitcase was his commission for the three trips.

Bourbonnais claimed he was only an errand boy for the syndicate. He rambled on vaguely about a mysterious Madame Simone, the wife of a doctor or dentist, whom he had met in Paris in the winter of 1960. Simone had asked him to collect $250,000 from a debtor in New York and to bring the money to her in Paris. He had made the delivery and she had paid him a commission of 1 per cent. Then Simone had asked him to meet a man in New York who would be standing on Fifth Avenue across from St. Patrick's Cathedral at 3 P.M. on October 2. This man would be wearing a gray suit and brown hat. He would hand Bourbonnais a package which he was to deliver to Tarditi, who would be in New York at this time.

Bourbonnais said he had met the stranger, received the package, and had arranged to have the package delivered to Tarditi, who passed it on to Rosal. Even if the story were fiction, at least it was one explanation of where the money came from to pay Rosal for the use of his diplomatic immunity.

The heroin in Rosal's luggage weighed 49.25 kilos. And four days later, agents located another 51.89 kilos of heroin which Tarditi had cached in a trunk on Long Island. It was the largest seizure of heroin ever made in the United States, and Narcotics officials estimated it was worth $20 million on the underworld market.

The Guatemalan ambassador to the United States announced that his government had disavowed Rosal. His trip to the United States had not been authorized, nor had it been sanctioned in any official manner—therefore he was not entitled to the diplomatic immunity which he had claimed.

Rosal was indicted along with Tarditi, Bourbonnais and Calamaris on charges of violating the narcotics laws of the United States. The four pleaded guilty. Rosal and Calamaris were sentenced to fifteen years in prison. Bourbonnais and Tarditi were given nine years each. And in passing sentence, the Federal judge said:

". . . I think the death sentence would not be an inappropriate sentence. Under the statute, I can imprison them for up to twenty years. If it had not been for pleas of guilty, I think I would have done so. . . ."

It was only then that the Customs Bureau closed its files on The Case of the Crooked Diplomat.

13

A STRANGE LITTLE ROOM

On a hot July day in 1941, gray-haired Adrian Grasseley sat at a small table in a room whose window overlooked Fifth Avenue, peering intently through a microscope at a large diamond.

Crowds strolled the streets below. Traffic rumbled along the Avenue. Pigeons sailed about the spires of St. Patrick's Cathedral. Grasseley saw and heard none of this. All of his attention was concentrated on the diamond lying on the table before him—a fabulous stone the likes of which few men had ever seen.

This was the Vargas diamond, discovered two years earlier in Brazil. The stone weighed 726.6 carats. It was Grasseley's job to divide it into twenty-three smaller stones which would be worth $2 million if he did his job well. The Vargas was one of the largest and most valuable diamonds ever to pass through Customs.

For forty years, Adrian Grasseley had cut, sawed and cleaved diamonds in Antwerp and in New York City. But this slender man with the thin, tapering fingers had never had the responsibilty of splitting a Vargas. Few men ever had.

Diamond Merchant Harry Winston had purchased the stone for $700,000. He had turned it over to Grasseley to divide, and the cutter's first important move would be to split the giant stone with a blow on the blade of a knife. If the diamond split smoothly, then the rest of the job would be relatively simple.

For weeks, hour after hour, Grasseley studied the Vargas, searching for the "grain" of the diamond. He looked for a hidden flaw which might cause the stone to burst into fragments, but he could find none.

At last Adrian Grasseley knew what had to be done. He would cut a small V-shaped notch at the precise point at which he intended to split the stone. Into this notch he would place a dull-edged knife. If his calculations were correct, a blow on the knife would cleave the diamond as truly as a piece of fine wood splits along its grain. If the blow were too heavy, or if he had misread the diamond's structure, then the Vargas might shatter and a fortune would be lost.

On the night before the blow was to be struck, Grasseley did not feel any undue nervousness. His hands were steady and he congratulated himself on being relaxed. But he could not sleep. He turned and twisted in his bed, and he listened to the grandfather clock in the hallway toll the quarter hours.

"What is the matter with me?" he muttered irritably. "I am not nervous and I have not been worrying about the Vargas." It was almost dawn before he dropped off to sleep.

The diamond cutter slept for only two hours. Then he hurried to the small room at Rockefeller Center where the diamond waited. All morning he worked to cut the small notch. He had lunch. And at 2 P.M. he was ready.

Only Harry Winston and a diamond polisher were in the room with Grasseley when he placed the diamond on the table. He carefully inserted the edge of the knife into the notch and, holding his breath, he rapped the knife with an iron bar. The only sound was the ring of the bar on the knife.

The Vargas didn't split. In that instant Adrian Grasseley felt only numbness. His calculations had been wrong.

Winston grabbed the stone and examined it under a magnifying glass. He saw at the point of the V-notch a small fracture in the stone. It wasn't deep. But it was straight and true along the grain as Grasseley had planned.

Winston handed the stone back to Grasseley. "Strike it harder," he said. "It's all right." It was a decision which could cost him a fortune but he had confidence in the gray-haired man beside him. Winston had seen Grasseley involuntarily soften the blow when he struck the knife with the iron bar and he could understand the fear that must have gripped him.

Again Grasseley placed the knife in the V and struck it with the rod. The fracture deepened. And when he struck the third blow, the Vargas split cleanly without even the loss of a fragment of the stone.

Winston heaved a sigh of relief, and when he looked at Adrian Grasseley he saw that the little diamond cutter was crying. The reaction to the weeks of strain had been too much.

The story of the Vargas diamond is only one among thousands of stories of suspense, excitement, glamor and intrigue in the world where diamonds fire the imagination of men and women and form the basis for a giant industry. And because the diamond trade is big business, it becomes the concern of the Customs Bureau.

The Vargas entered the country through one of the most unusual workshops in all the country, located in the nondescript, sprawling Customs building on Varick Street in lower Manhattan. The door to this room is never left unlocked. No one is permitted to enter the room unless he carries a pass or has special permission.

The reason for the extraordinary security is that the room is one of the most important clearing points for diamonds in all the world. It is the workshop of the Customs experts whose job it is to appraise the value—and determine the duty—on the diamonds, rubies, sapphires, and other precious and semi-precious stones which are brought into the United States.

Approximately $75 million worth of cut and polished diamonds enter the United States each year, along with $75 million to $100 million worth of rough diamonds and other precious stones. Each shipment of cut and polished diamonds—with few exceptions—must pass through the obscure little room presided over by Chief Examiner Leroy N. Pipino, a slender, dark-haired, young-looking

man who maintains a remarkably detached view toward the treasures that are spread before him each week. In the past ten years,
Pipino has appraised diamonds worth more than $1 billion.

Soon after joining the Customs Service in the mid-Thirties,
Pipino was assigned as an under clerk to the diamond office. As
he watched the flow of gems arrive from abroad and as he listened to the discussions of their good and bad points, he became
fascinated with the trade in precious stones.

Pipino began to read all he could about gems in New York
City's libraries. He learned much from the Customs Bureau's own
experts and each day's work was an education in itself. At night he
attended Columbia University to take courses on gems and gem-
ology, and often he talked to some of the country's leading experts,
learning from them.

Pipino advanced to the post of assistant appraiser during the
war years, and then in 1949 he was appointed chief examiner. In
the handling of so impressive a fortune in jewels, one might expect
to find him in the elegant surroundings of a Tiffany showroom. But
in Pipino's rather drab-looking workshop, the gems are spread ir-
reverently on a battered table for examination. Around the room
are laboratory aids commonly used by gemologists—the diamond-
scope, a binocular microscope with a special attachment for con-
trolling light source; a dichroscope which reveals color variances
in stones; a refractometer for measuring light rays; equipment to
test the hardness of stone; and the most-used instrument of all, a
ten-power microscope.

Ninety-five per cent of all the diamonds coming into the United
States pass through the port of New York and are brought to
Pipino's office for examination. Most of them come from Europe,
South Africa, Israel or Brazil. They are weighed and their value is
appraised. If there is no discrepancy between the weights and the
values listed on the importer's invoices, the gems are released to
Customs brokers for delivery to the persons or firms to which they
were shipped.

In this small room also are made the examinations of the modern gold and platinum jewelry and all the antique jewelry. The
cut and polished diamonds are subject to a 10 per cent duty.
Rough diamonds arrive duty-free. Diamonds which have been
incorporated into industrial tools or processed for industrial use

are dutiable at 15 per cent of their value. There is no duty required on antique jewelry.

Antwerp is the largest diamond-cutting center in the world, and has been for many years. Most of the cutting of small diamonds is done by the Antwerp craftsmen, although in recent years Israel has developed into an important diamond-cutting center.

The birth of the Israeli diamond industry was part of the chain reaction of the Nazi invasion of the Lowlands in World War II. Many of the best diamond cutters in Europe were Jews. When the invasion came, they fled from Belgium and from Holland. As Hitler's persecution of the Jews became more and more oppressive, reaching further and further, they scattered across the world to places of asylum. Many of these wanderers later went to the new state of Israel and with their skills they founded an industry that has been growing steadily in importance.

Diamonds—like gold—are sensitive to economic and political instability. There is a constant shifting of these treasures about the world, seeking havens of safety or places of the greatest profits.

Leroy Pipino and his associates didn't even have to read the newspaper headlines back in 1938–1939 to know that trouble was brewing in Europe. They could read the warnings in the increasing volume of diamonds and other precious stones which were being imported into the United States. The flight of jewelry from Europe was a measure of the fears of millions of people.

Most of the jewels arriving in New York at that time were carried by refugees fleeing before the threat of the Nazis. Families brought with them their treasured and often priceless heirlooms. Many had converted their property and life savings to the currency of diamonds.

As non-residents, the alien refugees were permitted by law to bring all of their personal jewelry into the country without paying a customs duty. But if they intended to sell any of the jewelry within a period of three years from the date of their arrival, then the jewelry had to be declared and duty paid on it.

There was, and still is, a provision in the law which allowed these people to manipulate their jewelry and to take advantage of the lowest customs rate in cases where they intended to sell the gems. They could do this by removing the stones from their settings.

Gems imported in their settings automatically become subject to a 30 per cent duty, based on the total value of the gems and the settings. But if the stones were separated from the mountings, then the importer paid only a 10 per cent tax on the stones and a 30 per cent tax on the mountings. Since most of the value of jewelry was in the stones, the refugees were able to reduce the duty roughly 20 per cent by this manipulation.

Americans travelling abroad today may take advantage of this law when they bring home a fine piece of jewelry. They are permitted to separate gems from setting and then have them appraised separately.

The flight of jewelry to the United States from Europe was great before the war, but it was even greater in the years immediately following the conflict. Pipino's office handled a record-breaking 10,000 packages of gems in 1947. And the rise in diamond shipments was a gauge of Europe's economic desperation.

In the postwar years, Europe's economy was shattered. Factories were in ruins. People were digging out of the debris of war to repair the ravages of the long struggle. They needed money not only to rebuild, but to survive.

Men and women took their gems from vaults, cupboards, and from secret burial places and forwarded them to the United States to exchange them for U.S. dollars. The demand for diamonds and other precious stones was strong in the United States and prices were high. The flow of gems became a flood.

The weakness of Britain's pound sterling in the postwar years also had a strong influence on the movement of diamonds. Countries with a large accumulation of sterling were willing to give discounts of up to 10 per cent on diamonds if the purchasers agreed to pay for them in dollars. And in this juggling of currencies and discounts, diamonds were moving about the world in strange patterns.

Diamond shipments would leave South Africa and go to Holland, for example. There they would be re-addressed and shipped to the United States so that payment could be made to Holland. Holland would accept dollars in payment and transfer pounds sterling to South Africa. The same thing was happening in Japan and other countries in the Far East where the currencies were weak.

Black market operators also found ways to evade currency controls. Some of them shipped their diamonds to Switzerland and then used that country as their base of operations to take advantage of Switzerland's total secrecy in banking operations. In this manner they were able to mask the origin of the diamonds.

Through the postwar years, the United States was the financial magnet drawing jewels from all parts of the world. But as the economies of the European countries improved with the support of American foreign aid programs, the tide began to turn in the 1950s. The purchasing power of the West Germans, British, French and Italians had improved to the point where the flight of jewelry was from the United States to Europe. The time had come when the baubles were more important to the buyers than American dollars.

Despite the ebb and flow of the diamond trade, diamonds remain one of the most tightly controlled commodities in the world. Each diamond-producing country tries to police the production to maintain price stability—since diamonds are an important means of earning dollar exchange.

The Diamond Syndicate, based in London, each month allots the rough diamond material to buyers in Belgium, Holland, Israel and the United States. Each country's share depends on the Syndicate's appraisal of what the world market will absorb without disturbing the price structure. The list of dealers permitted to purchase the rough stones remains relatively constant and there is rarely room for new members.

The tight monopoly held by the Syndicate has created a black market supported by dealers who look to sources other than the Syndicate for their merchandise. This market is called, in polite terms, the "open market." It also is the market of the underworld, operating illicitly and in defiance of the Syndicate controls.

Liberia in recent years has become an important source of diamonds for the "open market." It is whispered in the diamond trade that all of the diamonds which come from Liberia actually were stolen from the neighboring diamond-producing country of Sierra Leone where the production is controlled by the Syndicate. There are some who claim these diamonds were mined on Liberian soil near the Sierra Leone border.

One enterprising European dealer years ago started a mail-order business with individual diamond miners who would smuggle diamonds from the mines and mail them to him at various post office boxes. From a small beginning, these shipments reached the point where a $50,000 shipment was not uncommon.

This flow of bootleg diamonds has created a problem for Customs. The illicit material cannot be officially acknowledged by the merchants and no record can be made by the cutters in those countries where the production is carefully policed. The result is that these diamonds find their way into the hands of smugglers, who constantly are seeking ways to slip them past Customs without payment of duty.

With the rise in popularity of the marquise and teardrop diamonds, the demand for the emerald-cut diamond has waned. Cutters look for rough material which can be shaped into the marquise, teardrop, or the round diamond. The round stone has never lost its popularity and continued year after year among the fashion leaders. The oval diamond fell from popularity for a period of time but it, also, has staged a comeback.

Determining the value of a gem is often a controversial task for Pipino and his aides, who must study such factors as size, the quality of the cutting, the color of the stones, their cleanliness, and the imperfections left by nature. A diamond may be "ice white" or it may be any shade of yellow from "top silver cape" to "canary" or any one of several hues of brown. The colors may vary with the location of the window through which the light falls on the stone. The imperfections may range from a speck smaller than a fleck of dust to sizable fissures, crystals or carbon spots. It may be slightly off-color or the color may lack a clear definition.

Basically, the value of a diamond is determined by what is known in the trade as the Four Cs—color, cleanliness, cutting and caratage. As far as Pipino is concerned, the most important of all of these is the color, even though color often can be extremely deceptive in certain diamonds. Stones which come from the Premier mine in South Africa have a bluish cast in daylight, but when placed under an artificial light they have a yellowish glow. However, the Customs experts usually can look at a diamond and make an educated guess as to its origin—whether it came from Brazil, South Africa or French Equatorial Africa. Very seldom are these guesses wrong.

The standards used in judging the value of a diamond are the same as those used in determining the value of other precious stones. The finest of the rubies, sapphires, emeralds and many of the semi-precious stones have a deep, rich, velvety color instantly recognizable by the expert. In addition, the better stones have a glow which comes from within the stone itself.

Most of the fine gems imported into the United States in recent years have been those which came from famous jewel collections of the past. A tiara which Napoleon I reputedly presented to Empress Marie Louise was brought into the country as an artistic antiquity—free of duty. Then the jeweler, quite legally, removed the gems from the tiara and placed them in pieces of modern jewelry. Other fine stones have come from the collections of Indian maharajas.

To qualify as an artistic antiquity—free of duty—a piece of jewelry (or any other object) must have been produced prior to 1830. This arbitrary date for determining antiquity is a sensitive point in the import trade. As Pipino explained it to one puzzled inquirer: "Anything that was produced before 1830 is permitted into the country free of duty as an artistic antiquity—and not as an antique. We don't presume to tell a dealer or a curator what is to be considered antique and what is not. But an antique is not necessarily an artistic antiquity. To qualify for this legal description, it must have been produced prior to 1830—the date fixed by Congress for determining which cultural objects shall be free of duty and which shall not."

Many in the import-export trade angrily take exception to the law, passed in 1930, which refuses to recognize any object under 100 years old as being an artistic antiquity. But most will agree that the date 1830 marked the beginning of industry's mechanization, which permitted mass production of many items. Mechanization came to the jewelry trade around 1850 in the Victorian era, and a great deal of mass-produced jewelry was made in this period of prosperity in England. Customs does not permit its importation as an artistic antiquity—and it cannot do so unless Congress changes the date which controls the legal definition.

To the casual observer, Customs' little diamond room on Varick Street would appear to be far removed from anything but the dollars and cents value of precious stones arriving from abroad. But to Leroy Pipino it is a place where an adventure story unfolds every day for those who can read the meaning behind the ebb and flow of jewels.

14

THE DIAMOND SMUGGLERS

Richard X, an American dealer in diamonds, sat at the desk in his hotel room in Antwerp, Belgium, in June, 1953, scribbling figures on a sheet of paper. Even allowing for an unexpected drop in prices on the diamond market, his figures showed that this day's work eventually should bring him a net profit in the neighborhood of $100,000—a pleasing 50 per cent on his investment and no taxes on profits to be paid to the Internal Revenue Service.

Long before this, Mr. X had decided it was foolish to bring $200,000 worth of cut diamonds into the United States, to declare the gems on his customs declaration, to pay the government the required 10 per cent duty, to pay the Federal luxury tax on retail sales, and then to pay another tax on the profits from the sale of the diamonds.

He had learned there was a more profitable way to do business. True, it had its risks—but no one ever made money without risks. The trick was to buy insurance which guaranteed duty-free delivery of the diamonds in New York City. The risks were minimized. The system was about as foolproof as any system could be because you dealt with a reliable syndicate. By buying and selling secretly the profits were enormous.

Three years earlier Mr. X had arrived in Antwerp on his first buying trip, carrying a letter of credit for $200,000 from his bank in New York, and had fully expected to carry his diamond purchases home with him on his return.

Soon after his arrival, he had called a business acquaintance in the Antwerp diamond trade and asked him to dinner at his hotel. He had met the Belgian in New York City and the Belgian had insisted that they should get together on his first trip to Antwerp. The friend had arrived at the hotel and they had enjoyed an excellent dinner that evening. Over a brandy, they had discussed business. Mr. X had confided that the next day he intended to purchase $200,000 worth of diamonds in the market. And then he had complained of the customs duties and the taxes that he would have to pay on the profits.

After several more brandies, his friend had said to him: "Listen to me. It is silly for you to pay such taxes when it is unnecessary. Let me tell you how you can avoid the taxes. Tomorrow, go to any of the regular diamond houses, any that you prefer, and make discreet purchases. After you have selected the stones, go to the coffeehouse on the corner of (and he named the street). Order a cup of coffee and then tell the waiter that you wish to speak to the manager. When the manager comes to your table, ask him to have a cup of coffee with you. Tell him that you have purchased some merchandise and you wish to contact someone who will deliver the merchandise to you in New York City. The manager, quite naturally, will say he knows nothing of such affairs, but in a short time you will be approached by a stranger. This man will say he understands you wish the delivery of certain merchandise to the United States. He will ask you, 'How do you wish to pay for this?' And you say, 'By cash.' "

Mr. X had interrupted to say, "Can you give me the name of this man who will approach me?"

His friend had shaken his head. "No. You will never know his name—and you will never know the names of anyone with whom you deal. You must trust these men because they are reliable. They have to be reliable to stay in business."

"Now," he had continued, "the man who approaches you will take you to an appraiser's office somewhere in the city. You carry your diamonds with you to be appraised. When the value of the stones is confirmed, you will be asked for a cash payment of six or seven per cent of the stones' value as insurance which guarantees their safe delivery to you in New York. The insurance rate varies from six to ten per cent depending on circumstances. I think it now is about six or seven. After you pay the fee, you leave the diamonds with the gentlemen. They will tell you when to expect delivery."

Mr. X remembered his amazement. He had exclaimed, "Do they give me a receipt for the diamonds? Do I just walk out the door with nothing—not even knowing the names of the men I'm dealing with?"

His friend had said, "You get nothing. Believe me, this is the way the syndicates operate. It is done every week. You understand they cannot have a record of these transactions."

Then his friend had explained the syndicates. In Antwerp there were many wealthy businessmen who could not break into the tightly controlled, legitimate diamond business, which was in the hands of five old-line diamond clubs. Closed out of this market, they had turned to the only diamond business open to them—the insuring of diamonds smuggled into the United States and other countries. They had formed loose syndicates and had organized rings of men and women to act as carriers.

Members of these shadowy syndicates frequented certain coffee-houses in and near the diamond market. When advised that some-one had prepared a shipment of diamonds, and wished insurance, the group would meet to prorate the risk. One man would take $20,000, another $30,000, and so on, until the full value of the diamonds was covered. They would agree to pay the appraised value of the stones if the stones were lost, stolen, or seized by Customs officers.

Mr. X had lain awake for hours after the conversation with his friend, trying to decide whether he should make such a gamble. He had decided finally that the risk was worth it. The next day he had gone to the diamond market, purchased the stones, and then gone to the coffeehouse as his friend had suggested. He had talked to the manager. The stranger had approached him. He had been taken to an office in a part of the city which he could never find again. His gems had been appraised. He had paid the insurance fee—seven per cent of the appraised value—and had walked out of the office with nothing to show for any of the transaction.

Before he left the office one of the men had asked him, "When are you leaving for the United States?" He had said that he intended to leave the next day, which was Saturday. Then the man had said, "We will deliver the stones to you on Tuesday night next. You will receive a phone call at your home and be given further instructions."

Mr. X had returned to New York City and had waited at his home for the expected call on Tuesday night. The call came, finally, at 10 P.M. A voice had said, "Mr. X? Were you expecting delivery of a package?" Mr. X had eagerly assured the caller that he was expecting a delivery. The voice had said, "Can you be on the corner of 57th Street and Third Avenue at 11 P.M.?" Mr. X had told the caller that he would be there. Then the voice had said, "So that I will not make any mistakes, please stand on the southwest corner of the street and have a copy of the *Chicago Tribune* under your left arm."

Mr. X had taken a cab to the corner of 57th Street and Third Avenue. He had purchased a copy of the *Chicago Tribune* at a newsstand selling out-of-town papers, and he folded it under his left arm. As he stood on the corner, a man walked up and said, "Mr. X?" And he had replied, "Yes, I am Mr. X." The man had said, "Here is your package." Then he had walked away.

Mr. X had taken the diamonds back to his apartment. He had ripped the paper from the box and had opened it to find every gem that he had purchased in Antwerp and turned over to the syndicate representatives. It was as simple as that. There was not a scrap of paper on record anywhere showing that he was liable for taxes.

The second time he had made the trip to Antwerp he had followed the same procedure, although he had dealt with different men. The second delivery had been made safely also. And now he was ready for the syndicate to make its third delivery. All he had to do was wait. . . .

After Mr. X's return from his third trip to Antwerp—on July 12, 1953—a Belgian Sabena Airlines plane glided to a landing at Idlewild International Airport in New York City with Capt. Robert Edmund Deppe at the controls.

The passengers debarked. Members of the plane's crew came down the gangway with Deppe bringing up the rear. Deppe carried in his hand a shoe box tied with a string. He saw one of the airline clerks near the ship and he tossed the box to him.

"Hold this for me, Joe," he said. "It's a little gift I brought over for a friend. He'll be calling for it."

The clerk said, "Sure, Captain. I'll put it in the crews' baggage room." No one paid any attention to the incident nor did anyone later give a second look at the shoe box when the clerk tossed it onto a shelf in the baggage room.

There was considerable excitement in the terminal when the crew checked in. "What's going on?" Captain Deppe asked. An airline employee replied, "The Customs people are searching everyone again. You might as well get in line yourself."

Deppe got in line. He watched the agents and inspectors go through his luggage and then one of them ran his hands lightly over his clothing.

"What is it all about this time?" he asked.

The inspector grinned. "Just another one of those routine checks, Captain. I'll admit it's getting monotonous."

But it was more than merely another routine check. Several weeks earlier Tom Duncan, chief of the Customs Service's Racket Squad, had received a tip from an informer in Antwerp that diamonds were being smuggled into the United States by crew members of a trans-Atlantic airline. The informer didn't know which airline was involved. All he knew was that the carriers were airline employees. The chances were, however, that the carriers were employees of the Belgian airline, Sabena.

Duncan called in several agents and told them the story. "Let's start shaking down the crew members on those Sabena planes," he said. "We can't search them on every flight. But we can make it so rough maybe somebody will crack."

The searches had been underway for more than a month when Duncan received a telephone call from a Sabena representative.

"What can I do for you?" Duncan asked.

"We're pretty upset about these searches," the caller said. "One of our crew members is in my office now. He wants to talk to you. He believes he has some information that may be helpful. Will you see him?"

"Of course I'll see him," Duncan said.

"He'll be at the Henry Hudson Hotel in one hour," the Sabena representative said. "Room 301. He's one of our radio operators."

Duncan went to the hotel with Agent Harold Smith, another veteran investigator with whom he had worked on scores of cases. The Sabena radio operator was waiting for them in his room.

"You have some information for us?" Duncan asked.

"I think so," the operator said. "I want you to understand why I'm giving you this information. I'm damned tired of being under suspicion every time I come into New York. I'm fed up with being searched and questioned and delayed. I want to see this thing cleared up."

"We don't like it any more than you do," Duncan said. "We'll let up on the pressure as soon as we can."

The operator said that earlier in the year he had been approached in Belgium by a pilot with whom he had flown as a member of the Belgian air force. This man had told him he could earn a large sum of money if he would merely wear a pair of specially made shoes into the United States and then turn the shoes over to a man who would call for them. It was obvious to the operator that he was being asked to smuggle diamonds into the United States.

"I turned them down," he said to Duncan. "I didn't want to get mixed up in anything like that."

"Do you know anyone who is carrying diamonds?" Duncan asked.

"No," the operator said, "I don't. But I presume the same offer was made to someone else. Probably another Sabena crew member with whom this man had flown in the past." He gave them the pilot's name.

The conversation tended to support Duncan's suspicion that the smuggling was being done by a person connected with Sabena. He sent a cable to the Treasury representative in Antwerp, Bill Beers, a gregarious, bilingual agent with a remarkable talent for cultivating sources of information in Europe. He asked Beers to furnish a list of the names of Sabena employees who once had been fliers in the Belgian air force. He got the list, but at the time it wasn't much help, even though one of the names was Robert Edmund Deppe.

When the search of Deppe's luggage was completed at the airport, an agent said, "That's all. You may go now."

Deppe collected his luggage and walked outside to hail a cab. He was driven to the Henry Hudson Hotel on 57th Street between Eighth and Ninth Avenues, where Sabena Airlines personnel were quartered on their stopovers in New York.

When he reached his room, he tried to make a phone call, but no one answered. For the next few hours, he tried again and again to get an answer from the number. At last he took a shower, changed into light sports clothes and left the hotel to get a late dinner.

The telephone which Deppe heard ringing was in the apartment of Julius Falkenstein at 58 West 72nd St. The reason Falkenstein didn't answer at the time was that he and his wife were being detained and searched by Customs agents at the Canadian border.

As far as Falkenstein's friends knew, he was merely a hardworking employee of a New York furrier whose place of business was in the Manhattan garment district. He was a quiet chap who minded his own business. Customs agents had never heard his name until Friday, July 10—two days before Deppe's plane landed at Idlewild—when Duncan received an urgent trans-Atlantic call from Beers in Antwerp.

"Tom," Beers said, "I've got a good line on a smuggling ring. My informant here tells me that their New York contact is Julius Falkenstein. He has a brother in the business in Antwerp."

"Maybe this is what we've been looking for," Duncan said. "We'll get right on it."

Two agents called at the furrier's shop where Falkenstein worked but were told that he had left for the weekend. This news was relayed to Agents Harold F. Smith and John Moseley, who had been sent by Duncan to watch the Falkenstein apartment building. The agents had obtained a description of their man from an apartment employee.

At 6 P.M. on that muggy afternoon, Falkenstein and his wife Ann came out of the building carrying suitcases. They walked around the corner and climbed into a car. Then they headed across town to the elevated West Side Highway and turned north. The agents followed them for several miles but finally lost them in the heavy weekend traffic. When the agents reported by radio to Duncan that they had lost contact, Duncan said, "Let 'em go. They are probably headed for the Catskills. We'll pick them up again Monday."

That night Duncan had another call from Antwerp. He was told that an informant had reported two shipments of diamonds were enroute to New York, one by way of Canada.

Duncan played a hunch. He called Agent Abe Eisenberg, the Customs' representative in Montreal. Eisenberg was about sixty years old, a chunky man with graying hair who had been matching wits with smugglers for almost forty years. He was one of the best undercover men in the Service; he had an actor's ability to look like a dignified banker or a bum. A man of meticulous honesty, he had one obsession: he hated crooked Jews. Being Jewish himself, he regarded every dishonest Jew as a disgrace to his race.

When Eisenberg answered the call, Duncan told him of the tip from Antwerp and the suspicion that Falkenstein was involved. He explained that the Falkensteins had left Manhattan that afternoon and had headed north.

"Keep a check on the hotels, Abe," Duncan said. "They may be headed your way to pick up the diamonds."

"Remember, I'm up here all alone," Eisenberg said. "I can't do my job and watch them too."

Duncan laughed. "Don't worry. You'll get reinforcements. I'll send Harold Smith up on the next plane. Julius Zamosky and I will come up by car. We may need the car to tail them when they start back this way."

Duncan called Smith and told him to get to Montreal by plane as quickly as possible to give Eisenberg a helping hand. Then he called Zamosky, another of the veterans on the Racket Squad, and at dawn they were headed out of Manhattan for the Canadian border.

All day Saturday and Saturday night the agents, working with Canadian police, kept Falkenstein and his wife under surveillance. Falkenstein made several telephone calls to friends and visited them in their offices. Then at 9 A.M. on Sunday, he and his wife checked out of the hotel. They stowed their luggage in the car trunk and headed south.

Duncan, Smith and Zamosky followed the Falkenstein car out of Montreal. When it was evident the couple intended to cross the border at Champlain, New York, Duncan radioed a request to the Champlain Customs station asking that the Falkensteins be detained.

Julius and Ann Falkenstein were seated in an inspector's office when Duncan and his aides walked in and closed the door.

Falkenstein came out of his chair with a display of outraged innocence. "What is the meaning of this?" he shouted. "Why are we being held here?"

Duncan said, "We happen to think you went to Montreal to pick up a shipment of diamonds."

"We have no diamonds," Falkenstein said. "Go ahead and search us."

"That's what we intend to do, Mr. Falkenstein," Duncan said.

A search of their persons revealed nothing. Duncan ordered their automobile and luggage searched. Nothing was found.

Duncan felt certain that Falkenstein had gone to Montreal to pick up the diamonds. There must have been a hitch which prevented delivery. He questioned the couple at length. And then reluctantly, late in the afternoon, he told them they could go.

It was during this questioning that Captain Deppe was sitting in his room at the Henry Hudson Hotel listening to the telephone ring in the apartment of the Falkensteins.

When Duncan returned to his office the next morning, he found a cable from Beers congratulating him on the "seizure" of the diamonds. A telephone call to Antwerp cleared up the mystery of the cable: rumors were afloat in the diamond market underworld that a shipment of diamonds to the United States had not been acknowledged—and the diamonds were presumed to have been seized by Customs agents. There were reports, too, that Falkenstein was "in trouble."

The following day, Beers advised New York that Falkenstein was supposed to have received one shipment of diamonds in Montreal on July 11 and another shipment in New York on July 12. The shipment to Montreal had been delayed—but the shipment had arrived in New York and presumably was "safe."

Duncan could not know that the New York shipment at that moment was lying in a shoe box on a shelf at the Sabena Airlines baggage room. On the day of Captain Deppe's arrival, the room had been turned upside down in a search for contraband, with no one noticing the box. Duncan later said ruefully, "The box was in plain view, just sitting there. I suppose that's why it was never opened. It was too obvious."

A few days later another Sabena pilot would casually enter the baggage room, pick up the box, and deliver it to Mr. X—completing the job which Deppe had started.

At this point Duncan decided to drop the searches at the airport and to take another tack. A good starting point seemed to be the Henry Hudson Hotel. Agents Smith and Moseley were ordered to obtain from the hotel all records of outgoing telephone calls made by Sabena personnel over a period of several months. Hotels normally keep such records for as long as four or five years—or until there is no further need for them in verifying accounts.

The checking of the telephone calls was slow, tedious work. At last one of the agents came up with the record of two interesting calls—both made to Trafalgar 3-8682, the telephone of Julius Falkenstein. The calls had been placed from the room occupied at the time by Capt. Robert Edmund Deppe. "I think we had better keep a check on this gentleman," Duncan said.

From that day forward, each time Captain Deppe arrived in New York he was under surveillance by Customs agents. They checked him in and out of the hotel, in and out of restaurants, and in and out of movies, cabs and subways. Wherever he went, he had an agent as a shadow.

It was a boring surveillance. Captain Deppe was a methodical and unimaginative man who stayed pretty much to himself. He made few outside calls, and the incoming calls usually were those from the airline's flight operations office relaying routine instructions.

At last Deppe strayed from his normal routine. After bringing his plane into Idlewild International Airport on September 27 he left the airport and headed for the Henry Hudson Hotel, followed as usual by the Customs agents. When he arrived at the hotel he did not go directly to his room as he customarily did. He slipped into a lobby telephone booth and made a brief call. Then he went to his room to change into civilian dress.

A short time later, Deppe left the hotel. He walked to the subway and took a train to Columbus Circle. He changed trains and rode into the Bronx, where he left the subway and strolled to an apartment building on Bennett Avenue. He was reaching for the pushbutton at the door of Apartment 1A when the agents closed in on him.

"We are U.S. Treasury agents," Smith said. "We want to talk to you." He asked Deppe why he had come to this particular apartment.

Deppe made no pretense of innocence or outrage. He said calmly, "I came here to deliver a package." He reached into his pockets and pulled out two envelopes. Inside each of them was a package containing dozens of diamonds whose value was later appraised at $233,230.

"Go ahead and ring the bell," Smith said. "Give this package to the person who opens the door and don't try any tricks."

The agents stepped to one side and Deppe rang the doorbell. The door was opened by Mrs. Julia Michelson, a dark-haired, plump woman whose husband operated two neighborhood grocery stores.

"Here is the package I was to deliver to you," Deppe said.

Mrs. Michelson accepted the package with a nod of thanks and started to close the door. At this moment the agents moved quickly to block the closing of the door.

"We're Treasury agents, ma'am," Smith said. "We would like to talk to you about this package."

While Deppe was being taken to headquarters for questioning, Mrs. Michelson explained that her brother-in-law in Paris had written to her asking that she accept a package from a friend who would deliver it to her apartment. She was to hold it until someone else called for it.

"What is this all about?" she asked. "What is in the package?"

"Diamonds," Smith said. "Smuggled diamonds. I'm afraid you are in trouble."

Mrs. Michelson was permitted to call her husband, and when he arrived, the agents explained the situation. The couple readily agreed to cooperate in helping trap the receiver who would call for the gems.

For two days, Agents Abe Eisenberg and Harold Smith remained at the Michelson apartment, waiting for the telephone call from the receiver. But no call came and no one knocked at the door asking for the package.

Late in the third day the telephone rang and Mrs. Michelson answered. The caller asked if she were holding a package for him and she replied that she was. "I'll be around for it tomorrow morning," he said.

At 10 A.M. the Michelson doorbell rang. Mrs. Michelson went to the door and admitted a short, plump, well-manicured man dressed in conservative clothes. As he entered the living room he must have sensed the nervousness of Mrs. Michelson because he suddenly turned and started toward the door. But Eisenberg and Smith stepped from a bedroom doorway and halted him. He was Samuel Liberman, a Fifth Avenue dealer in diamonds.

Julius Falkenstein was arrested at his place of business and taken to headquarters on Varick Street to be questioned. He confessed his smuggling role. He admitted he had gone to Canada in July to receive a shipment of diamonds. Something had gone wrong and the diamonds were never delivered to him. He had been hurrying back to New York to meet Captain Deppe when he was halted at the border. It was this delay which had prevented him from meeting Deppe and reporting to Antwerp the safe arrival of the diamonds. After the experience at the border, he had been afraid to try to get in touch with Deppe.

Deppe also confessed. He told agents he had carried diamonds into the United States on six occasions. He told them of the diamonds hidden in the shoe box which he had left in the Sabena bagage room. He was supposed to have delivered it to Falkenstein as he had the others—but when he found the Customs agents searching crew members he made no effort to retrieve the box. Later, he said, he had asked another Sabena pilot to pick up the box and make the delivery to Mr. X.

Deppe was deported for his role in the smuggling operation and turned over to Belgian authorities who were investigating the smuggling ring. Julius Falkenstein and Samuel Liberman were fined $2,500 each and sentenced to one year in prison. The sentences were suspended because of their cooperation with Customs agents.

Before the investigation ended, others involved in the United States and Belgium included a chauffeur with the French Consulate in New York, a French Diplomatic courier, an employee in the French Foreign Office, and an officer in the Belgian air force.

As for Mr. X, Customs agents know that he was successful in

smuggling three shipments of diamonds into the United States even though they have no proof other than the word of informers. Mr. X is on their list, and one day, they are certain, he will make a false move that will land him in prison.

Diamond smuggling is one of the most lucrative of the illicit operations because diamonds are so easy to dispose of and so easy to conceal. Diamonds are found hidden in hollowed-out heels of shoes, in the running boards of automobiles, in rubber contraceptives inserted into body cavities, in false bottoms of suitcases, in fountain pens, in hollowed-out books, in women's corsets and brassieres, and in toy animals. They come by plane and they come by ship. Communications between the contact man in the United States and the syndicate in Europe is so swift that often the syndicate knows within minutes what has happened to a shipment.

Such was the case when the Racket Squad began a surveillance of Reginald John Morfett of Rainham, England, who was the purser and chief steward of the liner *Assyria*. Morfett was fifty-eight years old and looked more like a Bond Street merchant than an inveterate smuggler. He was a slender man with thin, black, wavy hair brushed back from a high forehead. He wore his clothes well.

Agents were watching Morfett when he left the *Assyria* early in the evening of October 16, 1955, and stepped onto the North River pier at 95th Street. An informer in London had reported that Morfett was carrying eighteen pieces of platinum and gold jewelry, set with diamonds, rubies, sapphires and jade, in addition to 34.41 carats of cut and polished diamonds. The jewelry had a total value of $48,135. Delivery was to be made to two brothers in a hotel room in New York City.

Morfett rode buses from 95th Street to Seventh Avenue and 50th Street, where he left the bus and walked to the Taft Hotel. He went into a drug store to a public telephone booth and made a telephone call.

A short time later, Morfett was joined in the lobby of the Taft by an attractive, black-haired woman who greeted him warmly. He took her into a bar where they had a drink, and then they left the Taft and began strolling up Seventh Avenue.

Agent John Rainey, a ten-year veteran with Customs, was in

charge of the surveillance. It had become apparent to him that Morfett did not intend to make delivery of the diamonds on this night. He would not be walking around the streets carrying gems worth more than $48,000. He reasoned that the jewelry was still aboard the *Assyria.*

"Let's grab him," he said, and he signalled to other agents nearby.

Morfett's frightened companion was released when agents were satisfied that she was only his date for the night. Morfett was taken back to the *Assyria,* where the agents began a search of his quarters and the other places aboard the vessel to which he had easy access.

Throughout the night the agents searched without finding the gems. The next day a fresh squad took over the search, which was continued in relays until a short time before the *Assyria* sailed for Baltimore in the early morning hours of October 18.

The *Assyria* was hardly three hours out when the New York Customs office received a trans-Atlantic call from London. The Customs representative in London said his undercover source had advised him that the search of the *Assyria* had failed—and that the gems were still aboard the vessel.

The *Assyria* returned to New York on October 27 and docked at Pier 90 on the North River. Racket Squad Chief Tom Duncan led a squad of agents aboard to continue the search—they knew this was their last chance because the ship was due to sail at 7 o'clock that evening.

The search was continued until late in the afternoon. Duncan finally said wearily, "It's no use. We might as well knock it off." He asked one of the agents to call Tom Rainey and tell him to drop the surveillance of the brothers to whom Morfett was supposed to deliver the jewels.

"Tell Rainey we'll wait for him here," Duncan said. "Then we'll all go to dinner together."

It was 6:30 P.M. when Rainey walked into Morfett's quarters. Morfett sat in a chair looking bored with the whole proceedings. Duncan said, "The ship sails in thirty minutes. Let's go and get something to eat."

Rainey said, "Mind if I take just one more look around?"

"No," Duncan said. "Go ahead, if it will make you feel better."

Rainey walked into Morfett's office and stood studying the room. He and the others had gone over the place thoroughly. But somehow he had the feeling that this was the room that held the secret of the jewels—if there were a secret.

Almost without thinking, he began to measure with his hands a small safe that sat in a bulkhead cabinet. Then he realized there was a space of about two inches between the top of the safe and the shelf of the cabinet, concealed by a strip of molding.

He pried loose the molding and discovered a package. When he opened it, he saw the sparkle of diamonds.

Rainey walked to the door and as Duncan looked up he tossed the package to him. "Here are your diamonds," he said.

Within the next few minutes, the agents found other gems tucked into envelopes in the hiding place. And then they confronted Morfett. He shrugged. "That's it," he said. "That's what you have been looking for." He lit a cigarette as calmly as though the agents had called on him to have tea.

As John Reginald Morfett was led from the *Assyria,* Tom Duncan looked at his watch. It was 6:56 P.M. Four minutes later the ship began to ease away from the pier.

Morfett was sentenced to three years in prison for his role in the smuggling effort.

Within a period of three days in 1951—on January 21, 22 and 23—Customs agents and inspectors seized smuggled diamonds worth more than $1 million. A traveller from Antwerp named Elijah Whiteman was discovered carrying $300,000 worth of gems in the false bottom of a suitcase. Lesser seizures totalled $200,000. And then more than $500,000 worth of diamonds were discovered in a strange scene enacted at Idlewild airport.

Over the years, many Customs inspectors develop a sixth sense for spotting travellers who are trying to conceal valuables they do not want to declare. Perhaps it is the way a man or woman walks, or the nervous manner in which a cigarette is lit. It may be slight hesitancy in answering a particular question—or nothing more than a general impression which the inspector himself cannot explain.

Inspector Joseph Koehler did not know at first what it was that drew his attention to Etta Hoffman. Koehler was a dark-haired, studious-looking, middle-aged officer who had joined the Service as a young man. He had watched travellers by the tens of thousands pass his inspection post. There was no reason why he should have paid special attention to Etta Hoffman when she approached his station along with other passengers arriving from Brussels.

Etta was a tall, neatly dressed, round-faced young woman who waited placidly in line for her baggage to be examined. A perky hat sat on her dark hair and there were touches of fur on her dark cloth coat.

Her baggage declaration showed she was alone. Her baggage consisted of a handbag and two suitcases of inexpensive make. The woman answered all of Koehler's questions calmly and without nervousness. She gave no sign of apprehension when her bags were opened for examination. Yet Koehler simply could not shake a feeling that there was something wrong. Something about this woman triggered a small alarm in his subconscious.

Suddenly, Koehler realized what was bothering him. Etta Hoffman was too tall. Many tall women came through his inspection lane day after day. But Etta Hoffman's tallness was unnatural. Her tallness was emphasized by the extraordinarily thick-soled shoes she was wearing. It simply wasn't reasonable for a woman trying to look attractive to deliberately make herself unattractive.

Koehler quietly signalled a woman inspector, Mathilda Clark. Miss Hoffman was taken to a room set aside for questioning passengers. The soles of her shoes were hollow. When the inspectress pried them open, a handful of diamonds spilled out on the floor. Other gems were found in a false bottom of a suitcase. The diamonds weighed 3,377 carats, and were one of the largest diamond hauls ever made by Customs.

Etta Hoffman broke down in tears and poured out her story. She had dreamed for years (so she said) of coming to the United States and obtaining citizenship. She had come to Belgium as a refugee from Czechoslovakia and had succeeded at last in getting her name on the immigration quota.

After months of waiting and suspense, Etta received the necessary papers from the American Consulate. Then a strange man called at her apartment and offered to pay her fare to the United States and give her $100 in cash if she would smuggle the diamonds past Customs. He provided her with the trick shoes, the suitcase with the false bottom, and a plane ticket. Before she boarded the plane, he had given her a sealed envelope which he said contained the $100 which he had promised her.

Etta Hoffman handed the envelope, still sealed, to a Customs inspector. He tore it open and found that it contained only $80. She had been shortchanged by $20, and, to pile injury on insult, she was sentenced to eighteen months in prison.

Abraham Winnik was another of the more successful diamond and gold smugglers. This thin-faced Belgian was an expert procurer of carriers for an Antwerp syndicate. He arranged for diamonds to be brought into the United States, and after they were sold he engineered the smuggling of gold to Europe. The gold was carried in the false bottoms of suitcases fashioned by an expert leather worker in Brooklyn—who received $30 for each suitcase he altered.

One of those enlisted into Winnik's ring of carriers was Mrs. Adele Meppen, a stocky Brooklyn housewife who gave Customs agents this story:

"I first met Abraham Winnik sometime in 1949 when he was visiting in Brooklyn. My husband and I became friendly with him, and whenever he visited this country he would come to see us at our home.

"Late in 1949 Marion Strokowski, a friend of Winnik's, visited us. He asked me how I would like to make a trip to Europe. I told him I didn't have the money. 'Don't worry about expenses,' he said. 'If you will do me a favor, I'll pay your expenses. All you have to do is take two suitcases to a friend of mine.'

"I agreed and Mr. Strokowski bought my ticket. He brought two suitcases to my home which I packed with clothes. I left New York from Idlewild airport by KLM Airlines, sometime in May, 1950. When the plane reached Amsterdam, Mr. Winnik met me at the airport and drove me in his automobile to his home in Brussels.

"I stayed there for about three weeks. I met Mr. Winnik's wife, Anna, and Mr. Strokowski's wife, Janka. I brought back two suitcases they gave me, and a couple of days after I got home Mr. Strokowski called for them and took them away. He gave me my plane fare both ways and expenses. . . ."

Five months after her return from this trip, Mrs. Meppen received a call from Winnik asking her to meet him in Montreal. He wanted her to "bring something into the country" for him. He said he would pay her expenses—and a little extra.

Mrs. Meppen flew to Montreal and went to the Laurentian Hotel, where she found Winnik and Janka Strokowski. They told her they wanted her to carry diamonds into the United States—and there would be no risk whatever.

Mrs. Meppen protested she didn't want to get involved and, besides, she was scared. They convinced her there was no danger. Janka Strokowski helped her insert two rubber-covered packages into her anus.

This smuggling effort perhaps would have gone as smoothly as the others engineered by Winnik except that somewhere along the line an informer had tipped Canadian Customs officers that Winnik had entered Canada carrying a small fortune in diamonds.

Winnik had been searched when he arrived at the Gander airport in Newfoundland and Customs officers there had found nothing. But the Canadians continued to keep Winnik under surveillance and they notified the U.S. Customs of the information they had received. The American agents joined in the surveillance in Montreal.

U.S. Agents were watching when Winnik and Mrs. Strokowski placed Mrs. Meppen aboard a train enroute to New York—and two agents were on the train when it pulled from the station. At Rouses Point, on the Canadian border, Mrs. Meppen was taken from the train and searched—but the search revealed nothing.

That night Mrs. Meppen obtained a room at the Holland Hotel. The following morning when she came from her room she saw several Customs agents lounging in the lobby. They, too, were waiting for the next train to New York—no longer interested in Mrs. Meppen because the previous day's search had been futile.

But Mrs. Meppen was frightened. She hurried to the public toilet near her room. . . .

A few minutes after Mrs. Meppen boarded the train for New York the manager of the Holland Hotel called in a plumber to unstop a toilet in the ladies' room. He found in the trap a rubber-covered packet stuffed with diamonds. Three days later the same toilet became stopped again. Again the plumber found a package of diamonds blocking the drain, a coincidence so unusual that the plumber became a local celebrity.

The hotel manager turned the diamonds over to Customs agents, and Mrs. Meppen was soon taken into custody for questioning. She confessed her role in the abortive smuggling effort, and a few days later Winnik was arrested as he was trying to board a plane for Amsterdam. He broke down and confessed, too.

Mrs. Meppen pleaded guilty and as a cooperative witness against Winnik was placed on probation for five years. Winnik was sent to prison for two years. Marion and Janka Strokowski were indicted, but since both were outside the jurisdiction of the United States courts, the indictments were dismissed.

The diamonds which Mrs. Meppen tried to flush down the toilet were worth $121,000.

15

A FOOL'S DREAM

From long experience U.S. Customs agents and inspectors know the methods of professional smugglers. But the non-professional smuggler is a problem, too. One of the more bizarre cases of jewelry smuggling in Customs history, involving the fabulous crown jewels of Hesse, was engineered by non-professionals. They were two lovers and their accomplice, who looked at the sparkling gems and were overwhelmed by avarice.

This plot began to unfold one cold November day in 1945 in the gray old Kronberg Castle at Wiesbaden, Germany, near Frankfurt. The castle was the home of Prince Wolfgang and the Countess Margarethe of Hesse, a daughter of Emperor Frederic of Germany and granddaughter of Queen Victoria of Britain. Now it was

requisitioned as a recreation and rest center for the men and
women of the U.S. Armed Forces.

The hostess in this royal setting was trim, attractive WAC Captain Kathleen Nash of Hudson, Wisconsin, a divorcee who told
friends that she had gone into the WACs to "get away from it all."

One evening there was a knock at Captain Nash's door and
Mess Sgt. Roy Carlton stepped into her room, his eyes wide with
excitement.

"Captain," the sergeant said, "there's something I think you
ought to know about. You know the old German janitor? Well,
he told me a few minutes ago that when the war began, the old
lady of the castle came to his house late one night and told him
to come with her and to tell no one where he had gone. She took
him into the basement of the castle, that little room that is used
for coal storage, and told him to dig a hole in the floor. He broke
through the concrete and dug a big hole in the floor and then she
sent him away. But when he came back to the room several days
later he found the hole had been covered with new concrete. He
figures that something was buried there by the old lady."

Captain Nash told the sergeant to bring the janitor and they
would go to the basement room and investigate. They made their
way down the winding stairs into the subterranean rooms of the
castle to the coal room. The old janitor pointed out the spot
where he had dug the hole. Captain Nash ordered him to dig into
the floor and see if anything had been hidden there.

The German broke the concrete with a sledge and then began
digging. He uncovered a wooden box. The box was lifted out of
the hole and when the top was ripped off they saw a lead box
inside. The lead box contained several packages, carefully wrapped
in heavy paper, weighing about 10 pounds each.

"You had better take them to my quarters," Captain Nash told
the sergeant.

When Captain Nash opened the packages in the privacy of her
quarters her eyes must have glittered with excitement. She was
gazing on one of the fabulous treasures of Europe—jewelry worth
at least $1,500,000, if in fact a money value could be placed on
the historic items at all.

Part of the jewelry belonged to the House of the Kurfursts and
to the Kurhessen Foundation. Most of it belonged to the Count-

ess Margarethe and to Prince Wolfgang. Some of it was the personal property of Princess Christoph and Prince Richard of Hesse.
The owners, who lived in less pretentious quarters at this time,
rarely visited the old castle, and none was aware that the treasure
had been discovered.

Captain Nash was enchanted. She took from the boxes diadems
and necklaces of diamonds, pearls and amethysts; rings of diamonds and other precious stones; a diamond-studded onyx badge,
made in the eighteenth century: the badge of the Order of the
Garter, which had been presented by King George II to his son-
in-law; necklaces of gold and platinum; bracelets of diamonds and
emeralds and pearls and topaz; buckles studded with diamonds;
large and small brooches studded with diamonds and other stones;
pendants with large and small diamonds; earrings made of diamonds and emeralds and pearls; tiaras delicately fashioned of gold
and studded with diamonds and other gems; a large necklace of
gray pearls and diamonds; an English decoration of the Victoria
and Albert Order, including a cameo with portrait of Queen
Victoria and her Prince Consort, surrounded by small diamonds;
diamond stick pins; diamond earrings; diamond-studded watches;
diamond studded cases; and golden chains studded with large
stones.

This, then, was the treasure which the girl from Wisconsin
picked up, piece by piece. At some period as she looked at the
glittering jewels, the idea was born that she would not give them
up.

One of the most frequent visitors to Kronberg Castle was slender, handsome Air Force Colonel Jack Durant, who was Kathleen
Nash's boy friend and constant companion. Colonel Durant had
been an attorney in the U.S. government's Interior Department
before he went into the Air Force at the outbreak of the war. He
was attached to the Adjutant General's office and therefore was
not unaware of the rules governing the conduct of the armed
forces.

Captain Nash invited Colonel Durant and her friend, Major
David Watson, to her quarters. She showed them the treasure
which had been dug from the coal room in the basement of the
castle. And then it was they began to talk of stealing the Hesse
jewels.

These three sat behind the closed and locked door of Captain

Nash's quarters and pried the jewels from their settings. They decided it would be much easier to smuggle the loose jewels into the United States rather than leave them in their settings.

Why they thought they could escape undetected with one of the great treasures of Europe remains a mystery. It was a monstrous game of "losers weepers, finders keepers." In their greed they began to look upon the Hesse jewels as legitimate loot. Because they were on the winning team in the war, they reasoned they were entitled to share in the spoils. If their share happened to be a fortune in gems, then that was merely their good luck.

Colonel Durant casually made inquiries among his fellow officers about the customs procedures in the United States and whether or not the inspectors of military personnel were very thorough in going through luggage.

One officer who had returned from a recent trip home said, "There's no sweat. The inspectors clear you as fast as they can. They didn't even look into my baggage. I guess they figure a guy who has been fighting a war should not be delayed in getting home."

Durant persuaded a former secretary to carry home for him several pieces of the jewelry. She innocently believed they were nothing more valuable than costume jewelry which he had picked up in Europe.

Captain Nash turned over her share of the loot to Major Watson, who packed it in an ordinary wooden box and then mailed it to her in care of her sister, Mrs. Eileen Lonergan, in Hudson, Wisconsin. The box arrived in New York along with several thousands of other shipments from Europe. A Customs examiner accepted the statement on the box that it contained only personal belongings and nothing of dutiable value. And so the box went on its way to the house in Wisconsin.

Colonel Durant arrived at Westover Field by plane on March 12, 1946, aboard ATC Flight 9076, which had originated in Paris. He wrote on his customs declaration that he carried one watch worth $60, perfume worth $83, a $2.50 purse, and two cigarette lighters worth $17. He stated he had no other articles on which he should pay duty.

No one questioned the colonel's declaration and within a short time he was on his way to Washington, D. C., to visit his brother, James E. Durant, who lived in Falls Church, Virginia.

Colonel Durant showed his brother a good many of the unset stones and articles which he had brought back from overseas, and his brother helped him remove several diamonds from two tubes of shaving cream. Durant explained that while travelling to Italy a German had sold him more than one hundred diamonds for 3,000 German marks.

Durant gave one of the diamonds to a Washington, D. C., automobile dealer—a diamond appraised at $500—as part payment for a Hudson automobile. Another automobile dealer in Falls Church, Virginia, purchased two of the diamonds for $400, and Durant—using the assumed name of J. W. Gable—disposed of three of the diamonds to a jewelry firm in Washington for $357. Then he drove to Chicago to meet Kathleen Nash.

A few days after arriving in Chicago, Colonel Durant put in a call for his friend, Dr. Reuben Mark, at the Embassy Hotel. Dr. Mark was a dentist who had struck up a friendship with Durant a few years earlier in Washington, D. C. As Dr. Mark related the story of their meeting later:

"It was around April of this year. One evening he called and he said, 'Ruby, this is Jack.' I said, 'When did you get in?' He said, 'Just today.' I asked him how long he was going to be in town and he said he did not know. He was on thirty days leave and he had already spent a few days.

"Then he asked when we would get together. That was on Saturday night. He said something about a girl friend of his coming in from the coast. He said it was a girl that had been overseas with him and she was a divorcee. He said she was pretty and had been married to a wealthy man in Arizona and had just joined the WACs to get away.

"We arranged to meet in a day or so. A couple of days later we met after office hours at Isbell's restaurant on Diversey. That was the night I first met his girl. Katy, as I began to call her, was a nice girl. Nothing unusual.

"It was there that Jack asked me, 'Ruby, do you know any jewelers?' I said, 'Sure, I know some jewelers.' Just about that time he pulled out a tissue paper. He opened it up and I saw three stones. I asked, 'Where did you get them?' He said he picked them up overseas in Frankfurt.

"At that time nothing occurred to me about anything being

wrong. I know lots of boys who brought things from overseas and I felt, well, so what, he was overseas. I said, 'Yes, I know some jewelers.' And he said he would like to call them. I told him I would call the following day.

"I called a Mr. Horwitz, whom I had known for some time, and I asked if he was interested in buying some diamonds. He said yes. . . ."

Dr. Mark accompanied Durant to the jeweler's place of business and introduced him. Durant took a small cloth sack from his pocket and when he upended it, a shower of diamonds cascaded onto the desk. There were 102 stones in the lot.

Horwitz looked at the stones under a magnifying glass, examining each of them carefully. Finally he said, "These are fine stones, Colonel. We don't see diamonds like these very often. They're beautifully cut."

Durant explained he had been able to get them at a bargain price from a German badly in need of cash. "How much do you figure they are worth?" he asked.

"I'll pay you $125 a carat," Horwitz said. "It's a fair price."

"That's okay," Durant said. "But there's just one thing. The deal can't be made in my name. I'm in the Army and I'm not supposed to transact any outside business. It will have to be a cash transaction."

Horwitz shook his head. "I'm sorry," he said. "We only make purchases by check. In buying outside the regular channels I would have to call the police to make certain there is no violation of regulations."

"That's all right," Durant said quickly. "Go ahead and call."

Horwitz made a telephone call and then said, "The police say there's nothing wrong with making a purchase from an Army man who has returned from overseas—provided the customs duty has been paid. Has the duty been paid on these stones?"

"I mailed them into the country," Durant said. "All the boys were mailing stuff back and I did too." Then Durant added, "But, look, I'm not here for business particularly. I'm going to take a trip to Mexico. If it's only a question of duty, I'll stop off someplace and take care of the duty part of it and I'll see you when I get back."

Horwitz then said to Mark, "Why don't we make out the check

in your name, Doctor? You can cash it and give the money to the colonel."

Mark hesitated. "I suppose the check could be made out to me on a tentative basis," he said. "But I'll have to call my auditors and see that I don't get fouled up with them."

Horwitz had his secretary draw a check for the purchase of the diamonds. When Durant and the doctor had left his office, he called his lawyer. He explained the situation and asked his advice.

"There's nothing wrong about buying diamonds from a member of the armed forces," the lawyer said, "but you'd better be certain the diamonds were declared and duty paid on them when they were brought into the country. If they were not declared, it is not a proper transaction and I'd advise you to stop payment on the check."

Horwitz immediately called his bank and stopped payment on the check. The following morning he called Dr. Mark and advised him of what he had done on the advice of his attorney. "I can't go through with the transaction," he said, "unless the colonel will produce a customs receipt showing the diamonds were declared and the duty was satisfied."

Mark and Durant returned to Horwitz's place of business to retrieve the diamonds and to hand back the check.

Horwitz suggested, "Why don't you go to see Mr. Meiners at the customs house? He's assistant collector of customs and he could clear this thing up for you. I'd even be willing to pay half of the duty."

Durant mumbled something about having to hurry to the airport to make a flight. He said he would be back in Chicago in about ten days and he certainly would go and see Mr. Meiners at the first opportunity.

After the collapse of this deal, Durant and Captain Nash left Chicago by automobile for a vacation in the Southwest and Mexico. But even as they were leaving Chicago, Federal agents were on their trail.

The theft of the gems had been discovered by the Countess Margarethe in Germany. She had gone to the basement to check on the safety of the jewels. She had found the hole in the basement floor. The conspirators had not even refilled the hole or re-covered it with concrete. The theft was reported to Army

authorities and the matter was turned over to the Army's criminal
investigation division.

The Army's agents began questioning everyone who had been
employed in any capacity at Kronberg Castle. Finally they came to
the old janitor who told them of digging up the boxes in the basement coal room. He didn't know what was in the boxes. He only
knew they had been taken to Captain Nash's quarters. He had
never heard any mention of them again.

Customs agents were called in to help with the case. They
traced Captain Nash's movements from the time of her arrival in
New York until she left Chicago accompanied by Colonel Durant.
They learned of Durant's visit with Dr. Mark to the jeweler,
Horwitz, and the collapse of the diamond deal—because the customs duties had not been paid on the gems. But no one knew the
destination of the couple when they left Chicago.

Through calls to friends and relatives, Dr. Mark located Durant
in Texas—and advised him he was wanted by the Customs people for questioning. On April 19, 1946, Durant appeared at the
office of the Supervising Customs Agent in Chicago with the air
of an innocent man who was shocked that anyone should question
his integrity.

"You did bring diamonds into the country without declaring
them and without paying duty on them, didn't you, Colonel?" an
agent asked.

"Yes," Durant said, "but I was doing only what everybody
else in the armed services was doing. I didn't know a declaration
was required."

"Where did you get the diamonds?"

"I bought them from a German civilian. I gave him my Elgin
wrist watch and 3,000 German marks."

The agent said, "How did you get them into the country?"

"I put them in a cigar box and mailed the box to myself in care
of my brother in Falls Church," Durant replied.

"Where are the diamonds now?"

Durant reached into his pocket and pulled out the sack of diamonds. "There they are," he said, tossing the sack onto the desk.
"That's all of them."

"We're going to have to hold these diamonds until our investigation is completed, Colonel," an agent said. "But of course you

have the right under law to petition for a return of the diamonds and for remission or mitigation of any penalties."

"I certainly do want to petition for their return," Durant said angrily.

He was handed a blank petition. And he wrote: "I am the sole owner of said diamonds. . . . At the time I mailed these diamonds into the United States I assumed that it was not necessary for me to declare them to any governmental agency. . . . At no time did I intend to import into the United States and thereafter make any disposition of said diamonds in violation of any statute of the United States. . . . Therefore, I petition for (their return). . . ."

Immediately after this meeting with Customs agents, Durant and Captain Nash drove from Chicago to Washington, D. C. Durant hurried to the home of his brother in Falls Church. After nightfall, the brothers drove to a spot on a country road halfway between Lee Highway and Route 50.

They parked the car and walked into a woods to a large oak tree. At the base of the tree, Durant buried an ink bottle which contained fifty small diamonds and two large emerald-cut diamonds—together with a roll of gold wire which weighed 8 ounces.

"For God's sake, don't forget where we buried this stuff," Durant said to his brother. And then the two returned to the car and headed back to Falls Church. A few days later, Colonel Durant began his terminal leave prior to being mustered out of the armed services.

Less than a month later, on May 18, Colonel Durant drove into Washington accompanied by Kathleen Nash. They went to a hotel and that night Durant again visited his brother James in Falls Church. Again the brothers drove to the woods on Lee Highway, where they walked to the big oak tree. Durant took a large jar from a leather handbag and buried it at the base of the tree. The jar contained loose amethysts and white envelopes which Durant told his brother contained loose diamonds.

As they drove from the woods, Durant said, "Don't forget where we buried the jars. There's enough in them to set us up for life. If anything happens, I want you to have what's there." The next day, Durant and Captain Nash left Washington and headed for Chicago.

Now the net was tightening and Durant sensed it. He had heard the disturbing news in Washington that his terminal leave might be cancelled—and this could mean only one thing: the Army didn't want to lose its hold on him. Then he and Kathleen learned that she, too, might have difficulty in getting out of the Army.

Two weeks after burying the large jar in the woods, Durant telephoned his brother from Chicago.

"Listen, Jim," he said. "Go to the big tree and get the large glass jar. Bring it to me in Chicago. It's urgent."

James Durant went to the woods and searched for the tree. But this night they all looked alike. He called his brother. "I can't find it," he said. "I can't even find the tree."

Jack Durant cursed softly. "I've got to have that jar," he said. "I'll have to get it myself."

Durant caught a late plane from Chicago, arriving at the Washington International Airport at 4 A.M. He took a taxi to his brother's home, awakened him, and they drove to the woods, where the colonel walked unerringly to the tree and unearthed the jar. Then he returned to the airport and bought a ticket for the 8 A.M. flight to Chicago. But before he left, he gave his brother two small packages containing $28,000 in cash—with instructions to place the money in a sealed jar and bury it at a place he wouldn't forget. The brother buried the money that same afternoon.

During this frantic activity, the War Department cancelled the unexpired part of the colonel's terminal leave and ordered him back on active duty. Similar orders went forth for Kathleen Nash.

It was after they received these orders that Colonel Durant and Captain Nash were married. Some cynics suggested later that the colonel married her because once the marriage vows were said, she could not be made to testify aginst him. But there was nothing in the record to indicate that the two were not in love and had not planned marriage all along.

Early in June, Army and Customs agents began questioning the couple in Chicago. For several days Durant maintained a stubborn silence, but finally he broke. He told of the gems and the money hidden near Falls Church—and he took full responsibility, clearing his brother of any complicity.

Agents found the hiding place in the woods. They dug up the

money and the gems—but these were only a part of the treasure taken from Kronberg Castle. Durant was pressed to tell what had happened to the other gems.

"The situation is complicated," he parried. "I might be able to get the stuff back if you will let me make some telephone calls—in private."

Durant was permitted to make the calls. After each call he made excuses and talked vaguely of "complications." He refused to disclose with whom he had talked.

On Friday, June 7, the agents permitted Durant to see his bride alone. What they discussed no one except themselves ever knew. When Durant came from this meeting he told the agents, "I'm sorry. I haven't been trying to get the jewels. I've been stalling for time. But now I'll try to get them for you."

"Where are the jewels," he was asked.

"They are in the hands of a fence. I think I can get them—but it will take some more telephoning. This time I'm not fooling." He continued to insist that the calls had to be unmonitored.

Durant was permitted to make telephone calls from a public pay station—and to wait for a return call. The return call came within a few minutes, and when he had hung up the receiver, Durant said, "Everything looks all right. I think we can get the stuff this evening."

That evening the colonel's mysterious contact called for him at the pay station. This time Durant said, "We can get the jewels any time we wish. They're at the Illinois Railroad Station."

Two agents accompanied Durant to the station. He walked to an electric wall fixture near the luggage lockers, reached up, and removed a key from the fixture. He opened a nearby locker and removed a package which he handed over to the agents. The package contained a large number of emeralds, sapphires, pearls, rubies and other stones.

Durant counted the gems carefully and then exclaimed, "Some of the stuff is missing. Let me make another telephone call." Again he called his contact and this time he reported, "We can't get the stuff until Monday."

On the following Monday, June 10, Durant again called his unknown contact. This time he told agents the remainder of the jewels were checked at the North Western Railroad and the claim check was hidden in a telephone booth across from the parcel room.

When Durant and the agents reached the station, Durant searched the telephone booths without finding a claim check. "It doesn't matter," Durant said. "I got the number of the check in case anything should go wrong. It's number 110."

But there was no parcel numbered 110 at the North Western Station. Durant hurried to a phone booth and placed another call to his contact man. When he completed the call, he said, "I misunderstood the instructions. We should have gone to the LaSalle Street Station."

At the LaSalle Street Station, Durant went to the sixth telephone booth and took from behind the instrument panel a slip of paper. He read it and handed it over to the agents. On the paper was a handwritten note which said: "Too bad. My hat knocked your ticket off. Guess I have a right to keep the baggage."

An inquiry at the check room disclosed that a parcel had been left there the day before under the number 110—but it had been removed that morning by a man who had presented the proper claim check.

"I don't remember what the guy looked like," the attendant said. "I didn't pay any attention. All I know is the guy had the right check and I gave him the package."

At this point, Durant refused any further cooperation. He insisted that his mysterious contact had nothing to do with the missing jewels—and he refused to disclose the name of the contact or to make any further effort to locate the jewels.

The investigators had better luck with Kathleen Nash Durant. She admitted to officers the agreement in Germany between herself, Colonel Durant and Major Watson. She told of removing the numerous stones from their settings and sending a large number of them to her sister's home in Wisconsin, concealed in boxes. Her sister was instructed not to release the boxes to anyone unless she heard or read the code word "Cemetery." She turned over to Army officers the following note:

To Eileen, Jack, or David,   June 3, 1946
    I have confessed to having the box of jewels, Bibles and fan that I hid in the attic. Will you please give same to officer presenting you this note, Major John D. Salb, our code "cemetery"—goes—sorry to

cause you so much grief and I don't deserve you to worry over me anymore.

Love,

Vonie (Kathleen B. Durant)

When agents flew to Hudson, Wisconsin, and presented the note to Mrs. Lonergan, she readily turned over the boxes hidden in the attic.

Kathleen Nash Durant and her husband were sentenced by a military court martial to fifteen years in prison. Major Watson was sentenced to three years for his smaller role in the conspiracy.

Most all the jewels of the Hesse treasury found in old Kronberg Castle were returned to their rightful owners. But some of the priceless pieces still are missing. The settings—many of them fashioned by Europe's greatest artisans—were lost forever. They had been cut to pieces and melted into gold wire.

16

THE CHISELERS

Chiselers are constantly seeking ways to avoid paying customs duties. And the female of the species is just as clever and persistent as the male—or, as is more often the case, just as dumb. In the early 1930s, the chiselers found it extremely profitable to smuggle watch movements into the United States from Switzerland. Smuggling reached such proportions that it helped to virtually destroy the American watch industry. The situation became so grave that the Federal government appealed to the Swiss government to cooperate in a program to control the illegal traffic in watch parts. An agreement finally was reached on a treaty whereby the Swiss devised a system of numbering the watch parts and assigning code numbers to importers as a means of discouraging illegal imports.

The treaty helped to wipe out much of the commercial smuggling of watch parts. Despite these efforts the traffic continued through the years to be a profitable venture for smuggling gangs who often persuaded housewives, businessmen, and tourists to act as carriers.

Mrs. Elizabeth Schmidbauer, the plump, middle-aged wife of a restaurant owner in Munich, Germany, was one of those who became a dupe for a watch smuggling gang in 1954. And her trip to the United States to visit a relative—a trip for which she had planned so eagerly and for so long—became a nightmare for her and her family.

The nightmare began in Munich when Mrs. Schmidbauer told friends at her husband's restaurant that she was going to America with an aunt, Mrs. Anna Obermaier, who was then visiting in Germany. She talked of the clothes she would need and her intention of buying two new suitcases for the trip. Among those in the restaurant who listened with interest to Mrs. Schmidbauer's excited chatter was a regular customer named Moritz, with whom the Schmidbauers had been on friendly terms for many years.

Two days before her departure from Munich, Mrs. Schmidbauer answered a knock at her door and found that the caller was Moritz, who was carrying two new suitcases. "I heard you say you needed luggage for your trip," he said, "and here it is."

Mrs. Schmidbauer invited Moritz into the living room. Over coffee and cakes he told her that he was willing to pay her fare to the United States if she would do him a favor: deliver the suitcases to a friend in New York along with a small parcel.

"What is in the parcel?" Mrs. Schmidbauer asked.

"Watch movements," Mortiz said. "If you will take them through customs it will save quite a bit of money. I am ready to pay your fare to the United States if you will do this favor for me."

"But what about the police and the American Customs?" Mrs. Schmidbauer exclaimed. "I may get into trouble if I do this thing."

"Nonsense," Mortiz said. "Nothing can happen to you. All you have to do is sew the watch parts into your corset and no one will be the wiser."

The lure of free passage to the United States was too great a temptation. Mrs. Schmidbauer agreed to the scheme. That night she obtained strips of cloth and sewed most of the watch movements into her corset. The others she placed in her large handbag.

Mrs. Schmidbauer felt that Moritz was telling the truth when he said that she would have no difficulty. If he thought there would be any trouble, then he would not take such a risk himself.

The plan was very simple. When she arrived in New York and was safely through customs, she was to send a cable to her husband saying, "Gut angekommen," indicating that all was well. Mortiz would keep in touch with her husband. After the receipt of the message, he would cable his friend in New York and instruct him to pick up the suitcases and the watch movements. Once the delivery was made, then she would receive payment for her fare to New York.

Mrs. Schmidbauer left Munich with her aunt, Mrs. Obermaier, and travelled to Southhampton, England, where she boarded the SS *Queen Elizabeth* for the Atlantic crossing. The big liner reached New York harbor on December 14, 1954, and docked at Pier 90 on the North River at 8:15 A.M.

On the pier everything seemed to go as smoothly as Moritz said it would. The Customs people were courteous. Mrs. Schmidbauer's luggage was examined by Inspector Abe Pokress. He did not ask to see the contents of her handbag after she told him it contained only personal belongings. And he inquired amiably about her voyage.

"It was a wonderful trip," Mrs. Schmidbauer said, watching Pokress' hands move swiftly through her belongings.

She was immensely relieved when Pokress told her she could close her luggage. She quickly strapped the bags shut. The luggage was placed on a handcart by a porter and Mrs. Schmidbauer thanked Inspector Pokress for his courtesy.

But when the handcart was rolled beside an electronic detection device, Pokress saw a warning light begin to blink. The light indicated the luggage contained a quantity of metal—and Mrs. Schmidbauer's declaration did not list any metal objects, nor had the casual examination revealed any.

Pokress ordered the luggage returned to his station. He asked Mrs. Schmidbauer to open the bags once more.

"What is wrong?" Mrs. Schmidbauer demanded. "You have inspected the suitcases. Why am I being detained like this?"

"You aren't being detained," Pokress said. "But I'm afraid we must take another look at your luggage."

Pokress began to make a thorough examination of the contents of the smaller of the two suitcases. He was unable to find anything which could have caused the electronic device to trigger the alarm signal.

Mrs. Schmidbauer stood watching the search with tears welling in her eyes. She made no further protest as Pokress removed the clothing from the bag and began to measure the inside depth of the suitcase against its outside depth. The measurement disclosed a discrepancy of approximately three-quarters of an inch.

Pokress was reasonably certain the suitcase had a false bottom. He placed the suitcase on a small platform between two metal cabinets standing nearby. The cabinets housed an X-ray device called an inspectroscope, which Customs inspectors and agents frequently used in peering into luggage and boxes suspected of containing contraband made of metal.

Pokress opened the door of one of the cabinets and squeezed into a seat before a small screen similar to a fluoroscope. He turned a few dials and switched on the X ray. And then on the screen appeared in clear outline the metal fastenings, screws and other hardware used in the construction of the suitcase. In addition the screen showed several rectangular metal objects in the bottom of the suitcase.

Pokress switched off the inspectroscope and emerged from the cabinet. He had Mrs. Schmidbauer taken to an inspection room. And there inspectors discovered that both her suitcases had false bottoms which concealed several thin tin containers. The containers were packed with 759 Swiss watch movements.

A woman inspector led the weeping Mrs. Schmidbauer into a room where she was searched. It was found that she had 167 watch movements sewn into her corset and 26 movements in her handbag. The 952 watch movements were estimated to have a wholesale value of more than $10,000.

Mrs. Schmidbauer tearfully told Customs agents of being approached by Moritz in Munich. She told them of his offer to pay her fare to the United States if she would bring the watch parts through Customs hidden on her person. She said that he told her he had put something in the suitcases but he did not tell her what it was and she did not know that there were watch movements hidden in false bottoms of the luggage. She also told of the arrangement whereby she was to send a message to her husband if all went well.

It was obvious to agents that Mrs. Schmidbauer was only a dupe in the smuggling plot. Mrs. Schmidbauer was asked to co-operate in trapping Moritz's accomplice. She quickly agreed.

Mrs. Schmidbauer dispatched a cable to her husband saying, "Gut angekommen." Then two agents, Harold F. Smith and Abraham Eisenberg, accompanied Mrs. Schmidbauer and Mrs. Obermaier to Mrs. Obermaier's apartment to await the call from Moritz's accomplice.

They did not have to wait long. Mrs. Obermaier received a call from a man who identified himself as Hans Berger. Berger said, "I understand Mrs. Schmidbauer is visiting you and that she has something for me."

Mrs. Obermaier said that Mrs. Schmidbauer was ill and could not talk to the caller herself. She added that she did have something for him if he would call at the apartment the next morning at ten o'clock.

The agents were hidden in the apartment the following morning when a knock came on the Obermaiers' door. Mrs. Obermaier opened the door and a man stepped in.

"You are Hans Berger? You called yesterday?" she asked.

The caller said, "Yes. May I see Mrs. Schmidbauer?"

Mrs. Obermaier invited him into the living room. She asked him what he came for and who had sent him.

Berger said he was sent by "Moritz." He handed her a slip of paper which said, "Dear Mrs. Schmidbauer—I hope you arrive safely in New York. I beg you to be kind enough when you receive this piece of paper to turn over the things. Best regards, Your Moritz."

At this point the agents stepped from hiding. Questioning of Berger convinced the agents that he had called to pick up two suitcases and a package from Mrs. Schmidbauer without any knowledge that he was getting involved in a smuggling plot. He thought he was merely doing a favor for his friend, Moritz, who would show up later to claim them.

But Moritz never showed up in New York. Berger was not prosecuted, and Mrs. Schmidbauer was given a six-months suspended sentence.

One of the largest smuggling rings dealing in Swiss watch movements was broken up by customs agents in 1956 on a tip received from customs officials in Germany. This ring involved a foreign shipping firm working with an American importer, an American shipping official, and a dishonest customs broker in New York.

This case began to develop when four packing cases of roughly the same dimensions arrived in the foreign trade zone in Germany from Switzerland. Two of the cases, documented as containing camera tripods, were consigned to a firm in the United States. The other two cases were documented as containing 4,488 Swiss watch movements.

A German customs officer became suspicious when he saw two men transferring the watch movements from their original cases into the cases marked as camera tripods. The Customs officer made no move at that time to interfere with the transfer of the merchandise, but he notified his superiors and an investigation was begun. The Germans at that time believed that it was an effort to avoid payment of German customs. When they realized that the transfer was being made as part of a scheme to violate American customs laws, the U.S. Customs agent stationed in Bremen was informed of the facts in the case. These facts were forwarded to agents in New York, who were alerted to be on the lookout for the arrival of the boxes labelled as carrying "camera tripods." Several days later a German customs official advised the Customs agent in Bremen that the two suspect boxes, marked IH74 and IH75, were being shipped aboard the SS *Black Falcon* manifested as camera tripods valued at $200.

The SS *Black Falcon* arrived at the port of New York on January 23, 1956, and docked at the Smith Street Pier in Brooklyn. Customs agents kept the two boxes under surveillance. They were watching as the boxes were moved from the pier by a trucker to a warehouse. Agents hidden in the warehouse saw the trucker and the broker switch the watches from the cases and replace them with camera tripods.

Had this scheme succeeded, the chiselers would have paid duty on camera tripods valued at $200 rather than on watch movements valued at more than $50,000.

Stephen Schrieber of New York City was one of the cleverest of the chiselers. He was a tall, thin, balding man in his middle years who was engaged in the import-export business. Customs had no reason to suspect Schrieber of wrongdoing until agents got a tip that he was smuggling gold out of the United States, selling it on Europe's black market, and then smuggling diamonds into this country.

On April 29, 1952, Customs agents learned that Schrieber was preparing to make another trip outside the country and that he had booked passage for Cherbourg, France, aboard the SS *Queen Mary*. Schrieber also had arranged to export a car on the *Queen Mary* as "accompanying baggage."

After Schrieber delivered his car to the pier to be taken aboard the liner, agents made arrangements to examine the vehicle, a 1949 Pontiac. The examination began at approximately 4 P.M. They searched the car for ninety minutes without finding any contraband.

At last one of the agents said, "Why don't we weigh the car and check its weight against the Blue Book weight that is listed by the manufacturer."

With the cooperation of Customs inspectors and Cunard Line officials, the car was removed from Pier 90 to the scale house at Pier 84. The automobile Blue Book listed the Pontiac as weighing 3375 pounds. But when it was put on the scales, it registered 3840 pounds. There was a discrepancy between the listed weight and the actual weight of 465 pounds. It was obvious that something was concealed somewhere on the vehicle and that the hiding place had not been discovered.

The car was then moved back to Pier 90 and driven to a service station at the corner of 51st Street and Eleventh Avenue. It was run over a grease pit in order that the searchers could take a better look at the underside. One of the searchers began tapping the gas tank of the Pontiac and then tapping gas tanks on other automobiles in the station to compare the sound. He called to an agent, "There's something wrong with this gas tank. It doesn't sound like these other gas tanks when I tap on it."

With the help of service station personnel, the searchers removed the gas tank. As soon as it was loosened from its fastenings, they knew that they had discovered hidden contraband: the gas tank was so heavy that it took the combined efforts of four men to lift it out of the grease pit. It was specially built of heavy steel.

Inside the gas tank, the searchers found a cleverly concealed compartment which contained thirty-three individually wrapped packages of gold bullion, valued at $110,000.

Apparently Schrieber became suspicious that he was suspect or he was tipped that the gold hoard had been discovered. At any rate, he did not show up as a passenger before the Cunard liner sailed. He was reported to have fled from the United States on a phony passport. After that, he was reported variously in Canada, in South America, and in Europe.

Saul Chabot of New York City was also one of the chiselers. Chabot was a slender, middle-aged man with graying sandy hair and bushy eyebrows who had built up a large-scale business in used rags. But the profits from his rag business weren't enough for Chabot—and he decided to expand his operations into gold smuggling.

Chabot might well have smuggled a fortune in gold from the country had it not been for the alertness of Matthew Jake Berckman of Jersey City, New Jersey. Berckman had joined the Cunard Line's police force in 1937 and he had remained on this job until 1947, when he was employed as a pier checker, checking automobiles to be shipped abroad.

On February 15, 1951, a 1950 Buick sedan bearing a New York license drove up to the pier where Berckman was checking the cars to be taken aboard the *Queen Elizabeth,* which was sailing for Cherbourg. The driver of the car identified himself as Saul Chabot. He showed Berckman his contract receipt for shipment of the car aboard the liner. He turned over his keys to Berckman, who assured him that the automobile would be handled carefully.

Berckman told Chabot to remove the cigarette lighter and the contents of the glove compartment and to lock the articles in the automobile's luggage compartment. When Chabot opened the compartment, Berckman saw there was nothing inside except tools and a spare tire.

He also noticed that although the compartment was virtually empty, the car looked as though it were heavily loaded because it sat low in the rear.

As they were talking, there was a banging from underneath the car. A longshoreman was having difficulty removing the tap from the gasoline tank. Chabot seemed extremely nervous and said, "What's the matter? What is he doing?"

Berckman replied, "He's loosening the tap on the gas tank. We can't take a car aboard the ship until the gas tank is empty." Then he added, "This is a very heavy car, isn't it?"

Chabot said, "Yes, these Buicks are very heavy."

Berckman gave Chabot his receipt. He told him that he would look after his car and he need have no further worry. But Chabot said, "Well, I'll stay and see that he gets the gas out all right."

Chabot remained until the gas had been drained from the car and then he walked across the street. Berckman noticed that Chabot hung around for another fifteen or twenty minutes watching his automobile. It was Chabot's nervousness which aroused Berckman's suspicions. He decided to inspect the other cars and to show no further interest in Chabot's car as long as he was around.

After lunch, Berckman went back to Chabot's automobile to look at it more closely. He saw what appeared to him to be a new welding on the inside of the trunk near the rear fenders. The welding was odd because the car did not look as though it had been in a collision. There was no sign of any damage to the front or rear of the car and the original paint was unmarred.

Berckman went to the office of Customs Inspector Howard Walter and reported his suspicion that the car had been tampered with and that it might be loaded with contraband. Inspector Walter dispatched Inspector Mario Cozzi and James P. Dalton, along with three port patrol officers, to investigate.

The preliminary examination revealed nothing unusual about the car except that it did seem to sag heavily on the rear springs and there was no apparent explanation for the welding near the rear fenders.

Cozzi began rapping on the sides of the car with his knuckles. It seemed solid enough until he rapped on the body just above the rear fenders—and then the rapping gave forth a hollow sound.

"Let's unbolt one of these fenders and take a look," Cozzi said.

Three bolts were loosened near the left rear door post. The fender was pried away from the body far enough to reveal a piece of gray cardboard. When Cozzi poked into the cardboard with a screwdriver, he could see it covered a package wrapped in heavy black cloth.

The fender was removed and the searchers found that it concealed a secret compartment containing several parcels—all of them packed with sheets of gold. Two secret compartments yielded eighty-two packages of gold valued at $171,197.

Customs agents were alerted. They kept Chabot's apartment under surveillance. They were following when he and Mrs. Chabot left the apartment at 9:30 A.M. enroute to Pier 90. The couple boarded the *Queen Elizabeth* and went to their cabin, D291. And it was there that agents questioned Chabot.

Chabot protested that he knew nothing of any gold hidden in the automobile. He claimed that two weeks earlier a man he knew only as "Carl" had given him $1,900 and told him to go to a used car lot and buy a certain automobile. Chabot said he bought the car for $1,750 and that he turned it over to Carl. Then Carl had brought the car back to him and he had delivered it to the steamship line without any knowledge that the gold had been hidden behind the fenders.

Chabot's story was not very convincing. He was tried and found guilty on a charge of smuggling and was sentenced to five years in prison.

As for Matthew Jake Berckman, the car checker whose suspicions led to the gold seizure, he was given a reward of $16,119 by the government for his alertness.

Unfortunately, the chiselers sometimes have been found in the ranks of Customs employees. The bad ones have been the exception, but occasionally there have been those who were tempted to make a racket of their places of trust. In one such case an importer of Italian-made men's wear built up a booming business with smuggled merchandise—acting on the advice and with the connivance of Customs inspectors who drifted into a conspiracy which wrecked their careers.

Giuseppe Battaglia, an enterprising merchant of Milan, Italy, had not the slightest intention of entering into a smuggling operation when he first arrived in the United States in 1952 seeking a market for silk ties, robes, sweaters, pajamas, shirts, scarves, and other men's wear and accessories.

Battaglia operated a retail haberdashery in Milan which was popular with American tourists, Hollywood movie celebrities, and businessmen who liked the distinctive and expensive Italian styling. Business was so good that the darkly handsome Battaglia decided the time was ripe to develop outlets for Italian-made merchandise in the United States.

He arrived in New York in February, 1952, after making arrangements to act as sales agent for three firms manufacturing ties, gloves and scarves. He was to pay all expenses and receive a straight 15 per cent commission on sales in the United States.

Battaglia had no difficulty in finding a market for his merchandise. Sales of Italian-made clothing and accessories were increasing throughout the country. Business was so promising, in fact, that he expanded his line of men's wear and became agent for such respected and well-known Italian houses as Galliene, Ratti, Salterio, Longhi and Caelli. He opened an office in the Empire State Building (later moved to 15 West 37th Street) and took a partner, Domenico Guarna, into the business. The partnership arrangement permitted Battaglia to travel throughout the country calling on retail outlets. He also was able to return to Italy on buying trips while Guarna looked after the New York end of the business.

On each return trip from Italy, Battaglia listed on his declaration the samples of silk materials and other merchandise he was carrying with him. He paid the required duty without question.

The partnership of Battaglia and Guarna operated honestly and aboveboard, Customs files show, until January 18, 1954. On that day, Battaglia arrived in New York harbor aboard the SS *Vulcania*. He handed over his declaration to Inspector Benjamin Danis, who was a short, pudgy man who soon impressed Battaglia as an extremely courteous and helpful officer. Danis made only a casual inspection of Battaglia's trunks and luggage, which was not unusual on this particular day because the inspectors' instructions were to make only a spot check of travellers' baggage.

After clearing all the baggage, Danis hinted amicably that if Battaglia had not listed the samples of merchandise on his declaration, he could very easily have overlooked them and there would have been no need to pay the duty.

"Is that so?" Battaglia said in surprise. "I was told to list everything."

Danis grinned. "It's simple if you know the right people."

Battaglia reached into his pocket and pulled out a business card. "Take this card and drop around to see me at my place of business," he said to Danis. "And would you give me your name and address? I would like to send you a few Italian ties as a gift. You have been very courteous."

Danis gave Battaglia his name and address. "I'll be around to see you," he said. "I can give you some tips that will help you in clearing Customs."

A few days later, Danis visited the shop of Battaglia and Guarna and chatted with the partners for several minutes about the problems of Customs clearances. Battaglia asked him to take his choice of several expensive Italian ties. But after Danis selected them Battaglia realized that Danis expected more than a gift of ties. He handed him a $20 bill, which Danis accepted.

As he stuffed the bill into his pocket, Danis said, "Let's get down to business. If you will let me know in advance when you or your representatives are arriving from Europe, I can arrange to handle the inspection of your baggage. I won't ask any questions if all your merchandise is not listed on the declarations."

Battaglia said, "But what if we arrive and you are sick—or for some reason can't handle the inspection?"

"That's no problem," Danis said. "If I can't handle the inspection myself, then I'll arrange for someone else to do it."

"What if we're caught bringing in merchandise which is not on the declaration?" Battaglia asked.

Danis laughed. "The worst that will happen to you is that you'll have to pay the duty. So what have you got to lose?"

It seemed so simple to the partners that they decided to give it a try on the next trip that Battaglia made to Italy. If Danis could arrange the clearance of sample merchandise so easily, then it was reasonable to assume he would have no difficulty with larger shipments of merchandise as well. If they could save the payment of duties, then the partnership's profits would rise in spectacular fashion.

A few days after this conversation, Danis returned to the office of Battaglia and Guarna, accompanied by Customs Inspector William Lev, a tall, fat man with a swarthy complexion. Danis advised the partners that Lev was a man they could trust. He said in the event one of them should arrive in New York and he, Danis, was not available to help them through Customs, then they could depend on Lev to help them just as they could depend on him.

Battaglia returned to Italy in June, 1954, on another of his buying trips. He remained there until January 17, 1955, when he returned to the United States aboard the SS *Andrea Doria*. Prior to his arrival, Guarna telephoned Inspector Danis and advised him of the time of Battaglia's arrival.

Danis was on the pier when Battaglia walked from the ship, and he handled the examination of his baggage. The examination and clearance proceeded smoothly. None of the samples which Battaglia brought from Italy was listed on his declaration. And there was no reason why Danis' perfunctory inspection should have aroused the suspicion of any other inspector because again that day the inspectors had orders to make only a spot check of the travellers' luggage. On some days, the inspectors were required to inspect all luggage. On other days only spot checks were ordered.

In testing the scheme proposed by Danis, Battaglia carried merchandise valued at something over $1,000, on which the duty would not have been more than $300 even had he declared the imports. He took the merchandise from the pier to the office on West 37th Street, and shortly thereafter Danis appeared to receive his payment. Battaglia gave him $100 in cash.

Both Battaglia and Guarna were elated over the discovery that they could bring merchandise into the country so simply without the payment of duties. They began planning to bring even greater quantities of merchandise from Italy on future trips.

In the months that followed, Battaglia and Guarna brought from Italy trunks packed with expensive men's wear which they were able to slip through Customs without the payment of duty. When unable to make a trip themselves, they arranged to have acquaintances and relatives bring the merchandise. In each case, there were prearranged inspections, with Lev having taken over the inspection end of the operation.

Inspector Theodore Rider, a tall, long-nosed, sallow-faced man, became involved in the operation quite by accident. On one of his many trips, Battaglia was standing on the pier waiting for Lev to make an inspection of his baggage when Rider approached and asked if he could help with his clearance.

"Thanks," Battaglia said, "but Inspector William Lev is a good friend of mine and I'm waiting for him to handle the clearance. He'll be along shortly."

Rider said, "Whatever Lev can do, I can do."

"Well," Battaglia said, "go easy on the examination, will you?"

Rider took only a casual look at a couple of small suitcases and then stamped all the baggage for clearance. For their cooperation in this case, Rider received $100 and Lev was paid $300. Battaglia and Guarna saved $6,185 in duties.

By midsummer of 1957, Battaglia and Guarna were convinced that the U.S. Customs Service was riddled with corruption and that there was no further need to worry. They were so certain that their system was foolproof that Guarna went to Italy and arranged the purchase of $41,000 worth of merchandise, which normally could be imported only with the payment of $13,325 in duties. The partners were not worrying about the duties because they had received a communication from Lev that when Guarna returned "everything will be all right."

But everything was not "all right." Earlier in the year a dapper, dark-haired man had called at the Varick Street headquarters of the Customs Special Agency Service and asked to see Agent Dave Cardoza, the big, amiable veteran of a thousand investigations, who headed the Bureau's New York Racket Squad.

This man, whose identity has never been disclosed by Customs, had an interesting story to tell Cardoza. He was a competitor of Battaglia and Guarna and he had become extremely curious about their sudden rise in the merchandising field. He also was intrigued by their peculiar ability to shave prices below a reasonable competitive level.

He had been making his own inquiries and observations over a period of many months. He knew the names of some of the people who had carried merchandise into the country for the partners. He had seen Customs inspectors visit the partners' place of business—and on one occasion he had seen Battaglia pass money to an inspector whom he identified from a picture as being Lev.

On the basis of this information, which was supported by names, places and dates, the Service opened a formal investigation. Agents sifted through thousands of declarations, seeking the names of the carriers for Battaglia and Guarna, and the names of the inspectors who had signed the suspect declarations.

A study of the declarations convinced the agents that Lev's name appeared far too frequently on the documents relating to the partners' travels. And there were too few imports recorded for a firm as obviously prosperous as Battaglia & Guarna, which dealt exclusively in foreign haberdashery.

This investigation was underway when Guarna left for Europe in July. By mid-August, Cardoza had decided the time had come to crack down on the partners—and the best time would be when Guarna returned from the Italian trip. He was reasonably certain that if Guarna were engaged in smuggling, he would return from Italy with a load of merchandise which he would try to slip through Customs. For this reason it was important to know when and how Guarna planned to return to the United States.

The time of Guarna's return was learned by a telephone call to the office of Battaglia & Guarna, where a secretary—told that an old friend from Chicago was calling—disclosed that Guarna was due to return on October 1 aboard the Italian liner *Cristoforo Colombo*.

With more than a month in which to set his trap, Cardoza began making plans to keep Guarna within sight of a Customs agent from the time he set foot on the pier until he cleared his baggage with an inspector. But this surveillance had to be done in such a manner that it would not arouse the suspicion of Lev or any other inspector who might be involved in the smuggling.

Finally, it was decided to use a "zone defense," in which three agents would be stationed at strategic points commanding a view of the pier and the baggage examination area. No one was to leave his post and follow Guarna or show any undue interest in his movements. One out-of-town agent—unknown to any of the inspectors—was to be stationed on the pier under the baggage collection point "G" in the role of a visitor come to meet one of the passengers.

In September, the agents made a "dry run" of the zone defense to acquaint themselves with their posts. On October 1, they put the plan into operation.

Mario Cozzi, a chunky young man especially adept at surveillance, was sent down the Bay with the Customs boarding party to seek out Guarna in order that he could be pointed out to the other agents when he came ashore. None of them knew him by sight.

Cozzi was wandering about the ship wondering how to locate Guarna without arousing suspicion when he got an unexpected break. Cozzi saw the Italian Line's agent, Angelo Cappa, standing by the ship's rail talking to a well-dressed, middle-aged passenger. Cappa called him over and said, "Mario, I want you to meet Mr. Guarna, who is returning from Italy. Mr. Guarna, this is Mr. Cozzi."

Cozzi shook hands with Guarna and then hastily excused himself, saying he had work to do before the ship docked. From that moment he remained close to Guarna, and when the merchant walked down the gangplank, Cozzi discreetly pointed him out to the waiting agents.

Guarna hurried to the collection point "G" and paid little attention to the man who was standing under the sign holding a visitor's pass in his hand. He would have been intensely interested had he known the stranger was Agent Melvin Huffman.

Inspector Lev walked up and shook hands with Guarna. And then he turned to Huffman and said brusquely, "Do you have permission to be on the pier?"

Huffman handed over his pass and said amiably, "I'm waiting for a friend—Mr. Gardiner. He's supposed to be on the *Colombo* and he asked me to meet him here."

Lev examined the pass and then handed it back, satisfied that Huffman was only a visitor. He said, "It's all right. Mr. Gardiner should be along soon."

Lev then called over another inspector and whispered in his ear. The inspector nodded and shook hands with Guarna. He quickly examined four small pieces of luggage and then he pasted clearance stickers on a half-dozen large trunks without opening them.

This operation was witnessed by Huffman and also by Agent Carl Esposito, who was watching from a nearby telephone booth. The examination was in violation of orders, because the inspectors had been instructed that morning to make a thorough examination of all baggage. None was to be cleared without inspection.

As Guarna's baggage was being taken to a platform to be loaded onto a truck, Cardoza walked over to the telephone booth where Esposito sat.

"That's a lot of baggage," Cardoza said. "We'll have to hire a truck to get it to the office."

Esposito grinned maliciously. "Why don't we wait," he said, "and let Guarna hire his own truck. Then he'll have to pay the bill."

"Why not?" Cardoza said.

Porters were preparing to heave the trunks onto a truck at the loading station when Cardoza and Esposito approached Guarna. They identified themselves as Customs agents and asked to see the contents of the trunks.

Guarna said nothing. Perhaps he was too frightened to speak. He merely took several keys from his pocket and began unlocking the trunks. When the agents raised the lids, they saw that each was packed with expensive men's haberdashery which had not been declared.

Guarna and Battaglia talked readily. They identified the inspectors who had helped them in their smuggling. When agents completed their examination of the partners' books, they were able to prove that over a period of two and a half years, the two men and their accomplices had smuggled into the United States merchandise with a wholesale value of $147,613—and they had avoided payment of duties totalling some $56,600. They had paid out $6,000 to various inspectors, of which the lion's share—about $5,000—went to Lev.

Battaglia and Guarna were convicted and fined $10,000 and $5,000 respectively, and placed on five years' probation. Inspector Lev was fined $2,500 and sentenced to three years in prison, along with Inspector Danis. Six other inspectors were dishonorably discharged from the service.

17

THE INNOCENTS

Betty Warren and Harriet Davis—trim and attractive in their U.S. Army nurses' uniforms—were wide-eyed with excitement as they looked from the window of the airliner and saw Hong Kong for the first time. The clouds hung low over the peaks of the island jutting from the sea at the edge of Red China. In the harbor they saw great luxury liners at anchor alongside battered old freighters from the four corners of the earth. The harbor was alive with Chinese junks and sampans.

Their excitement grew no less as the plane landed and a bus carried them into the bustle of Kowloon to the Grand Hotel. The hotel would be their headquarters for several days of sightseeing and shopping before they returned to their posts at Yokosuka Army Hospital, and the end of a vacation tour which had included Manila, Calcutta and Bangkok. It was one of the standard tours arranged by the military for personnel stationed in Japan and other Far Eastern bases. And Betty and Harriet, both lieutenants, were only two among the hundreds who made the circuit each year.

Before leaving Yokosuka, a fellow nurse had told them: "When you get to Hong Kong, be sure to look up Mr. Chu in the Miramar Hotel arcade. He's terribly nice—and honest. He can tell you where to buy things at the cheapest prices and he'll show you

around Hong Kong. He gets a commission on anything you buy
—but it's worth it."

The next morning after their arrival, blonde, blue-eyed Betty
and dark-haired, brown-eyed Harriet headed toward the Miramar
Hotel arcade to find Mr. Chu. They were window-shopping in the
arcade when a voice said politely, "Excuse me, please. I am Mr.
Chu. Are you Miss Warren and Miss Davis?"

The two women exclaimed in surprise. Betty said, "Yes. But
how in the world did you know who we are?"

Chu, a smiling, dapper, middle-aged man, said, "Lieutenant
Bess and Lieutenant Marge were here last week. They said you
would be in Hong Kong soon. So I have been watching for you.
I would be happy to show you around Hong Kong if you wish."

The next morning, Chu called at the Grand Hotel with a chauf-
feur-driven car. Obviously to make the girls feel more at ease,
he had with him his three-year-old son—a cute, button-eyed boy
who stared at the two American women as though they were
creatures from another planet.

Soon the four of them were touring Kowloon and the New Ter-
ritories, the farm land stretching from Kowloon to the border of
Red China. Chu entertained them as they went along with a history of the countryside and of the people. They even stood at one
end of the bridge at the border, looking into Red China and watching the impassive Red soldier standing guard at the other end with
a Russian-made machinegun slung from his shoulder.

Before their Hong Kong stay had ended, Betty and Harriet
were as much impressed by Chu's courtesy and helpfulness as
other military personnel had been in years past. Chu had concentrated on building good will among the American military people,
with the result that he knew scores of Army, Navy and Air Force
men and women throughout the Far East. He carried on a lively
correspondence with them, acting as their agent in buying gifts
to be shipped to friends and relatives in all parts of the United
States. His reputation for fair dealing was impeccable.

On the last day of their stay, Chu called at the Grand Hotel to
bid the nurses goodbye. They thanked him profusely for his kind-
nesses and asked if there was anything that they could do for him.

"If you would be so kind," Chu said, "I would like for you to
deliver some gifts to a relative in Japan."

He explained that he would have a seamen deliver two suitcases to them at Yokosuka. The cases, which they would be free to open if they wished, would contain a few shirts, some dolls for his relative's children, and a few other inexpensive gifts. The nurses would not have to bother about delivering them, because his relative would call for them at their quarters. The nurses said they would be delighted to do him a favor. And they bid one another goodbye.

Betty and Harriet were not the only Americans who had sought the services of Mr. Chu that week of February, 1958. Air Force Captain Bob Hampton, a tall, slim young jet fighter pilot, also was one of his customers. Hampton had hitched a ride from Japan to Hong Kong aboard an Air Force transport. He had called on Chu to help him purchase several tailored suits and shirts, a camera, a watch and other gifts.

Before they parted Chu also asked Hampton if he would mind carrying a suitcase back to Japan for his relative, a Mr. Lee. The captain said he would be glad to do him a favor, whereupon Chu brought out a suitcase from the shop where he worked. He opened it to show his friend that it contained only a few dolls, several shirts, ties, and other inexpensive small gifts. Hampton bid Chu goodbye, carrying the suitcase with him as he hurried to catch his plane back to Tokyo.

Soon afterward, Chu once more ran into a friend, Seaman Leslie Brown, a broad-shouldered young native of Los Angeles who had come ashore from the SS *President Cleveland* when the big liner docked with its load of 'round-the-world tourists. Chu had met Brown on a previous visit, introducing himself to the lonely sailor he had noticed wandering through the streets of Kowloon and inviting him on a tour of the colony. Brown had repaid Chu by introducing him to other crew members on shopping expeditions.

When they met once again, Chu invited Brown to lunch at a restaurant where waiters brought to the table the most bewildering variety of Chinese food Brown had ever eaten. "This is the best and cheapest food in all Hong Kong," Chu said.

During the meal, Chu asked Brown if he would do him the favor of delivering a suitcase to a relative, Mr. Lee, in Los Angeles. He explained, as he had to the other Americans, that the suitcase contained only a few gifts.

"Sure," Brown said, "if there is nothing in it to cause me any trouble."

Chu assured Brown there would be no trouble. He took him to the home of a friend, Ting Ching-Tsoi, where Mrs. Ting brought out a suitcase. Chu opened it to show Brown that it contained nothing but the gifts he had described. And then he gave Brown $20 for his trouble in delivering the luggage.

That night, Chu also delivered two suitcases to a seaman aboard the USS *Kearsarge,* to be taken to Betty Warren and Harriet Davis in Yokosuka.

Unknowingly, these Americans were innocents in a plot to smuggle millions of dollars worth of narcotics into the United States, either directly or by way of Japan. Each of the suitcases contained a false bottom in which packets of heroin were concealed.

As American and British agents later pieced together the story, Chu himself was unaware that the luggage contained heroin, or that he was being used as a pawn merely because he had so many friends among the military people and seamen who visited Hong Kong.

The plot had its beginning when Chu's friend, Ting Ching-Tsoi, conceived the idea of using Chu as an unwitting agent in a heroin-smuggling ring. Ting approached Chu with a proposition that they could make a big profit by sending watch parts to the United States, hidden in the false bottoms of suitcases carried by Chu's American friends. Ting knew that Chu would have nothing to do with narcotics but that his code of ethics would not be violated if he thought he was having his friends smuggle a few watch parts.

Chu agreed to a deal. Ting sent a confederate, Kung Kee-Sun, to nearby Macao, where anything can be bought if one has the cash—and where heroin can be purchased by the pound as easily as a woman can be bought for the night.

Kung smuggled the heroin past the British customs patrol. Then Ting bought several good-quality leather suitcases. He took them to a friend in Kowloon, who inserted false bottoms, fashioned of thin plywood covered with leather. The packages of heroin literally were built into the luggage. The job was so well done that only a careful inspection by an expert would disclose anything wrong.

Then, quite by chance, the system broke down because an Air Force wife became suspicious. When Captain Hampton returned to his home near the Tachikawa air base outside Tokyo, he found that his wife was on a shopping trip into town. He put the suitcase Chu had given him in a closet and promptly forgot about it. He also forgot to inform his wife that a Chinese would be calling for the suitcase later. Then he was suddenly called away from home on a training mission.

While he was gone, a Chinese called at the Hampton home. When Mrs. Hampton opened the door, the Chinese introduced himself as Mr. Ling. He inquired about the gifts which Captain Hampton had brought from Hong Kong from his relative, Mr. Chu. He said he had come for them and would appreciate it if Mrs. Hampton would give him the suitcase.

But Mrs. Hampton knew nothing about gifts in a suitcase. She knew nothing about a Mr. Ling and nothing about a Mr. Chu. "I'm very sorry," she said, "but you will have to return when my husband is home. He has said nothing to me about it."

Mr. Ling was visibly upset and seemed not to understand why Mrs. Hampton would not give him the suitcase. But he left, promising to return.

When Hampton returned home, his wife told him of the strange Chinese who had called and how upset he had been when she had refused to turn over a suitcase to him.

"I'm sorry," Hampton laughed. "I put the suitcase in the closet and forgot all about it." He explained he had brought it home and was to deliver it to Ling as a favor to Chu. "There's nothing in it except a few cheap gifts," he said.

But Mrs. Hampton remembered the sudden distress she had seen in Ling's eyes when she disclaimed any knowledge of a suitcase. "I don't like the looks of this at all," she said. "That man Ling was actually frightened when I wouldn't give him the suitcase. The loss of a few cheap gifts shouldn't upset him like that."

Captain Hampton began to worry that perhaps something was wrong. He checked the contents of the case but saw nothing to get alarmed about. Nevertheless he decided to report the matter to Air Force intelligence officers. When the agents examined the suitcase carefully, they found the hidden narcotics.

The Air Force investigators turned the case over to Japanese

police. Ling was arrested and finally broke down. He confessed
the smuggling plot. He also told investigators about the shipment
of narcotics in the suitcases destined for the two Army nurses.
These bags were intercepted, and when the bottoms were pried
loose, the investigators found that each contained heroin valued
at $50,000 on the retail market.

The news of Ling's arrest reached Chu in Hong Kong. He was
appalled that he was being used as a tool in the smuggling of narcotics. He wrote a frantic note to Lieutenants Warren and Davis,
urging them to destroy the two suitcases as soon as they arrived,
in order to avoid trouble. He apologized to them for causing them
any embarrassment or trouble.

And then he wrote a letter to Seaman Leslie Brown. He mailed
one copy to Honolulu and another copy to Brown's home in Los
Angeles. He said:

Dear Leslie:

I hope this letter will catch you up in Honolulu or Los Angeles. If
in San Francisco too late. I want to tell you about the story of the
suitcase. It is a very dangerous thing. Please do not take it back to your
house. Please keep it board ship and return it to me in Hong Kong,
otherwise you will have big troubles. If you already took them home,
and have no trouble, please keep it. If some Chinese people try to
get it, please do not let any people have it. The best thing is to return
to Hong Kong. It is a very dangerous suitcase. Be careful of yourself.
You have family and I also have family. I don't want you and me to
have troubles.

I am very sorry for everything. Please take my word. Please return
me a mail. I am looking forward to hearing from you in the very very
soonest.

Sincerely yours,
Chu

The letter was waiting for Brown when the *President Cleveland*
arrived at Honolulu. Again he examined the suitcase closely, and
everything that was in it. But he could find nothing that was suspicious. He decided that the best thing to do was to keep the case
in his cabin and to take it back to Hong Kong on his next trip.

Brown wrote to Chu, saying:

Dear Chu:

Received your letter in Honolulu. Was quite surprised and hurt to
know you put me in such a spot after I asked you if there was anything

in the suitcase. We arrive in San Francisco today. I have the suitcase on the ship and will return it to you next trip when I come. That is if nothing happens to me. I have spent every night since then worrying about the spot you put me on.

Well, I will close for now. Hope you write and that your children are well.

Sincerely yours,
Leslie Brown

When the *President Cleveland* reached Los Angeles, Brown left the suitcase in his cabin and hurried ashore to his apartment. He was told that a Mr. Lee, a Chinese, had made several calls inquiring about his return. And within a few minutes after his arrival, there was a knock on his door. Brown opened the door and found that his caller was a Chinese about fifty-five or sixty years of age. He had thin, sharp features and a dark complexion. His hair was turning gray. He was wearing a brown suit and a topcoat.

"I am Mr. Chu's relative, Mr. Lee," the visitor said. He asked if Brown had brought the suitcase from Mr. Chu.

"I can't give it to you," Brown said. "I got a letter from Chu and he told me to hang on to that suitcase or I'd get in trouble."

Lee angrily accused Brown of trying to keep the suitcase in order to sell it. He demanded to know where it was.

To prove he still had it as he claimed, Brown took Lee with him aboard the *Cleveland* and showed him the suitcase in his cabin. But he refused to give it to him. Brown had the bag in his cabin when the *President Cleveland* sailed from Los Angeles on the return trip to Hong Kong.

The U.S. Customs agents in San Francisco and Los Angeles were informed by the Customs representative in Tokyo of the developments at that end of the line. By this time they had learned that Brown was involved in the smuggling operation and that he was to make delivery to a Chinese known only as Mr. Lee. But the message from Tokyo arrived after the *Cleveland* had put to sea.

When the *Cleveland* arrived in Yokohama, Treasury agents in Japan boarded the vessel and asked Brown if he still had the suitcase which had been given to him by the Chinese in Hong Kong. Brown said, "Yes. I know which one you are talking about." He took them to his cabin and showed them the case. "I have looked it over," he said, "and I can't find anything wrong."

A customs agent went over the suitcase carefully, discovered the false bottom, pried out the piece of plywood, and uncovered the cache of heroin. It was estimated to be worth $500,000 at retail prices.

Brown agreed to work with Customs agents when he returned to the United States and to help trap the Chinese who had called on him for the narcotics. The narcotics were turned over to the ship's captain and Brown was confined to the ship. When the vessel docked in San Francisco the heroin was turned over to Customs agents. Brown was taken in tow by Customs Agent Paul Samaduroff, a blond-haired, broad-shouldered man who had specialized in tracking down West Coast narcotics smugglers.

Samaduroff and other agents in San Francisco suspected that the "Mr. Lee" who had called on Brown in Los Angeles was actually Li Sheung, also known as Shin Lee. He fitted the description which Brown had given the agents when he was questioned in Japan. Li had been on the agents' wanted list for months—but they had never been able to trap him while he was buying or selling narcotics. Now the chance had come.

The agents placed fake packages of heroin in the false bottom of the suitcase and went with Brown to the bus depot, where the bag was checked in a locker. Then Brown was taken to a telephone, where he placed a call to Li Sheung's hangout at a shirt shop on Grand Avenue in Chinatown. The shop owner answered the phone and Brown asked if he could talk to Li Sheung. The shop owner said, "You call later, and I'll see if I can contact him."

Several times Brown called the shirt shop only to be told to call again. Late that evening the contact was made. A man who identified himself as Li Sheung got on the phone and talked to Brown. Brown identified himself as a seaman aboard the *President Cleveland* and said he had something which he was supposed to deliver to Li Sheung.

"Yes," Li said, "I remember you in Los Angeles. Why didn't you give me the suitcase when I was in Los Angeles?"

Brown said that he would explain the whole thing to him when they met. He added, "I have the suitcase here now and I'm supposed to give it to you."

They agreed to meet in a restaurant in Chinatown. Li Sheung was waiting for Brown when he arrived at the restaurant. Customs agents had placed themselves at strategic points outside the restaurant, and one was seated at a table in the rear of the room when the two men sat down together.

Li Sheung kept referring to the fact that Brown would not give him the suitcase in Los Angeles. He said he could not understand why the delivery had not been made.

Brown said, "That time you came to my house, I thought there was something hidden in the suitcase but I didn't know what it was. Now I know, and I want some money for my trouble."

Li Sheung agreed to go with Brown to the bus station to pick up the heroin and to pay him $100. They left the restaurant and got into a cab.

Customs agents, keeping contact with each other by radio, trailed the cab from the restaurant to the bus station, where other agents waited, lounging about the place as though they were travellers. They were watching as Brown went to a baggage locker, took out the bag, and handed it to Li Sheung. The Chinese then counted out $100 and handed it to the seaman. At this point Samaduroff and the other agents moved in and arrested Li Sheung. He was convicted and sentenced to five years in prison.

And Mr. Chu—the amiable, friendly little man in Hong Kong? The British were lenient with him because he was, after all, only the dupe, and he had cooperated in rounding up the smuggling gang. By now, he may have returned to his old job of being helpful to touring Americans.

The Customs files are fat with such cases, in which smuggling rings and individual smugglers have used innocent victims to help them bring jewels, heroin, watch parts, and other small but valuable items into the United States.

One of the innocents in such a plot was dark-eyed, attractive Countess Kyra Kapnist, who arrived in the United States aboard the SS *Champlain* on September 2, 1937, to join the exclusive fashion house of Marcel Rochas, Inc., of New York City as a model and saleswoman.

Before she left Paris, an official of the firm had informed her that two trunks and a hat box would be added to her baggage when it was delivered to the liner. It was nothing she was to worry about. She would be met on the pier in New York by Mr. Guy Fonte-Joyeuse, vice president of the firm and manager of its New York branch. He would take care of her customs declaration and the baggage inspection. All the countess had to do was to be her charming self and not worry her pretty head about such small details.

And so the countess arrived in New York. On the pier, she was met by Fonte-Joyeuse, a distinguished-looking man accompanied by a fashionably dressed woman. Everything seemed to go as she had been told it would in Paris. Fonte-Joyeuse was extremely solicitous about his new employee. "Give me your customs declaration," he said, "and I'll take care of everything."

He hurried away to find an inspector to examine her baggage. Within a matter of minutes an inspector appeared and peeked into one piece of the countess' luggage. Then he stamped all the baggage for clearance and the countess was whisked from the pier with her friends. Fonte-Joyeuse seemed unduly elated over her arrival.

Fonte-Joyeuse would not have been so happy had he known that a member of his own firm was an informer for the U.S. Customs Service—and that a letter was even then on its way to the Service advising them that Countess Kapnist's luggage included two trunks and a hat box containing seventy original gowns and hats valued at approximately $40,000.

Agents opened an investigation and found that Countess Kapnist's declaration made no mention of dutiable imports. They questioned the inspector who had handled the examination and found that—for a price—he had agreed to feign an examination of trunks and luggage brought into the country by the models and employees designated by Fonte-Joyeuse.

When agents confronted the countess, she willingly told them the whole story. She told them of the instructions given her in Paris, of being met by Fonte-Joyeuse on the pier in New York, and of her surprise when an inspector took the trouble to look at only one small suitcase among all the luggage which she carried with her.

Agents found in the house of Marcel Rochas 104 gowns of French origin, valued at about $60,000, which had been smuggled into the United States by models and others employed by the firm.

Fonte-Joyeuse was indicted on two charges of smuggling and conspiracy. He was sentenced to one year and a day in prison and fined $1,000. He served six months of his sentence and then was released on parole and deported to France. The Parisian fashions seized from the house of Marcel Rochas were sold at auction. They brought about $9,000 into the U.S. Treasury—of which $2,250 was paid to the Paris informer.

18

THE STORMY WORLD OF ART

The Korean War was still raging in April, 1951, when Sgt. Elverne Giltner left the American Army's Tenth Corps Headquarters for a stroll about the war-battered streets of Seoul. Four times in less than one year fighting had washed through the city as the United Nations forces battled the North Korean and Chinese Communist troops across the mountains and through the valleys of this unhappy land. Sergeant Giltner was only one of thousands of American soldiers in Seoul at this time.

Like most Americans overseas, the sergeant was a collector of souvenirs. Whenever he had the chance to get away from headquarters, he enjoyed poking about in the little shops in Seoul, searching for interesting knickknacks to send back to his parents, Mr. and Mrs. Hugh V. Giltner, in Pueblo, Colorado.

Not far from the parliament building—a gaunt structure bearing the scars of war—Sergeant Giltner halted to examine the wares of a street peddler. "I have nice rug you will like," the peddler said. He pulled back the edge of a bundle, revealing part of a leopard skin. "This rug was made from leopard skins. It is very valuable," the peddler said.

"How big is the rug?" the sergeant asked.

The peddler replied, "Very big." He indicated by stepping off several paces that the rug was probably 18 feet long by 8 feet wide. "In your country," the peddler said, "this rug would be worth several hundred dollars."

The peddler unrolled the bundle to give the sergeant a better look at this bargain he was offering. Giltner saw that it was, indeed, a large rug of leopard skins. It appeared to him as though it were not in the best of condition, but he liked the idea of surprising his folks in Pueblo with a genuine leopard-skin rug. "How much do you want?"

The peddler said he would sell the rug for 150,000 won, the equivalent at that time of about $25 in U.S. money. Then the peddler tugged at Giltner's sleeve and whispered, "This rug is from the old queen's palace. She was the last queen of Korea. It is worth $2,000 in United States."

Sergeant Giltner was impressed. He agreed to pay 150,000 won. He picked up his new souvenir and lugged it back to the barracks, where he tossed it into a corner. He would send it home later by mail, as he had such gifts as a black lacquer chest, a lamp fashioned from a beer can, and other souvenirs of his stay in Korea.

But Giltner's plans for shipping the rug were postponed. A lieutenant took a fancy to the rug and, pulling rank, persuaded the reluctant sergeant to part with his souvenir for the purchase price. That same evening, the lieutenant lost the rug in a poker game to Lieutenant No. 2, who sold it to Lieutenant No. 3 for $50. Lieutenant No. 3 was going to send the rug to his parents, but then he decided it was too much trouble. He sold it to Sergeant Giltner for $25.

The sergeant stuffed the rug into a carton and mailed it home. He wrote a note to his mother: ". . . I figure you won't have much use for this rug even after it gets there. But you can always sell it. . . . The rug like I said before is made of leopard skin—the real thing, and is mounted on red felt or something. . . . Just where you would put it beats me. . . ."

The rug was a sensation in Pueblo. Neighbors dropped by to see it. It was so large that it could not be used in any of the rooms in the Giltner home. For the best viewing, Mrs. Giltner had the rug hauled out into the back yard and strung over a clothes line. The exact measurements of the rug were 18 feet 11 inches by 8 feet. It was embroidered at the four corners and had a red felt backing.

Mrs. Giltner told neighbors, "It's too pretty to walk on and too big for my living room. I don't know what in the world we'll do with it."

The Giltners sent the rug to a local firm for cleaning and storage. They valued the rug at $25,000 and had it insured for $16,000. The Pueblo *Star-Journal* carried a picture of the rug with a pretty girl seated on it. The accompanying story said: "Owners of the rug are contacting museums and big-game hunters, with a view to selling it, since they feel it is too valuable for their use, and their home will not accommodate it."

Denver's Collector of Customs Harry A. Zinn saw the news story in the Pueblo paper. He thought it odd that an American sergeant should be sending back a $25,000 rug to the United States. He forwarded a copy of the clipping to the Supervising Customs Agent in Chicago, saying, "Enclosed is a newspaper clipping, the subject of which you may consider warrants some investigation." The Customs agency certainly was interested in investigating the importation of a rug of such value.

At the same time, the Korean Consul General in New York, David Namkoong, was displaying interest in the report of the rug shipped from Seoul. Namkoong realized that the rug was one of the national treasures which had been stolen from the palace in Seoul at the outbreak of the Korean War. The rug had hung in the Chang Duk palace, the home of Queen Min. The palace had been made into a national museum where the Koreans displayed historical treasures of the ancient kingdom. Many of these treasures had been among the loot taken by Communists and civilians during the first invasion of Seoul. Mr. Namkoong told a reporter for *The New York Times,* "The rug is worth about $100,000, if such a priceless national treasure can have a price tag."

The Korean government and the United States government took the view that young Giltner was an innocent purchaser of the rug and that he had knowingly violated no law in sending the rug home. A Customs agent hurried to Pueblo from Chicago to impound the rug. It was placed in storage for safekeeping in Denver pending its return to Korea. The Korean government reimbursed the Giltners for all the expenses involved in the shipment, cleaning, storage, and insuring of the rug. And thus the case of the souvenir-hunting sergeant and the leopard-skin rug ended on a note of international good will.

The case of the leopard-skin rug presented no difficulty for Customs in establishing the historic and artistic authenticity of the rug. But classification in the field of fine art is not always so simple. Customs has become embroiled in some hilarious and notable cases of this sort.

Early in this century, Congress decided in the interest of promoting culture to permit, free of duty, the importation of paintings, sculptures, and other art objects which could be classified as "fine arts." It was when Congress began defining fine arts in legal language that the trouble began. For example, a sculpture was defined as something which is representative of an animate object in nature that is in its true proportion of length, breadth, and thickness. When this definition was written, members of Congress did not take into account the abstractionists and the modernists, who hardly view their subjects in their "true proportion of length, breadth, and thickness."

With the passage of this law, Congress automatically converted every Customs appraiser in the United States into an active critic and judge of the arts. This was so because—whether the appraisers liked it or not—they had to decide whether an import was a work of fine art and thus free of duty. No shilly-shallying about it. It was or it was not subject to duty. Juries of eminent art critics might enjoy the luxury of disagreement; the Customs appraiser had to say yes or no.

This was the situation in 1927 when the distinguished sculptor Constantin Brancusi sent from Europe a highly polished bronze figure called "Bird in Flight." The bronze was about 4 feet 6 inches high and stood on a cylindrical base about 6 inches in diameter and 6 inches in height.

In his effort to describe the sculpture, Justice Waite of the Customs Appeals Court would write: "The importation . . . terminates at the top in a point which might be caused by the cutting of the piece diagonally across and upward until it terminates in an edge. It increases in size as it descends with a slight curve to the middle, from which point it decreases and terminates about ten inches from the pedestal, where it is cylindrical, and from that point it increases in size on a conical shaped base which rests upon a pedestal. . . .

"The piece is characterized . . . as a bird. Without the exercise of rather a vivid imagination, it bears no resemblance to a bird except, perchance, with such imagination it may be likened to the shape of the body of a bird. It has neither head nor feet nor feathers portrayed in the piece. . . . It is extremely smooth on its exterior which is a polished and burnished surface. . . ."

When a Customs examiner first saw this objet d'art, he decided that it could not, from his viewpoint, be called even a reasonable facsimile of a bird. As he studied it further, he was unable to detect the "true proportions" which were necessary to meet the requirements of the law laid down by Congress for duty-free statuary.

His ruling that the famed "Bird in Flight" was not a work of fine art touched off a storm in the art world, with much derisive comment aimed at Customs. Edward Steichen, the importer of the Brancusi work, appealed the examiner's ruling, and when the case came to trial in 1928, he was flanked by an imposing list of witnesses ready to testify that Brancusi had indeed produced a work of fine art in "Bird in Flight."

The witnesses who came to the defense of Brancusi were Sculptor Jacob Epstein, Forbes Watson, editor of the *Arts* magazine, Frank Crowninshield, editor of *Vanity Fair* magazine, and William Henry Fox, director of the Brooklyn Museum of Art.

After hearing all the evidence, the court conceded that "under the earlier (court) decisions, this importation would have been rejected as a work of art, or, to be more accurate, as a work within the classification of high art." However, it noted that opinions of what constituted high art had undergone changes under the influence of modern schools of art.

Finally the court said of the statue: "It is beautiful and symmetrical in outline, and while some difficulty might be encountered in associating it with a bird, it is nevertheless pleasing to look at and highly ornamental, and as we hold under the evidence that it is the original production of a professional sculptor and is in fact a piece of sculpture and a work of art according to the authorities above referred to, we sustain the protest and find that it is entitled to free entry. . . ."

The storm kicked up over the Brancusi bird created little more uproar than the arrival in New York in May, 1955, of an abstract painting by the European artist Dr. Alberto Burri. It was a most unusual work of art, as it consisted of several pieces of burlap sewn together and affixed to a board, stencilled with letters, and decorated with birds painted in oils. The artist said the effect of the whole was to convey a spiritual sense of the order in life. He valued his work at $450.

However the Customs examiner, failing to perceive the artist's message, ruled that the importation was not a work of art. He held that it was a manufactured object whose chief value was in the vegetable fiber, or burlap sacking. Under this ruling, the import was dutiable at 20 per cent of the value placed upon it by the artist.

The examiner's ruling posed an unusual problem. Art experts agreed that Dr. Burri's work was not a painting—but a collage. And Congress had failed to mention collages in the categories of art held to be duty free, an oversight thought by some to reflect no credit on the Congressional artistic sense.

Alfred H. Barr, Jr., director of museum collections of the Museum of Modern Art, and Leo Castelli, owner of a New York art gallery, were among those who came to Dr. Burri's defense in court. They agreed his collage was an original work of free fine art and they described Dr. Burri as one of the first half-dozen artists to emerge in postwar Italy with a world-wide reputation. His works had been exhibited in the New York Museum of Modern Art, the Carnegie Museum in Pittsburgh, the Allbright Gallery in Buffalo and other well-known museums.

The court reluctantly held, however, that since Congress had failed to include collages in the the free fine arts, an import duty of 20 per cent would have to be paid—a ruling which later led to Congress amending the law to permit collages to be imported free of duty.

These cases and others moved leaders in the world of art to petition Congress to change the tariff laws governing the entry of works of art, and to remove the absurdly restrictive language which had caused so much embarrassment not only to the artists and to museums, but also to Customs and the government itself. As a result of these petitions, Senators Jacob Javits of New York and Paul Douglas of Illinois introduced in 1959 a bill to amend the tariff laws to permit free duty for all fine art and to eliminate the old definitions which had bemused Customs examiners. The bill was passed by Congress.

Actually, the slings and arrows hurled at the Bureau in the disputes over abstract art obscured the fact that over the years the Bureau had developed a good many experts whose opinions were valued highly by museums and leaders in the world of art. The Bureau also has some of the country's leading experts on appraisals of a wide range of imports. It even boasts that it has a man who can look at a hog's bristle and tell whether the hog was raised on the China slope of the Himalayas or the Indian side of the mountain, a bit of esoteric knowledge which is not as useless as it might seem. Little is heard of the fact that almost daily these men protect American dealers, collectors, and the buying public from forgeries, fraud, and unfair trade practices.

Thirty years ago the country was being flooded with fake antique silverware from England. In many cases an old hallmark—authentic in itself and perhaps 200 years old—would appear on a beautiful teapot. To all outward appearances the teapot was an authentic antique 200 years old. But what had happened was that an expert silversmith had lifted the hallmark from an inexpensive spoon and then soldered it into the teapot so smoothly that only an expert could detect the fakery.

There is little chance for such fraud today, even though dealers and collectors import each year more than $2 million worth of antique silver and old Sheffield, largely from England. Much of the credit for this protection is due to a dapper little man named Nathan Nathanson, who is one of the world's leading experts on silverware. Nathanson is a small, bouncing man with a bristling black moustache and an infectious enthusiasm for his work. He was reared in Brooklyn and as a boy served as a jeweler's apprentice. He became fascinated with metals and gems. The youth haunted museums, art galleries, antique dealers' showrooms, and libraries, studying everything he could find on the subject of silver and old jewelry. He pursued his interests with study at Columbia University and then joined the Customs Bureau, where he quickly became recognized as an authority in his field. As a result of these years of study, Nathanson usually can tell within five years when an antique piece of silverware was made, the name of the artisan who made it, the city in which it was made, and the original owner of the piece. This he is able to do through his knowledge of the hallmarks on the silver—the symbols which were first stamped into silver pieces by the ancient guilds of England during the reign of King Edward I in the year 1300.

During the last 200 years, hallmarks have been an important guide to those versed in the lore of old silver. But of equal importance is a knowledge of the patina of old silver—that mellow coloration which is given to silver only by time and which no one yet has been able to duplicate. The expert must also know the distinctive designs from each period.

Unscrupulous silversmiths have several methods of faking antique silver. The most commonly used fraud is the transfer of a famous hallmark from a small piece of silver to a large tray, coffee pot or teapot, a process known as "sweating."

One simple method to detect such a graft is to breathe on the hallmark. The warm breath in most cases will make the graft lines show up. The infallible method is to heat the silver—and this can only be done safely by an expert. Under strong heat the graft lines come into view.

Another method of forgery is to take a valuable and authentically old piece of silver, make a cast of it, and from the casting create a duplicate. The new silver piece is "aged" with an artificial patina. But no matter how good this job might be, the forgers always leave after casting tiny marks and other imperfections which the expert is able to spot by close study. Nathanson insists that even if the job were so well done that an expert missed the telltale marks, he could not be fooled by a phony patina.

Nathanson and his colleagues have their own quiet moments of triumph when they pit their knowledge against that of well-known importers. In one case a New York importer objected to paying duty on a loving cup which obviously was much more than a century old and qualified in his opinion for free entry. He argued that this loving cup was absolutely authentic and that all Nathanson had to do was look at the patina of the silver and also at the hallmarks. "Anyone can recognize those hallmarks and see that they are legitimate," the importer said.

But Nathanson was quite sure there was something wrong with this piece of silver. The design was not quite right for its period. The hallmarks were genuine. There was no evidence that they had been tampered with. The patina, without doubt, was that of a very old piece of silver, and the sheen could not have been imparted by any chicanery.

Finally he suggested to the importer that they take the loving cup to the workshop of the importer, where his own silversmith could heat it to a near-melting point without doing damage. As they watched the silversmith carefully heat the silver, Nathanson saw that his suspicion was justified. The heat showed up definite lines where a spout had been removed from the "loving cup" and the hole patched over very expertly with silver to change the shape of a teapot and convert it to a loving cup.

Under the law, this piece of silver—even though it was far more than a century old—could not meet the requirements for free importation because it had been changed from its original form.

Many antique dealers are upset by the fact that they import what appears to be a legitimate antique only to find that it does not qualify for free entry because it has been tampered with at some time in the past. For example, one importer brought into the country a very old Oriental panel which had been made into a modern coffee table. He declared the table was entitled to free entry because the panel was an antique. Customs did not agree with the dealer's viewpoint. While the panel alone would have been permitted to enter free of duty, once it became a part of a modern piece of furniture then it no longer met the legal requirements. This meant that the importer not only had to pay the regular rate of duty but also a penalty of 25 per cent—a penalty which is used by the government to discourage the practice of mislabelling imports.

In the eighteenth century in England it was common practice to use a pole screen while sitting in front of an open fire. The pole screen, sometimes made of painted wood and sometimes of fabric, stood on a tripod base and was placed in front of a person to shield his face from the fire. The top part was adjustable and could be raised or lowered as the person wished while toasting his legs.

Dealers in later years got the idea of converting the pole screens to other uses. They cut the screen from the pole and used the tripod as a base so that the old pole screen became a coffee table. While all the parts actually were antiques in themselves, Customs

held that it did not qualify for free entry because the character of
the article had been changed over the years. It was not being imported in the same form in which it originated and for which it was
primarily intended. The fact that the parts were antique did
not qualify it for free entry any more than the table fashioned
from an Oriental panel.

Even the best and most reputable of dealers sometimes make
mistakes in judging the age of art objects. There was one case in
which such a misjudgment cost the dealer $6,300 in duties. A
New York art gallery in 1953 paid $4,300 for porcelain vases
which it believed to be early eighteenth-century Chinese. They
were purchased from importers, who had bought them from a corporation which was disposing of several art objects for an estate.
The vases originally had been owned by the royal family of Russia and had been brought to this country after the Russian revolution.

The gallery sold the vases for $9,000 to a woman who main-
tained her residence in Paris. One evening she boasted to her dinner guests that the vases were early eighteenth-century discoveries
which once had reposed in the palace of the late Czar of Russia.
One of her guests, an antiquarian, suggested discreetly to her later
that possibly her purchases were not eighteenth-century Chinese
but were from the nineteenth century.

The woman indignantly demanded an explanation from the gallery, which replied that they would gladly refund her money if she
were dissatisfied, but they could not admit that a mistake had been
made in dating the vases. The woman shipped the vases back to
the United States labelled as antiques, free of duty, and valued
at $9,000. When the vases arrived at Customs in New York, one
of the Bureau's experts studied them and declared that the vases
were not Chinese eighteenth-century vases, but in fact had been
made in France in the nineteenth century.

The Customs examiner's judgment was upheld by other authorities in this field. The gallery was required to pay duty of $6,300.
The tariff law states "if any article . . . is detected as unauthentic in
. . . the antiquity claimed as a basis for free entry, there shall be
imposed, collected, and paid . . . a duty of 25 per cent of the
value . . . in addition to any other duty." And in this case the
"other duty" amounted to 45 per cent of the value.

Cultural growth can hardly be reduced to statistics, but Customs' statistics are at least persuasive in support of the argument that the United States is now enjoying a cultural boom. Ten years ago American collectors were purchasing original paintings at the rate of $8.5 million a year. The purchases have increased to $33 million a year, with indications that the country is on a prolonged art-buying binge. It has been a profitable investment for many, as the values of the modernists' paintings—particularly popular in this country—have spiralled.

The increase of interest in art has created a problem for Customs because—with the huge sums of money involved—there have emerged in Europe several "factories" producing bogus paintings in Paris, Amsterdam and Rome.

The appearance of the forgeries moved the Customs Bureau to issue this warning in its monthly bulletin:

Dealers and experts must approach all shipments with extreme caution and employ modern scientific testing methods because of the skill that has developed in the forging of scenes and signatures.

A recent purchase of a Modigliani, described merely as a "Portrait of a Woman," as so many of his works are, demanded much time and research. A well-known American collector obtained the picture for $25,000—a bargain, considering the quality of the painting. Our appraisers and examiners set to work. They delved into the very elaborate history of the painting and discovered that the canvas actually was 2 inches smaller than the original—also there were color differences. To the dismay of the importer, this import was appraised at $150 and returned for duty as a copy.

Many of the fakes are discovered through the use of X-ray and infrared and ultraviolet lights, which reveal overpainting, restorations, and flaws not visible to the naked eye. Chemical analysis of the paints and varnishes used by the artists often give a clue to the period in which the work was done.

Over the years, the Customs examiners have learned that any decision they make on a work of art is potentially explosive. They have learned, too, that on some days they can expect to appear very dumb—and on other days very smart. And that very few people seem to hear of the smart days.

19

SEX AND THE CENSOR

Censors are unloved creatures. They are damned by writers, artists, and liberal thinkers wherever men cherish free expression. They are regarded generally as crude conformists who wear their righteousness as proudly as a Boy Scout wears his merit badge.

Every rule is likely to have its exception. The exceptional censor in the United States is a tall, good-natured, erudite lawyer named Huntington Cairns, who might justifiably be called the nation's watchdog against the importation of obscene books, pictures, and other items of a questionable moral character. It would be too much to call Cairns "the beloved censor." But if a department of the government were capable of affection, then the Treasury Department (and the Customs Bureau) at least should feel this warm emotion for the man who has kept them remarkably free from foot-in-mouth embarrassment for more than a quarter of a century.

Since 1934, Cairns has advised the Treasury and the Customs Bureau in their decisions as to what constitutes obscenity in foreign imports. Since his arrival on the scene there has been no significant public controversy over his decisions, even though the dividing line between genuine art and pornography is often no more than one man's prejudice.

Officially, Cairns is secretary, treasurer, and general counsel of the National Gallery of Art. His headquarters is a large, secluded and attractive office in a wing of the National Gallery on Constitution Avenue in Washington, D. C. It is from these improbable surroundings that Cairns advises Treasury and Customs on what is obscene and what isn't, what should be refused entry into this country as plain trash, and what should be permitted to enter. The Treasury is under no obligation to follow his advice, but it does.

Cairns is a big, dark-haired, distinguished-looking man in his early sixties who is far more interested in Plato than in pornography. He is convinced that the ancient Greeks were the greatest people, intellectually, who ever trod the earth. Even their pornography, in his view, was superior to the modern product.

Cairns assumed the role of censor because of a curious chain of events, which began when he successfully opposed government censorship banning George Moore's translation of *Daphnis and Chloe*—a book which shocked the sensibilities of many people, including the Customs collector who read it and ordered it banned.

A Baltimore book dealer had imported Moore's translation with high hopes for a large and lucrative sale in Baltimore and in other cities. But Customs ruled the book was obscene under Section 305 of the Tariff Act of 1930. This act says: "(a) Prohibition of importation—all persons are prohibited from importing into the United States from any foreign country any book, pamphlet, paper, writing, advertising, circular, print, picture, drawing, or other representation, figure, or image on or of paper or other material, or any cast, instrument or other article which is obscene or immoral. . . . No such article, whether imported separately or contained in packages with other goods entitled to entry, shall be admitted to entry. . . . Upon the appearance of any such book or matter at any Customs office, the same shall be seized and held by the Collector to await the judgment of the District Court as hereinafter provided; and no protest shall be taken to the United States Customs Court from the decision of the Collector."

Thwarted by this formidable language, the book dealer took his problem to Cairns, who was then practicing law in Baltimore. Cairns appealed the ruling by Customs to the Customs Court of Appeals. Then he cannily persuaded the judge to hear the case without a jury—and to hear the testimony of expert witnesses, including a psychiatrist, a professor of English, and a newspaper editorial writer then with the Baltimore *Sun*. Cairns tried to persuade a classics scholar from Johns Hopkins University to testify for him, but the professor replied, "No, I will not testify in defense of such a worthless book as George Moore's translation of *Daphnis and Chloe*."

The trial procedure broke legal precedent. Previously the rule had been that expert witnesses could not testify because they would usurp the function of a jury. But Cairns was permitted to put his witnesses on the stand.

Cairns wasn't too sure of his psychiatrist and how he would react to cross-examination by the government attorney on the question of what effect the book would have on immature adults and children. The psychiatrist handled himself very well under direct questioning, but then the prosecuting attorney at the close of his cross-examination said to the psychiatrist, "Would you recommend this book to be read by everybody?"

At this point Cairns literally held his breath waiting for the reply of the psychiatrist. His heart sank when the psychiatrist replied, "No, I would not."

The prosecuting attorney turned triumphantly and said, "That's all, your honor."

Cairns simply could not leave his case in that precarious position. He said to his witness, "Well, Doctor, would you recommend that everyone read the Bible?" The psychiatrist replied, "No, I would not."

Cairns won this case. The book ban was lifted. The result of the trial, headlined in the daily newspapers, did not go unnoticed in Washington.

Soon after this case had been decided, Secretary of the Treasury Henry Morgenthau decided something had to be done about the adverse publicity received over the years by the Treasury Department and by Customs because of disputed rulings being made on books, art and other items being imported into the country. One of the most publicized cases had involved the attempt by an importer to bring into the country copies of James Joyce's controversial *Ulysses*. The book had created a tremendous stir in literary circles in Europe and among those in the United States who could get their hands on a copy. Joyce's use of four-letter words and his then-shocking treatment of sex brought howls of protest from many. There were outcries against any importation of the book into the United States. Likewise, there was an outcry against censorship among those who regarded Joyce's work as an outstanding work of literature, written in a style and with a realism which they said raised it to a high level of art.

Joyce's book went on Customs' banned list. The case was taken to court and the judge wrote a blistering opinion against censorship. The court held that the book had to be viewed as a whole, and that one could not judge it by picking out isolated passages from the text; when the book was viewed in its entirety, it was not obscene.

About this time, also, Customs found itself in hot water because an examiner refused entry for a shipment of photographs of sculptures of nude men and women. The examiner took one look at the photographs and ruled that they were pornographic. The trouble was that the pictures were photographs of sculpture in the Vatican —a point which did not seem to impress the examiner but which was noted acidly in the protest against his ruling.

This combination of events, among others, persuaded Secretary Morgenthau to look for someone who could bring the situation under reasonable control. As Cairns tells the story: "Of course, I don't know what went on in the Treasury or why they turned to me, except that I had beaten the government in the Baltimore case. I had been writing on books for the Baltimore papers for a number of years and Eli Frank, the chief counsel of Customs, knew about my work and my interests. The story I heard was that after the chain of adverse publicity, Secretary Morgenthau called on his counsel, Herman Oliphant, and said, 'Find me a lawyer who has read a book.' So Oliphant called up the chief counsel of Customs and passed on the word, 'Find a lawyer who has read a book.' That is how I got into it."

Before "getting into it" Cairns decided to make a trip to New York to interview those who had had a voice in banning the controversial works. He wanted to know the Customs procedures and how those involved arrived at their decisions. He decided the best starting point would be to interview one of the Customs employees engaged in opening and examining packages from overseas.

Cairns opened the interview by saying, "Tell me on what grounds you act when you refuse entry for an item."

The clerk replied, "Well, if I see a book with a naked woman in it, a photograph, I hold it up."

"I can understand that," Cairns said, "but tell me about some other cases that are not so clear-cut as a book having a picture of a nude in it."

"Well, did you ever hear of this *Ulysses* case?"

"Yes," Cairns said, "I have heard of that case. Did you handle the book when it arrived?"

The man nodded. "Yes, I did. What happened was that when the book came in I admitted it. There was another shipment and I admitted it. There was a third shipment which I admitted, too. Then I began to get suspicious. Here's a book bound in paper and it was selling for fifteen dollars. So I said to myself, it must be a dirty book. So I got my knife and cut the pages. I cut the pages and when I got to the end of the book, I saw the dirtiest words I had ever seen in my life. So I held it up."

Cairns nodded. "Who was the book addressed to?"

"It was addressed to an actress. She came down to see me and said, 'I want my *Ulysses*.' I said, 'Lady, I ain't going to give it to you. It's a dirty book.' 'Well,' she said, 'at least let me look at it.' I looked at her and said, 'Lady, are you married?' She said, 'No, I am not married.' And then I said, 'Well, lady, I ain't even going to let you see it.' "

After this revealing interview, Cairns decided to work with the Treasury and Customs in an advisory capacity. A procedure was set up whereby questionable items were forwarded to him at Baltimore for his recommendation before the Bureau made any formal ruling. The procedure worked so well that it was continued through the years.

Cairns left Baltimore to join the Treasury in 1937 as the Senior Assistant General Counsel. He remained with the Treasury until December, 1942, when he came to the National Gallery in his present post. Over the years, Cairns' work as a "censor" has become less difficult as the courts have become more liberal in their interpretations of what constitutes obscenity and what does not. Cairns now receives only about 5 to 7 per cent of the questionable imports and he does not consider them to be difficult cases.

More than 90 per cent of the questionable items are what Cairns refers to as "junk," and "hard core" pornography. There never is any question about the hard-core pornography. It consists of filthy pictures and objects obviously manufactured with a lascivious and lewd intent; Customs examiners have learned over the years to recognize such shipments almost immediately by the wrapping of the packages, the names of the shipping companies, and the countries of origin. For a time France was the source of most of the pornographic material. Then it was Italy. Then the source shifted again back to France. Then to India. For a time Japan was the major supplier of pornography, and at present Sweden is a leader in this field.

In some cases, Cairns advised test cases so that the court might decide the issue and establish a legal precedent. One such case involved the importation of birth control items by a doctor in seeming violation of the law banning "any article whatever for the prevention of conception." Did the statute mean such items could not be imported for medical purposes? Cairns thought it a point for the court to decide—and the decision was that the statute was not intended to exclude such imports by a medical practitioner.

Another such case involved the importation of acknowledged hard-core pornography in 1950 by Dr. Alfred C. Kinsey, the Indiana University professor whose controversial "Kinsey Report" on human sexual behavior created a stir in the late 1940s.

The Kinsey case developed when Dr. Kinsey had shipped from Europe to the Institute of Sex Research of Indiana University a case filled with pornographic books, sailors' postcards, and photographs of males and females in the sexual act. Customs previously had banned such items with no voice raised in objection. But a nationwide interest was aroused when Collector of Customs Alden H. Baker at Indianapolis took one look at the Kinsey material and declared it "damned dirty stuff."

Baker refused to release the shipment to Dr. Kinsey and defended his position by saying, "There is nothing scientific about it. . . . If you saw some of these pictures, you wouldn't think they were scientific." He shipped the material to Washington, where Customs officials—and Cairns—agreed with the collector that it was unadulterated pornography specifically banned by law.

Kinsey protested the material was necessary to his research and that since it was for scientific study the government had no right to withhold it from him and from his colleagues at the Institute. He issued a statement saying, "You can use the Bible or almost anything for obscene purposes. Any material you can think of can be made obscene by perverting it to erotic stimulations. . . . The Institute of Sex Research at Indiana University considers this issue is one that concerns all scholars the world over who need access to so-called obscene materials for scientific investigations which in the long run may contribute immeasurably to human welfare."

Kinsey appealed to members of Congress for an amendment to the tariff laws which would permit him to have access to the material impounded by Customs. Then he went to see Cairns, to ask for his help. As Cairns recalled the meeting, "He came to see me about it and said that I had admitted the works of Havelock Ellis and he felt he was entitled to have the material on which Ellis based his studies. I said that may be, but before you came to see me, you had asked Congress to amend the statute to permit you to import hard-core pornography. How can I, as an administrator, say that the statute doesn't cover you when you have already asked for an amendment which they have refused to grant?"

In any case, the test case served its purpose. The court held that since the material was intended for scientific use, the statute barring pornography did not apply in this case. The ruling did not mean that the court was lowering the bars for importation of pornographic material to everyone who wished to import it into the country. It only meant that the bars were being lowered for the Institute of Sex Research in its investigations.

Cairns considers it no great accomplishment to separate the obscene from the artistic. "I have long been of the view," he once said, "that any man of letters can tell whether the impulse behind a book is literary or pornographic."

Once when asked if reading and viewing pornographic material over a long span of years had had any effect on his own morals, Cairns grinned and said, "According to the theory of censorship I should be fairly corrupted by now—but I don't believe I am. I just find the stuff boring."

20

OF TOY CANARIES AND PIRATES

One day in 1957 an examiner in the New York Customs Appraiser's Stores opened a packing case received from Switzerland. He lifted out a small brass object resembling a canary cage. On a tiny swing in the cage sat an extremely lifelike little bird. When the examiner wound a key in the bottom of the cage, the bird threw back its head, opened its beak, and burst into song. It ruffled its feathers and wagged its tail as it trilled its merry little tune.

The examiner called to a colleague nearby and said, "Hey, Joe! Come and look at this one."

He turned the key and they watched the little bird perform. The examiner said, "Cute, isn't it?"

"If my wife sees it, she'll want one," the other examiner replied. "It certainly is beautifully made. How are you going to classify it?"

There was the rub. What was this tiny cage with the singing bird? Was it a toy, dutiable at 50 per cent of its value? Was it a musical instrument, subject to a duty of 35 per cent? Or was it, as the importer claimed, simply a "manufacture of metal," subject to a duty of 20 per cent?

The examiner disagreed with the importer. He ruled that the little singing bird with the music box in the bottom of the cage was in fact a musical instrument. This opinion was sustained by the appraiser. The appraiser's decision was supported by the Collector of Customs.

The importer took the case to court. His attorney called one company witness who testified the imports were designed as ornaments for home decoration. He said they could be used as a nice toy—but they weren't toys. And he had "never known it to be used in an orchestra." Therefore it could not be held to be a musical instrument.

After the court heard the testimony and listened to the trilling of the tiny bird in its small brass cage, the court was moved to lyrical language in its decision, saying:

It may be contended that this bird does not emit a continuous melody, and that it is not an instrument upon which a chromatic scale can be played. . . . Music is the one harmonious science that dispells discord, softens the winds, and makes all nature kin. It has quickened the step for the warrior in the field of battle; has riveted the attention of the savage on the march of his enemy; has stirred the ambitions of men to higher ideals; and caused the beauty of the human heart to speak in friendliness and love. . . .

Indeed, if it was not for sweet music, human life would be so dreary as to be unbearable. It matters not whence it may arise, from the throat of the opera singer or of the bird. From the scintillating trills of the flute or the low notes of the Chinese gong, music is yet the curious and most harmonious succession of sounds conceivable. It is the anesthetic of life.

The instrument in question is a musical one, and the tuneful ear of the Collector was correct in thus classifying it.

The protest is overruled.

The case of the Singing Canary underscores one of the most important functions of the U.S. Customs Bureau—the classifying of millions of imports which arrive in the United States and the determination of their dutiable value. The Customs Appraiser's Stores—the port depots where the imports are examined—are sometimes a weird world in which things are not what they seem.

Every schoolboy is taught that a whale is a mammal. But when whale steaks reach the Customs examiners, they are classified as "fish cut to portions." A tomato is a fruit to a botanist. But to every housewife and the Customs examiner it is a vegetable. Botanists classify rhubarb as a vegetable—but in Customs' language it is a fruit.

Customs examiners are not just being arbitrary and ornery when they make these classifications in defiance of the botanist and the dictionary. The contradictions came about because the U.S. Court of Customs and the U.S. Court of Customs Appeals have made these rulings for the purpose of identifying imports so that a proper rate of duty may be paid upon them.

The courts have said over and over that in the language of commerce and in the everyday language of the streets, a whale must be considered to be a fish because it lives in the sea. Also, they have said the tomato is a vegetable because it is sold and eaten as a vegetable. And rhubarb in the legal world has become a fruit because it is bought and sold as a fruit.

In most cases, the appraisers have no difficulty in establishing the proper rate of duty to be paid on an import because the rate is fixed by law and the import is easily identified. But there are a great many imports not identified in any of the tariff acts or the amendments adopted by Congress, a lack which often creates difficulties, as it did when one importer brought in a shipment of Chinese mah-jongg sets.

The dominolike pieces used in playing the game were made of bone and bamboo. The importer and the government agreed that the material of chief value in the mah-jongg pieces was bone. The importer insisted that the duty should be 20 per cent of the value because the games were "manufactures of bone." However the Collector classified these sets as "dominoes" and set the duty at 50 per cent. He ruled that the mah-jongg pieces came under the paragraph 341 of the Tariff Act of 1913 which provided for a duty of that rate on "dice, dominoes, draughts, chess men, and billiard, pool, bagatelle balls, and poker chips of ivory, bone or other material."

This case also found its way into the Customs Court. The government attorneys argued that the mah-jongg pieces should be classed as "dominoes by similitude" even though they were not specifically listed under the acts passed by Congress.

The importer argued through his attorneys that the mah-jongg sets were not specifically named by Congress in any of the classifications established in the various acts and therefore the duty should be applied on the "component material of chief value."

In this case the ruling went against the government. The court held that the mah-jongg sets were properly classifiable at 20 per cent as manufactures in which bone was the "component material of chief value."

The appraisers' staffs make millions of classifications each year on imported items, and there is remarkably little dispute over their decisions. Out of these millions, no more than 700 are disputed and contested in the courts annually.

Sometimes a seemingly obscure and innocuous ruling on a classification will blow up a storm across the country. Such a case developed when an importer brought in from Europe do-it-yourself kits containing parts of a miniature electric train and engine to be assembled by the purchaser.

The locomotives, freight cars, cabooses, passenger cars, track, and other equipment were precision-made scale models of larger railroad equipment. They were all made to a standard "HO" scale of 3.5 millimeters to one foot. The trains were designed to run at the scale speed, which meant that at maximum speed they would travel 60 feet a minute. At that speed, they would simulate the operation of a full-size train.

All of the equipment was manufactured according to the strictest standards set up by the National Model Railroad Association. This Association has been described as "an organization of adult model railroad hobbyists founded in 1935 to make and promulgate standards for wheels, flanges, rails, switches, and other working parts of model railroads, with the purpose of achieving interchangeability of equipment from different manufacturers."

The examiner who inspected the imported miniatures classified them as "toys"—and as such subject to duty of 50 per cent of their value. In the Tariff Act of 1930, Congress had described a toy as "an article chiefly used for the amusement of children, whether or not also suitable for physical exercise or for mental development."

The ruling brought a pained cry from miniature railroad hobbyists across the country.

Toys, indeed! The hobbyists were outraged that this import should be put in the same category with playthings and that anyone should have the affrontery to think that such railroad equipment—even though Lilliputian in size—could be put together, and operated, by a mere child.

When the Collector at the Port of New York supported the ruling of the appraiser that the miniature railroad equipment should be classed as toys, the ruling was appealed to the U.S. Court of Customs. And when the case came to trial the importer had behind him ranks of witnesses from all walks of life ready to dispute the government's description of the equipment: dentists, technical consultants, salesmen in various lines of business, doctors, lawyers, editors, publishers, and writers.

One after another, the witnesses took the witness chair to deride this nonsense that the miniature trains were made "for the amusement of children." They gave technical testimony on the operation of these miniatures to prove that no child could be trusted with them and in fact could not operate them.

To prove this point one witness testified, "It requires a knowledge of electricity and requires a thorough understanding of how the trains operate. For example, our accessories all operate on alternating current; our trains run on direct current. It is necessary to know the two types of current which our power-packs provide to connect up the wires correctly. In the case of the alternating current, they have two leads; one would be a common terminal, connecting all the different accessories and switches, and another would be a specific one which would go to each individual switch. . . . The locomotive can also be operated from an overhead wire with pantographs they have located on the roof. This makes it possible to operate two trains on the same track under independent control. To do this, it is necessary to set up a catenary system, which is an overhead wire system, such as the Pennsylvania and New Haven Railroad use in this area. This, naturally, requires wiring."

The importer insisted that the miniatures should not be classified as toys but should be classified as electrical equipment subject to a lower rate of duty.

Under this barrage of expert testimony from adults who play with small trains, the court overruled the Collector. The court held that the model railroad sets were not "toys," because they were used chiefly by adults or by grown-up children and that they "do not come within the legal meaning of the word toy."

In years past, Customs officials tried to establish a detailed classification system in which the examiner could refer to a given page in a book and quickly come up with the answer as to classification and duty of any item. But the system broke down under the weight of a vast number of new products arriving on the market. Discussing this effort a Customs Bureau official said: "On tariff classification, a number of people, who call up and ask for rates, think there is a detailed, logical breakdown and that we just thumb through a book and come up with an answer. To someone who hasn't worked with classification, that seems like the way to do it. That is the way the old-timers used to try to classify. They used to try to set up categories with a place for everything, and everything in its place. But every time anyone set up one of these classification systems, along would come some new item which didn't fit anywhere. So the present tendency in classification systems is to set up a specific category for the more important items, and then to set up what might be called a basket category to catch everything else."

The impossibility of achieving an easy index for classifying imports was illustrated in recent years when a machine arrived from Europe described by the importer as "printing machinery."

The machine had the equivalent of a type font but, instead of type, the font contained pictures of type on a transparent plate. The type-setter, using a keyboard similar to that on a linotype machine, punched out sentences on a roll of perforated tape. Then the tape was fed into the machine, and as each perforation passed an electronic control, a transparent plate bearing the image of a letter dropped into place to be photographed by a high-speed camera. In this way a full sentence was formed with photographed characters. This process was continued, letter by letter, until a column of "type" was set up on a film. Then the film was developed and, by a photoengraving process, was reproduced on a metal plate ready for printing on paper. In all the process there was no actual type used.

Customs was baffled by this one. Was the machine to be classed as photographic equipment, printing equipment or as typesetting machinery? It did not set type. It did not actually print. And it was more than a mere camera. The Bureau decided this was a case in which the court should hear all the arguments and make a decision—and a decision has yet to be made.

When Congress passed the 1930 Tariff Act there were roughly 700 categories of imports. Since that time—with the adoption of the Reciprocal Trade Agreement Act—the number of categories has been increased by the thousands. Most of the increases were in categories created to help foreign countries expand their trade in the United States. The duty on a comparatively few imports has been revised upward as a measure of protecting some of the American industries from lower-cost foreign competition. In the vast majority of cases the revisions have been downward, following the trend toward removing tariff barriers by international agreement.

In arriving at the dutiable value of an import, Customs officials are bound by the Tariff Act, which lays down the rules under which they calculate the true value of an article. This system of appraisal is complex and varies from category to category. Congress has proclaimed that duty on certain items shall be fixed on the foreign value—that is, the selling price in the country of production. Some items are appraised on their export value—the price which the exporter pays for them. Others are valued on their United States value, which means the price at which the exporter sells them in the United States. Some appraisals are based on cost of production.

Duties based on the American selling price are designed solely to protect certain American industries from foreign competition. Among the leading industries receiving this protection are the rubber and coal-tar dye industries. For example, an importer may be able to purchase a pound of coal-tar dye in Switzerland for $2. But if that dye is competitive with a dye of a similar shade produced in the United States, then the import will be appraised at $5 a pound, notwithstanding the fact that the importer paid the Swiss manufacurer only $2 a pound for the product.

However, most appraisements are made on the basis of export value, the price charged by the manufacturer or the seller in the foreign country.

The imports brought to the Appraiser's Stores for examination form a cross section of the commercial treasures of the world and they are unbelievably varied. The examiners—trained by years of study and on-the-job experience—have become experts in appraising the quality and the value of a staggering number of imports. Whether the import is wool, cotton, silk, sugar, hog bristles, furs, diamonds, ore, chemicals, exotic foods, or an antique table, there is someone with a background of knowledge on the subject.

One of the largest single sources of Customs revenue continues over the years to be duties collected on raw wool which has not yet been processed for manufacturing. The wool examiner is one of the most highly trained of the specialists within the Bureau. He must be—because the Tariff Act of 1930 requires him to be able to identify by type thirty different wools from all parts of the world, in addition to being able to determine whether a shipment of hair is from the Angora rabbit, the Cashmere goat, the Bactrian camel of Central Asia, or the llama and vicuna of South America.

The Bureau has found that the only way to obtain these specialists is to recruit young men who are interested in this field of work, and to train them under the guidance of experienced examiners. The recruits must spend hours with books outside their regular work hours, in addition to attending technical training schools and visiting manufacturing and processing plants throughout the United States.

As far as the Tariff Act is concerned, the term "wool" includes not only the fleece from sheep, but the fiber from other animals. This is why the examiner must be able to distinguish Cashmere goat hair from the hair of the Angora goat raised in the southwestern part of the United States; and to learn the subtle differences betweeen two grades of coarse hairs as well as the variations between the finest of fleeces.

Wool is graded by numbers, starting with 36 for the coarsest and moving through the 70s to the very finest. A miscalculation in the grading can deprive the Treasury of revenues—or cause an injustice to an importer.

For years, examinations of wool were conducted on the piers by taking samples from the ends of the highly compressed bales, which were covered with burlap and bound by steel bands. The examiner had no way of knowing—except to have a bale of fleece opened—whether or not the outer fleece concealed a higher grade of wool in the center of the bale. In some isolated cases, examiners found that a coarse grade of carpet wool concealed extremely high-grade wool. Contraband such as narcotics also was found hidden inside suspect bales.

Perhaps of even greater importance, the examiner had no reliable method of determining the amount of dirt, vegetable fiber, grease and other foreign matter contained throughout the bale— and the duties were supposed to be assessed only on the "clean content" of the wool.

This haphazard method of examination drew the fire of Congress in 1930. To correct the situation, the Customs Bureau established the post of Wool Administrator in New York City. It was his job to coordinate the examinations throughout the country and to establish more uniform practices. Daniel J. Kelly was named Administrator, with three assistants—Morris Shuster in Philadelphia, Al Kelleher in Boston and John Walker in New York.

The Bureau assigned to Chief Chemist Louis Tanner of the Boston laboratory the job of finding a method to determine the "clean content" of wool shipments. He developed a special boring tool which enabled examiners to take samples, or cores, of wool from inside the bales, and to judge the uniformity of the fiber in an entire bale without disturbing the bindings. This method proved so simple and effective that it has been adopted by the commercial trade and by government agencies in other countries throughout the world.

Imports of all kinds and types reach the Appraiser's Stores in this manner: When merchandise is ready for export from a foreign country to the United States, the exporter prepares a special customs invoice describing the merchandise and giving its value. This invoice is sent to the American importer. When the importer is notified that the merchandise has arrived at a port of entry, he turns over the invoice to his customs broker. The broker calculates the estimated rate of duty, then proceeds to the Customs House. There he makes what is called a formal entry of the merchandise, filing the information he has received from the exporter and paying the duty.

In the Collector's office at the Customs House, the broker's estimates of value and duty are reviewed for any errors. Then the invoice is transmitted to the appraiser's office, where it is assigned to the expert who will examine this particular merchandise.

The Collector notifies the Customs inspector at the pier that he is to send a 10 per cent sampling of the imported merchandise to the Appraiser's Stores to be physically examined by the specialist in that field. The specialist examines the samples of merchandise to see that they are correctly identified by the importer. Then he determines whether the broker's estimates of value and duty are correct.

If the broker entered the merchandise at $100 a unit and the examiner believes that the appraised value should be $125 a unit, then the examiner makes the change. His report is then forwarded to the office of the Collector for final action, and normally the Collector accepts the examiner's judgment.

The Collector then notifies the broker or the importer of the action that has been taken. The importer and broker may accept the ruling or they may take issue. If they disagree, they may appeal to the United States Customs Court. If either the importer or the government is dissatisfied with the lower court's decision, an appeal may be taken to the U.S. Court of Customs and Patent Appeals. Usually the decision of the Appeals Court is accepted as being final, but either of the parties may carry the appeal further, to the Supreme Court.

It seems odd that piracy should be a concern of Customs in the 1960s, as it was in the days of Jean and Pierre Laffite. But piracy still exists in modern dress and is a troublesome problem. The only practical difference between the modern pirates and the cutlass-carrying freebooters of the past is that the pirates' methods have changed.

There was the case that might be called "The Pirates of Taiwan" —a case which created an incident of international embarrassment between the governments of the United States and Formosa (Taiwan) and a potential threat to the U.S. book publishing industry.

The "pirates" of Taiwan were the owners of small printing shops who engaged in the business of publishing—without the consent of the authors or the original publishers—almost every book of any merit printed in the English language.

With fantastically cheap labor, cheap paper, and a photo-offset printing process, the publishers in Taiwan reproduced such extensive works as the *Encyclopaedia Britannica,* dictionaries, sets of medical and scientific works, volumes of the classics, standard reference books, best-selling novels and popular non-fiction. The books were carbon copies of the originals, even to the U.S. copyright numbers and the phrase "Manufactured in the United States." Nothing was changed in the pirating process, not even the typographical errors. From a casual examination, there was nothing to indicate that the books had not been published in Philadelphia, Boston, or New York.

The pirating problem became acute in 1959 when the Chinese publishers arranged contacts with sales agents in the United States, men and women usually located on or near a campus of a university or college. These agents solicited orders primarily from professors and teachers, librarians, researchers, and students. A standard set of the *Encyclopaedia Britannica*—normally costing about $400—was offered for less than $50. The $35 *Columbia Encyclopedia* was listed at $7.13. Gray's *Anatomy,* a standard work for all medical students and normally costing $17.50, could be purchased for $2.50. Allen Drury's best-selling novel of political life in Washington, *Advise and Consent,* cost $5.75 in American bookstores—but was advertised by the Chinese publishers at $1.25.

In some instances, the Chinese publishers obtained lists of likely customers and solicited them by mail. The prospects usually were men, women and organizations with modest incomes who were forced to operate on a very limited budget. And here they were being offered the opportunity to obtain expensive volumes of literary works—which they had long dreamed of owning—for only a fraction of the price being charged throughout the United States.

The books were shipped from Taiwan in individual packages. Even when the packages were opened for inspection by a Customs examiner, there was nothing to arouse suspicion of any irregularity. The first hint which Customs had of fraud was when a complaint was lodged in 1959 by the American Book Publishers Council and the American Textbook Publishers Institute.

The book publishers appealed for help to the State Department, the Customs Bureau, Congress and even to the White House. The sales of pirated books in the United States had become a multi-million-dollar business which threatened to destroy the American book market.

In theory, at least, the publishers could have protected themselves from the sales of pirated books in the United States by registering each title with the Customs Bureau and paying a fee of $75. The registration would have banned any import of a similar title without the publisher's consent.

Such a procedure would have been prohibitive in its cost because each title produced is regarded by law as a different product.

A single publisher might well have had to register as many as 2,000 titles annually to obtain total protection—at a cost of more than $150,000 in fees and incidental expenses. This cost would have been in addition to the $300,000 paid to copyright the works, at $150 per title.

When Customs agents opened an investigation they discovered that in the first half of February, 1960, sales of pirated books at Iowa State University alone totalled more than $1,200. It was obvious that American publishers and authors were literally being robbed of millions of dollars. Not only were the books being mailed to the United States in large quantities, but a great many sales were being made on Formosa to military personnel, to students, and to tourists who could not pass up such a bargain in literature.

Action was taken by Customs to halt the importation of the books through seizure at the ports of entry. Then the U.S. Ambassador to Nationalist China, Everett F. Drumright, took up the problem with Foreign Minister S. K. Huang in Taipei, seeking a ban on the export of the books.

The problem was not one presenting an easy solution because the laws of Taiwan technically tolerated such piracy. Many members of Chiang Kai-shek's government were not entirely sympathetic to shutting off this lucrative trade which brought dollars into the treasury. There was the fact, too, that lack of any copyright agreement gave Chinese students access to cheap editions of technical books and famous works of literature.

However, an arrangement was worked out on the diplomatic level for a ban on the wholesale export of pirated books from Taiwan. The American publishers agreed to make available certain of their works to Chinese students. This agreement brought a halt to much of the illicit traffic, but the problem of pirated books continues to be troublesome.

Competition for world trade has also brought some sharp practices in which foreign manufacturers copy American-made automobile parts, tools, and other merchandise and then ship them into the United States. The articles are identical in appearance to the American-made product down to such small details as the American manufacturer's registered trademark. But the price—and quality—are far below the American level.

The piracy in the field of trademarks is a continuing problem for Customs. There are approximately 5,000 trademarks registered with the Customs Bureau, including those registered by foreign firms. And each manufacturer guards his trademark jealously.

Many foreign trademark owners, for the protection of their representatives in this country, will not permit more than one of their trademarked articles to be imported into the United States by a tourist. Many tourists will go abroad and purchase an unusual bargain in a camera, perfume or some other item. They are dismayed when they return to this country to find that Customs will not permit them to keep more than one of the articles.

In these cases, Customs is following the letter of the law in preventing more than one article from being imported bearing the restricted trademark. It is only the trademark which Customs is interested in protecting. If the importer of the articles should obliterate or remove the trademark from the items he is carrying, Customs inspectors would have no objections to allowing them into the country.

The trademark prohibitions sometimes create unique problems. One of these developed when a Mexican cattle raiser shipped a herd of cattle to the Mexican border and was preparing to bring them into the United States at Nogales, Arizona. Before the cattle could cross the border an American cattle raiser rushed to Nogales and demanded that Customs halt the importation of the Mexican cattle. He argued that he was the owner of the cattle brand seared into the hides of the Mexican cattle and that any importation bearing this brand would be a violation of the trademark laws.

An investigation by Customs officers revealed that the American cattle owner was entirely correct. By chance, the Mexican cattle raiser had the same cattle brand as the American rancher. The American's cattle brand was registered with the Customs Bureau, and his cattle brand was entitled to the same protection given to the trademarks of manufacturers. Eventually, the protesting American and the baffled Mexican got together and the American gave his consent for the importation of the cattle.

One section of the trademark law prohibits the importation of any articles which are marked in a manner to indicate a false country of origin. It also bans imports which are marked with false descriptions. To enforce this section of the law, Customs officers must police millions of imports to weed out the products of foreign manufacturers who engage in some shady and sharp practices.

In recent months there arrived from Japan a large shipment of boys' baseball bats which were boldly marked with large letters burned into the wood, "American Model." At the end of the bat in extremely small letters was stamped the word "Japan." The Customs Service felt that the purchaser of these bats could only assume, by looking at them and seeing "American Model" in large letters, that they had been made in the United States. It ruled that before the bats could be entered, the word "Japan" would have to be stamped onto the bats in close proximity to the words "American Model," to remove the taint of deception.

Another manufacturer shipped into the country flatware made of iron with a chrome plating. It was marked with the word "stainless," implying that it was stainless steel. The courts and the Federal Trade Commission have held that the world "stainless," when used in describing manufactured articles, has a very specific meaning: that the product has a great deal of resistance to normal corrosive elements and to wear and tear that other metals normally do not have. And to describe an article as stainless steel, it must be an alloy of steel mixed with chromium in approved percentages.

To protect the manufacturers of stainless steel products in this country, the Customs Bureau instituted a campaign to halt such sharp practices and to educate foreign manufacturers to the fact that they cannot mark products with the word "stainless" unless they meet the very severe test required for the use of this word. The shipment of cast-iron flatware was refused entry, and inspectors were alerted to guard against any such shenanigans in the future.

21

THE MIDDLE MEN

Mr. and Mrs. John Smith of Lima, Ohio, were strolling through the streets in Florence, Italy, enjoying their first European vacation, when Mrs. Smith noticed a beautiful, hand-blown glass bowl in the window of a small shop.

"John!" she exclaimed. "There is the bowl I've been looking for. It would be perfect for our Christmas eggnog parties. Let's go in and price it."

They stepped inside the shop and a clerk brought the bowl from the window to a table where Mr. and Mrs. Smith could examine it more closely. It was a lovely piece of glass and obviously the work of a fine Venetian craftsmen. After admiring the delicate etchings on the glass, Mrs. Smith asked, "How much is it?"

The clerk said the bowl was one of the best pieces in the house and that it was priced at $75.

"My goodness," Mrs. Smith exclaimed. "That bowl would cost double the price at home. It's a good buy."

Mr. Smith said, "But how will we ever get it home? We can't lug it all over Europe with us. We would be certain to break it."

The clerk interrupted, saying, "Pardon me. You don't have to worry about getting the bowl to your home. We will take care of everything for you—the packing and the shipping. And we will insure it against breakage. We ship hundreds of purchases every year for American visitors."

Mr. Smith asked, "How much do you charge for that service?"

The clerk shrugged. "There is no charge for our service, sir," he said. "There will be a small shipping charge which you can pay on receipt of the package, but as for the trouble of packaging and handling the shipment from here, that is merely a part of the service we give our customers."

"We won't be back home for another three weeks," Mrs. Smith

said. "What will happen if the bowl arrives before we reach home?"

"You need not worry about that," the clerk said. "I'll hold the bowl for several days and then ship it so that it will not arrive until after you have reached home."

"Well, that seems simple enough," Mr. Smith said. "As long as you can handle this for us, then we'll buy it." He pulled out his wallet and paid for the bowl. Then he carefully wrote out his home address in Lima, Ohio.

"Don't worry about a thing," the clerk said, smiling. "The bowl will arrive soon after you get home."

As the Smiths left the shop, Mrs. Smith said to her husband, "Well, the Italians certainly do make it easy for the Americans to buy something and send it home. I had no idea there would be so little red tape to sending a purchase home."

A month later Mrs. Smith was at home when the telephone rang. It was a long-distance call from New York. A strange man —someone she had never heard of—asked if she had ordered a glass bowl from a shop in Florence, Italy. He explained that he was a Customs broker, the bowl had been consigned to him, and he was prepared to clear the package and forward the shipment if she authorized him to do so. He explained there would be a nominal fee for his services in getting the package released from Customs and forwarded to the Smiths in Lima.

Mrs. Smith was so flustered she told the caller she would have her husband get in touch with him. What was this strange man doing with her bowl? The clerk in Florence had said he would take care of everything, and now this broker was saying something about having legal title to the shipment and that she would have to pay a fee to get her bowl shipped to her. He had explained that she could come to New York and arrange personally for the Customs clearance if she wished to do so.

Mrs. Smith telephoned her husband at his office and told him about the call from the broker in New York. She gave her husband the man's name and his telephone number in New York.

And then Mr. Smith exploded with anger. "It's a gyp deal of some sort," he said. "I am going to call the nearest Customs office and see what this is all about. We didn't tell that clerk to send the package to anyone in New York. I don't know how he got into this picture. There's something funny going on and I'm going to find what it's all about."

Within a short time, Mr. Smith learned—by checking with a Customs officer—that he was not being gypped. The broker in New York was a legitimate broker, licensed by the Federal government to act as a clearing agent for merchandise arriving in the port of New York. The call that had been made to Mrs. Smith was a routine call, because the package containing the bowl had been consigned to the broker in routine fashion either by the shipper in Florence or by the carrier which brought the package into the port of New York.

Mr. Smith asked why it was that Customs in New York could not forward the bowl directly to him without going through a broker. That seemed the easy way to handle the shipment without all this red tape and the payment of a fee to some stranger whose name he had never heard before this day. Mr. Smith declared heatedly that he didn't have time to go running off to New York for a $75 glass bowl. As a matter of fact the bowl wasn't worth all that trouble and expense. He and his wife wanted the bowl and they wanted it as quickly as possible.

The Customs officer explained that unless Mr. Smith or his wife went to the port of entry to clear the shipment with Customs—or unless they authorized the broker to act as their agent—the bowl would be held by Customs for five days. Then if it were not claimed, it would be sent to a warehouse. It would remain in the warehouse for one year, and if it had not been claimed within that period, then it would be sold at auction along with other unclaimed packages. The officer explained further that Customs was not authorized by law to act as the forwarding agent for anyone —except in cases where a shipment valued at less than $250 was received by mail from an overseas point.

"Now, if you had shipped the bowl by mail," the Customs officer said, "it would have been delivered to your post office and you could have obtained its release with no difficulty at all."

Smith retorted, "This is a fine time to tell me I should have shipped by mail. All I can say is it's a hell of a way to run a railroad." He slammed down the phone, cursing Customs and all of the government's red tape. Then, reluctantly and angrily, he called the strange broker in New York and authorized him to clear the glass bowl. Thus the day was ruined for Mr. and Mrs. John Smith of Lima, Ohio.

The story of Mr. and Mrs. Smith is not unusual. Similar cases occur daily throughout the United States as returning travellers discover that they could have saved themselves worry, time, and money by familiarizing themselves with the Customs procedures governing the importation of foreign purchases into the United States. Had Mr. and Mrs. Smith taken the time to read a few relatively simple instructions—available to travellers in pamphlet form —they would not have gotten into the difficulty they did.

In the first place, they would not have accepted the glib assurance of the Florence clerk that he would take care of everything. Instead, they would have instructed the clerk to mail the glass bowl by parcel post, marked as a "tourist purchase." When the package arrived in New York, the post office would have turned it over to Customs in routine fashion for examination. An examiner would have verified the contents and its value and then returned the package to the post office to be forwarded directly to the Smiths in their home town. If any duty were due, it could have been paid to the postmaster after filling out a simple entry form. No broker. No delay. No red tape.

But this is what happened to the Smith's glass bowl after it was purchased in Florence: the clerk turned the package over to a forwarding agent with no special instructions. The agent routinely consigned the shipment to a broker in New York with whom he had been doing business for years. The bill of lading was made out to the New York broker, which meant that when the package arrived in New York, the broker had legal title to the glass bowl because it was consigned to him.

What few travellers realize is that there is no automatic movement of merchandise arriving by ship from overseas. Someone has to be on hand to clear each shipment with Customs and pay any duties that might be due. Someone must see to it that the merchandise is moved from the piers to its destination. And this is usually the job of the broker, a point which many people do not understand and which causes considerable difficulty.

The broker is the expediter of the multi-billion-dollar flow of merchandise through the ports of entry in the United States. He is the legal representative of his client in dealing with Customs problems.

The Customs Service is not interested in merchandise until it arrives within the limits of a port of entry to be unloaded. At this point the merchandise legally becomes an import. And the merchandise passes through Customs under two types of general entries. One is called the "consumption entry" and the other is known as a "warehouse entry."

Most imports arrive and are passed through Customs under the consumption entry, which permits the importer to pay the duties, obtain a release, and get immediate possession of all of his merchandise.

When merchandise is brought into the country under a warehouse entry, the major part of the merchandise is sent to a Customs bonded warehouse for storage. No duties are deposited when the papers are filed except for that portion of the merchandise which is to be taken immediately by the importer. In other words, the importer is permitted to place his goods in storage without payment of duties and then is permitted the privilege of making partial withdrawals from the warehouse, paying duties on whatever he draws for consumption.

There is a continual movement of merchandise from one bonded warehouse to another. This is particularly true in movements of liquor from one part of the country to another. Liquors may move across the country and may be in six or a dozen different bonded warehouses before they are withdrawn for consumption and taxes are paid. This system permits merchants to move their merchandise freely to meet shifting consumer demands.

The normal period for bonded storage is three years, but this period may be extended. If no extension is granted and the goods still remain in a bonded warehouse beyond the three-year period, they are considered unclaimed and abandoned to the government. The government then puts the merchandise up for public auction.

A point of constant friction in the field of imports is the law which requires that imports shall be marked "legibly and conspicuously" with the name of the country of origin. It has been the Customs Bureau's position that if the marking can be reasonably expected to remain on the article until it reaches the ultimate purchaser, then that is all that the laws requires. But there are many exporters and importers who disagree with the Customs interpretation of the law.

As one Customs veteran explained: "The domestic people, of course, would like to have great big red letters 40 feet high on a 20-foot article spelling out the name of the country of origin. Of course, it frequently happens that the importer would like to have this name about as small as the Lord's Prayer on the point of a pin.

"The markings from some countries increase the value of the article. Chinaware from England, for example. The English are very happy to put their marking under the glaze, where it will remain. There are other countries that are just as happy to put this identification on by paper sticker, which may come off in the rain. So we always are in the middle in the argument over markings on imports."

The purpose of the law, of course, is to inform the ultimate buyer of the country from which the merchandise came. Normally the ultimate purchaser is considered to be the man who buys it across the counter—the last person to receive the article in the condition in which it was imported.

A great deal of merchandise is permitted into the country under what is known as the "informal entry procedure." The informal entry is used where the value of a shipment does not exceed $250. The entry was devised for the benefit particularly of persons passing across the borders of the United States from Canada and Mexico.

In such border crossings, there is no formal appraisement. The Customs officers on duty write up the entries, take a look at the merchandise and decide themselves whether the value is correct. Then the duty is paid on the spot and the merchandise is released.

This informal entry procedure is also used at the airfields to expedite shipments of merchandise by air. It is used in the clearing of baggage through Customs when travellers arrive from overseas, and in the clearance of non-commercial shipments which include personal and household effects.

In the vast majority of importations, the broker plays an important part. The broker may be an individual, a partnership, corporation, or association. In any case, those acting as brokers must be licensed by the Customs Bureau, meet certain standards, and submit to Federal regulation of their operations.

Applicants for individual broker's licenses must undergo an examination at the headquarters port in the Customs district in which the broker intends to operate. The purpose of this examination is to determine the applicant's knowledge of Customs laws and procedure and his fitness to render a service to importers and exporters. This knowledge must necessarily be quite broad in scope, and a grade of 75 per cent is required for passing.

However, those applying for a broker's license as a corporation, partnership, or association do not take an examination. Their applications are forwarded by the Collector to the Supervising Customs Agent, who conducts an investigation and then makes a report and recommendation. The agents verify the correctness of the statements made in the applications and the qualifications of the person or persons who will actually handle the customs business. The government requires that each broker keep current records reflecting his financial transactions as a broker, and these records must be available for government inspection at any time.

The Customs Service has no part in fixing the fees charged by customs brokers for their services. However, if a complaint is made against an individual broker or a brokerage house, then the complaint is investigated by Customs Service agents and if the fees charged by the broker are found to be excessive or "unconscionable," then action is taken by the Service to correct the situation. In cases where investigation discloses irregularities, the Secretary of the Treasury has the authority to suspend or revoke the license of a broker. Such action is taken, however, only after a quasi-judicial hearing in which the accused broker has the right of cross-examining witnesses. If the decision goes against him, then the broker may, if he wishes, appeal his case to a U.S. Circuit Court of Appeals.

The broker plays a prominent role as the middle man in the import-export business, but this does not mean that an importer must necessarily seek the services of a broker in bringing merchandise into the country. Under the law, any citizen may act as his own agent in clearing his own imports through Customs and no license is required.

One of the ancient devices to aid the importer is known as the "drawback" privilege. "Drawback" is a word which is found in customs language through the centuries, and it is another word for "refund."

In brief, the drawback works in this fashion: an importer brings merchandise into the United States to be used in the manufacture of certain articles. At the time of importation, he pays the normal duty. After the articles are manufactured, they are exported to another country. It is then that the manufacturer is entitled to a refund on that part of the imports which he shipped back out of the country.

The drawback plays an important part in the manufacturing operations of all nations. It enables manufacturers to meet competition in the export market. For example, an automobile manufacturer in the United States imports a large amount of steel to be used in the manufacturing of his automobiles. Ten per cent of this steel is used in cars which are shipped overseas. Thus the manufacturer is entitled to a drawback or refund of 10 per cent of the duties he paid on the imported steel.

Congress has liberalized the drawback provisions so that a manufacturer does not necessarily have to use the imported materials in his exports in order to qualify for a refund of duties. An automobile manufacturer may export automobiles made entirely of domestic steel. But if the steel he used in the exports is of "the same kind and quality" as the imported steel, then he is allowed to obtain a refund on that quantity of steel used in the exported automobiles.

Virtually every manufacturer who is in the export business takes advantage of this drawback material, and its value to the manufacturing industry in the United States is realized when it is noted that the refunds paid in recent years have been running about $9 million annually.

Oddly enough, there are some American manufacturers who do not even know that they have the privilege of a duty refund. They have been importing materials for years, paying duties, and then exporting the finished products without making any claim for a refund of duties on the materials shipped back overseas. One midwestern manufacturer in recent years discovered that he had paid the government in excess of $1,500,000 in duties—and he was entitled to a refund of the entire amount.

This situation developed as a result of the Korean War. Because of the tremendous devastation in Korea, the U.S. government entered into a program of rebuilding the Korean economy. The midwestern manufacturer obtained orders from the government to supply a quantity of heavy machinery and equipment, the contract running into many millions of dollars.

In that period during and after the Korean War, there was a shortage of domestic steel. For that reason the manufacturer imported virtually all the steel used in the machinery manufactured for the Korean government. When he discovered that he was due a refund of duties, he obtained all his records over the past years, and submitted them to the government. These records were verified and the manufacturer was paid more than $1,500,000.

The maze of tariff laws which has grown up over the years has developed some peculiar situations, and one of the oddest of these involves the Virgin Islands, the insular possession which has attracted many manufacturers in recent years.

One reason that the Virgin Islands is proving attractive to new industries is that under the present laws, manufacturers operating in the Virgin Islands pay an import duty of only 6 per cent on merchandise brought into the Islands for use in manufacturing. Their finished products are permitted into the mainland free of any duty—provided the foreign materials used are less than 50 per cent of the total value.

This quirk in the law has created extreme problems for some American industries, such as the watch industry. For example, a manufacturer in the Virgin Islands will import various watch parts from France or Japan and pay only a 6 per cent duty on these imports. The parts will be assembled into a finished watch, and if the watch meets the requirements fixed by law, then it enters the United States free. In other words, the manufacturer in the Virgin Islands pays a 6 per cent duty on watch parts on which the American manufacturer is required to pay a 50 per cent duty. And this variance extends to other fields of manufacturing.

There has been, in recent years, a growing opposition to the duty differential which is permitted manufacturers in the Virgin Islands. Discussing this situation before Congress in September, 1960, Representative Eugene J. McCarthy of Minnesota voiced the views of many when he said: "In recent months there has been a growing tendency for companies to establish themselves in U.S. insular possessions on a basis that results in their escaping the proper payment of duty on products they wish to import into the

United States. Section 301 of the Tariff Act of 1930, as amended, was intended to promote the development of employment opportunities in our insular possessions . . . (Instead, it) has become an avenue for the avoidance of very substantial amounts of duty. . . ."

The McCarthy argument is disputed by the Virgin Island manufacturing interests, but nevertheless the situation underscores the complexity of the laws by which the Customs Bureau is bound.

In the fourteenth and fifteenth centuries, free-trade zones were common throughout the world. There were no customs requirements, and merchandise moved through these ports with no restrictions. Gradually the free-trade ports disappeared as the various countries imposed tariffs on imports and exports for revenue and for protection purposes.

The nearest thing to the old free-trade port that exists in the United States today is the foreign-trade zone. It is a sort of No Man's Land which has been described as "a neutral stockaded area where a shipper may put down his load, catch his breath, and decide what to do next."

There are four of these zones in the United States, located at New York, New Orleans, San Francisco and Seattle. They are fenced and guarded areas into which importers may bring merchandise without payment of duties—excepting prohibited merchandise such as narcotics, subversive or immoral literature, or lottery matter. The merchandise may remain in the zone indefinitely, and once it is there it may be manipulated, processed or manufactured without being subject to any Federal or state controls.

The foreign-trade zones are used for many operations such as assembling machinery, dyeing and bleaching materials, bottling, weaving, printing, extracting oils and other components from raw materials, and for cleaning, grading, sorting, and repackaging materials for a specific market.

It is only when the finished product is removed from the zone that it becomes subject to commodity quotas, commodity standards, labelling and marketing requirements, licenses, fees, controls and taxes that normally apply to all imports. However, if it is to his advantage, the importer may ask for an earlier determination of the duties and taxes due—before the processing changes the classification of the goods involved.

The foreign-trade zones are intriguing areas because although they are physically within the United States, for all practical commercial purposes they remain outside the United States—reminders of an earlier day when trade through many ports of the world was unfettered.

22

THE RESTLESS AMERICAN

Inspector Leonard Simon, a tall man with faint crinkles about his eyes, stood at his post in the Customs baggage examination area late one August afternoon at New York's Idlewild International Airport. He was waiting for the rush of travellers who then were disembarking from a huge Pan American Boeing 707 jet which had just completed its swift flight from Paris.

Simon had arrived on the job early that morning and this was one of the few times he had been able to relax. Tourists returning from Europe had been pouring through the airport in droves. And before the day was ended, he and his fellow inspectors would have examined the documents and the luggage of passengers disgorged from more than 100 airliners—a restless army arriving from all parts of the world.

At the peak of the traffic, as many as 1,000 persons moved through the inspection lanes each hour. Fifteen years earlier—in the postwar years—only a handful of officers was needed to handle the international air traffic. The jet age had changed all this. A force of 248 men was now required, and each year travel by air was increasing.

They came in waves from the planes, laden with boxes, bundles, bags and cases—impatient to clear this last official hurdle which stood between them and their destination. There was a certain air of resentment about some of them when they entered the inspection lanes, as though they were being forced to undergo an unpleasant inoculation which was entirely unnecessary. Some showed their nervousness with self-conscious titters. Some were openly hostile to the inspectors. And some viewed the routine with bored resignation.

Nevertheless, most of the travellers accepted the examinations with good grace, answering with candor the routine questions about their purchases abroad, and paying any duties assessed without complaint when the purchases exceeded the duty-free exemption of $100.

A few of the travellers had voiced complaints, as did the fat, perspiring man who demanded in a loud voice, "Why is it that our government is the only one which treats a citizen as if he might be a criminal?" He looked about belligerently to see if anyone would take exception to the statement, but the inspectors acted as though they had not heard the remark. None of them was in the mood for an unnecessary argument.

With minor variations, the scene had been replayed over and over throughout the day. Now, as the crowd from the 707 jet moved toward the inspection lanes, Simon ground out his cigarette in an ash tray and nudged a fellow inspector. He said, "Here comes trouble."

"Which one?" the man asked.

"The Duchess," Simon said, the crinkles deepening about his eyes. "The tall woman with her nose in the air. I'll bet she comes to my station."

Sure enough, The Duchess bustled into Simon's lane and fixed him with a beady stare. "Young man," she said with a heavy British accent, "can you tell me why I must go through with this nonsense of having my luggage examined?"

"I'm sorry," Simon said, "but it's a routine precaution we must take with all travellers unless they have the immunity of a diplomatic passport. I'm just doing my duty."

The woman glared. "I still think it's a lot of nonsense. It's most inconvenient. What do you think I'm carrying that is illegal?"

Simon said seriously, "We were informed that you were smuggling twenty small Russians into the country in your suitcases. I've got to see if it's true."

It was a corny gag but, unexpectedly, The Duchess laughed. "All right, young man," she said. "Get on with your job and I'll not trouble you again."

The visitor from Britain had hardly left Simon's station when he looked up and saw a well-known film star entering his lane. He knew her immediately from her pictures in the newspapers and from the film he had seen a few days earlier at a neighborhood theater. The papers had said she would be returning to Hollywood from Europe, where she had been working for several months on a new picture.

There had been stories of her appearances in Paris, Rome, Madrid and Monaco, and the usual gossip about the men with whom she had been seen. Now here she was in person—dressed in a fetching suit which had a made-in-Paris look to it. She carried a handsome Italian-made handbag. On her wrist was a watch which Simon saw at a glance was worth several hundred dollars, because it was encrusted with small diamonds.

The actress handed Simon her declaration. It was signed with a carefree flourish—but there were no purchases listed, only personal belongings. Simon felt like groaning when he saw the declaration. It simply didn't make sense for a well-known actress to be in Europe for six months without making a single purchase of clothing or jewelry.

Simon said, "You are certain you understand the regulations? A good many people don't know that the declaration must include any wearing apparel purchased abroad, even though it has been worn." Simon was trying, tactfully, to suggest that if she had any undeclared purchases, she still could "remember" them and amend the declaration without penalty. He didn't want to make trouble for her because, as he explained later, "I really liked her pictures." And there was the chance that she didn't understand the regulations.

The actress snapped, "Of course, I understand. I took these things with me when I left the country."

It was the tone of voice that did it. Simon shrugged and asked her to open her suitcases. The top layers of clothing were dresses with California designers' labels attached, and Simon saw they were genuine California models.

Beneath these dresses there were other gowns with no labels on them. But Simon didn't have to rely on a label to know that these were creations from the houses of Dior and Balenciaga. He recognized their Paris origin from the distinctive stitching and from other small peculiarities of design which were more reliable identifications than labels. A label might be changed or removed —but the work of the French seamstresses could not be altered.

Simon had only to glance through the suitcases to see that the matter had gone beyond his authority. He signalled for one of his superiors. The actress was asked to step into a private room for questioning and for a more thorough examination of her luggage. She was found to be carrying undeclared clothing and jewelry worth $10,800. She was not subjected to criminal prosecution, but she paid into the Treasury the value of the purchases in addition to the stiff penalty for the smuggling attempt. She left New York for Hollywood a much wiser young woman, although she would never feel moved to voice any praise for the Customs Bureau and its employees.

The case of the Hollywood actress is only one minor example of why the Bureau requires that travellers' luggage be examined upon arrival in the United States. Each year roughly 150 million persons and 43 million vehicles cross and recross the borders. Among those millions are cheats, smugglers and conspirators seeking to evade the payment of duties on imports or trying to bring contraband into the country.

Baggage examinations have been made since the Republic was in its infancy. The system has been continued simply because no one yet has devised a better way to protect the Treasury from those who seek to avoid the payment of legitimate duties. The system remains much the same as it was in the days of George Washington—and without doubt just as annoying to travellers.

There is an old story that Napoleon once assembled his marshals, just before launching a long-planned campaign, to deliver a stirring address on the brilliance of his strategy, the weaknesses of the enemies, and the indomitable spirit of the Napoleonic legions.

"Nothing," thundered the little emperor, "can stop our march!"

Then a voice piped up from the rear: "Sire, you forget the French Customs!"

The U.S. Customs Service in its more than 170 years of operation has never achieved a position of such bureaucratic eminence as the anonymous storyteller attributed to the French Customs—even though some tired and disgruntled travellers returning from abroad might feel inclined to dispute this point. But there is no doubt that among governmental agencies, the Customs Service has —in Madison Avenue terms—projected a poor image of itself and the importance of the role it plays in protecting the Treasury.

Smuggling and attempts at fraud continue to be big-money problems. During the fiscal year 1960, Customs agents and inspectors made 13,531 seizures of merchandise, narcotics and other imports worth $8,238,649. From these seizures, the Treasury received a total of $1,402,084.24 in fines and penalties—of which $896,159.42 was collected by Customs agents.

While the value of the seizures reported by Customs in one year may seem high, Customs officers are certain that they intercept only a part of the contraband that is brought into the United States. They are equally certain that diligent inspection and enforcement work slow down the operations of the underworld operators, the one-shot smugglers, and the chiselers who—if this deterrent did not exist—would flood the country with illegal imports.

Unfortunately, there is no way in looking at passengers arriving by plane or by ship to separate the honest from the dishonest. The little gray-haired lady with a shawl about her shoulders, wearing steel spectacles and a shy, grandmotherly smile, may have two pounds of heroin concealed beneath her petticoat. And the square-jawed, blue-eyed, All-American business executive with the firm handclasp may be trying to bring into the country a diamond ring and several watches.

Frequently men of wealth try to smuggle purchases past the inspectors merely to see if they can get away with it. Such a case involved a Pittsburgh industrialist who arrived in New York from a trip to Europe. He was a man whose name was well-known in the business world and who was financially able to pay tariff duties on purchases costing tens of thousands of dollars. But when an inspector looked at his new hand-made alligator bags—purchased in Italy—he was reasonably certain the luggage was grossly undervalued on the businessman's declaration. The inspector called for an appraiser to check his judgment. The appraiser asked the businessman to open one of the bags, and the traveller said belligerently, "Why do you want to open it?" The appraiser replied, "Because I want to see inside. Any objection?" And he proceeded with an examination of the luggage.

Upon opening one of the bags, he found two expensive Patek Philippe watches—rated among the world's best. Not only did the traveller's declaration not list any watches, but more than one watch of this particular brand could not legally be imported without a special permit from the agency which handled them in the United States. Another handbag contained several other expensive watches.

When the watches were found, the businessman looked at the appraiser and the inspector and grinned. He said, "Well, now that you've caught me, how much is it going to cost? Let me pay you and get on my way."

The appraiser said, "I'm sorry but it isn't that simple. This could be a criminal case rather than just a matter of just paying for a mistake."

By this time the businessman had wiped the smile from his face. He was beginning to sweat. He lowered his voice and said, "Let me speak to you privately."

The inspector and appraiser took the traveller into a private office, where he apologized abjectly. He explained that he was trying to be a "wise guy." He said he thought it would be amusing to see if he could bluff his way past Customs and he hadn't realized the serious implications involved.

"He was a pretty shaken man when he left that office," the appraiser recalled. "No criminal case was made against him but he did pay a stiff penalty."

For the transgressions of the few, the great majority must undergo the inconveniences of delay in having their baggage inspected.

There is no doubt that the inspectors who arrive on the job out of sorts, grumpy and even rude make more enemies for the Customs Bureau in dealing with the public than a dozen Customs men could have made working in any other capacity.

Such an experience brought a protest from a Canadian, who

wrote *The New York Times* in November, 1958, complaining of rude treatment by a churlish airport inspector. The inspector curtly demanded the Canadian's bags be opened for inspection. Then without as much as a peek inside them, he ordered the bags to be closed in what the visitor termed "an exercise in official nuisance and an assertion of bureaucratic authority." He added, "The trip began with irritation from this first contact with a representative of the United States. . . ."

Baggage inspection—while it is only a small part of the overall Bureau operation—nevertheless is one of the most sensitive parts of the Bureau's work, and officials are painfully aware of this fact. They are trying to eliminate the kind of patently absurd situation which inspired a *New Yorker* cartoonist to picture a stern, arms-folded Customs inspector at the U.S.-Mexico border facing a very pregnant young lady and saying, "That's the rule, lady—if you got it in Mexico, you pay duty on it."

The keeper of the law can hardly hope to win popularity contests. But most of the complaints against Customs spring from the average American traveller's resentment of the baggage inspection. People simply don't like to have a stranger poking about among personal belongings.

The Bureau has been seeking ways to speed up the examinations and to keep the public at least tranquil, if not happy, over the operation. Conveyor belts have been installed at examination counters at airports in New York, Miami, San Juan and San Francisco, and are planned at other major points of international travel. They have helped to cut down delays. Campaigns are conducted among employees to promote greater courtesy in dealing with the travelling public.

Inspector Simon, discussing this situation, said: "We rarely have difficulty with seasoned travellers who know all the rules. It's the people who don't travel too often, the person who makes one trip in ten years' time, and the general tourist who are always apprehensive about Customs. One of the most difficult things is to settle them down and make them feel at ease so that you can get the answers to your questions without upsetting them too much. Once they feel that you understand their situation and you start to discuss with them what they have purchased and what they might have ordered to be shipped later and how they must go about clearing these articles, then they relax a bit and you find that it is easier to handle them."

To train new Customs employees in their duties and responsibilities, the Customs Bureau operates a school for inspectors and examiners in an old building at 54 Stone Street in lower Manhattan. Here the recruits are not only instructed in the proper way to meet the public and to inspect luggage, but also how to look for the tricks of the smuggler, how to obtain a sample from a shipment of wool for a laboratory analysis, the proper procedures for verifying shipments of merchandise to determine their dutiable value, and what items are on the forbidden list, such as narcotics and certain plants and vegetables. They also must familiarize themselves with an impost book on whose pages are listed more than 60,000 articles which are dutiable. And in hours of study there is instruction in other phases of the Bureau's widespread operations.

While the schooling is helpful for any future inspectors, only experience will give them the finesse and the tact necessary to avoid constant irritations in dealing with the thousands of people who pass through the ports each year from overseas, or from Canada and Mexico.

Customs inspectors have learned from long experience that elderly women returning from abroad for the first time and women who are travelling alone are apt to be the most emotional when approaching the Customs inspection lane. They require special attention by inspectors in filling out the proper forms and in getting their baggage prepared for inspection. Many of them regard Customs as a frightening barrier to entry into the United States —and not as an agency to help them comply with the laws which were written by Congress.

Actually, a close look at the record reveals that the Customs Bureau is one of the more efficient units in the Federal government. Even though the work load for examiners, agents, appraisers and other employees has increased more than 200 per cent over the past ten years, the Bureau does the job with fewer employees. In 1951 the Bureau had a total of 8,561 employees—8 more than were employed in 1962. The Bureau's operating budget had increased from $40,500,000 to $63,400,000 over that period, but most of the increase went into pay raises voted by Congress, employee retirement funds, increased health benefits, and employee insurance contributions.

In 1960, the Bureau won a commendation from the watchdog Bureau of the Budget for an impressive showing in management improvements effected by outgoing Commissioner Ralph Kelly.

Since that remote day in 1789 when William Seton paid the first $774.41 in duties into the U.S. Treasury, the responsibility for policing the imports has grown steadily.

The nerve center for the sprawling operation is located in the office of Commissioner Philip Nichols, Jr., in Washington, D. C., whose top lieutenant is a long-time government career man, Assistant Commissioner David B. Strubinger.

Management control is maintained through seven main divisions: the Division of Engineering and Weighing, the Division of Laboratories, the Division of Tariff and Marine Administration, the Division of Personnel, the Supervisor of Appraisers, the Division of Investigations and Patrols, and the Division of Fiscal Administration.

In the field there are forty-five collectors of customs in thirty-two Customs districts, thirty-two appraisers, nine chief chemists, seven comptrollers, thirteen supervising Customs agents, and nine chief laboratory chemists, in addition to the inspectors, enforcement agents, examiners, border patrolmen, technicians, and clerical workers.

In the fiscal year 1960, the imports reached $13 billion, and in 1962 they climbed to more than $15 billion—pouring through 350 ports of entry and Customs stations along the borders. The collection of duties soared in 1962 to more than $1.5 billion. International air travel at New York's Idlewild Airport increased more than 10 per cent over the preceding year, and air cargo shipments were up 20 per cent. Similar reports came from other points of international travel.

Perhaps one of the more notable achievements of the Service is the fact that with improved management controls, better auditing procedures, and swift action against crooked employees, the Bureau has not had a major household scandal in more than a quarter of a century.

For years, the Bureau has had one of the lowest personnel turnover rates of any of the government agencies. It is now in a period of rapid change. The reason is that many of the long-time employees, including those in top management positions, are reaching retirement age. They are the ones who came into the Service in the early 1920s and chose to remain.

Government employees may retire any time from age sixty-two on to the mandatory retirement age of seventy. Most of those retiring are stepping out at age sixty-five, and since 1960 the Bureau has been forced to seek approximately 400 new employees each year—with a heavy turnover in the upper management echelon.

The management vacancies are being filled by promotions within the Service. The upward move has left openings in the lower positions for young men and women interested in a government career and, more particularly, in the specialized work offered by Customs. This trend in employment will continue through 1965.

Why did they stay with the Customs Bureau in such numbers? One of the old-timers put it this way: "We came into the Customs Service as young people and it became a part of our life. We felt we had more than an ordinary job. We felt we were taking part in something important to our country—and for this reason we felt important. There never was time to get bored because there never was a day when you didn't run up against a new and interesting problem. I don't mean a gimmick problem—but a problem that might mean millions of dollars. Of course, no job can be perfect— but I don't know where I could have found another that would have kept me interested this long. . . ."

There is every reason to believe that the Customs Service—the gray old frontier sheriff among the Federal agencies—is improving with age.

ABOUT THE AUTHOR

Don Whitehead was born in Inman, Virginia, and studied at the University of Kentucky. He has spent most of his working life in newspaper work, and for twenty-one years was with the Associated Press, twice winning Pulitzer prizes. For a time he was chief of the Washington, D.C., bureau of the *New York Herald Tribune.* In 1956 he wrote the widely acclaimed *The F.B.I. Story,* and in 1960 he wrote *Journey into Crime.* He now lives with his wife in Concord, Tennessee, where he writes a column for the Knoxville *News-Sentinel* and does freelance writing.